# Equity Crowdfunding for Investors

The Wiley Finance series contains books written specifically for finance and investment professionals as well as sophisticated individual investors and their financial advisors. Book topics range from portfolio management to e-commerce, risk management, financial engineering, valuation and financial instrument analysis, as well as much more. For a list of available titles, visit our Web site at www.WileyFinance.com.

Founded in 1807, John Wiley & Sons is the oldest independent publishing company in the United States. With offices in North America, Europe, Australia and Asia, Wiley is globally committed to developing and marketing print and electronic products and services for our customers' professional and personal knowledge and understanding.

# Equity Crowdfunding for Investors

*A Guide to Risks, Returns, Regulations, Funding Portals, Due Diligence, and Deal Terms*

DAVID M. FREEDMAN AND
MATTHEW R. NUTTING

WILEY

*Library of Congress Cataloging-in-Publication Data Is Available*

ISBN 9781118853566 (Hardcover)
ISBN 9781118857847 (ePDF)
ISBN 9781118857809 (ePub)

Printed in the United States of America

10 9 8 7 6 5 4 3 2 1

# Disclaimer

The information in this book is intended for educational purposes only, not to be construed as specific investment advice for particular individuals. The authors are not investment advisers. Readers should consult qualified tax, legal, and other appropriate advisers prior to engaging in any business or financial transactions. Because the laws and regulations underpinning this book are new and ever-changing, please refer to updated information at www.wiley.com/equitycf.

# Contents

# Foreword

It is a rare privilege to have the opportunity to recognize a work of substantial merit and value, as I do in writing this foreword to *Equity Crowdfunding for Investors*. For over three years now, even before the JOBS Act was enacted into law in our country, I have been an ardent supporter of and an enthusiastic participant in the crowdfunding movement.

Although crowdfunding is a diverse collection of strategies and mechanisms for supporting fund-raising by innovative and entrepreneurial projects and ventures, my primary enthusiasm for the crowdfunding arena is that of an investor interested in the securities-based forms, as opposed to the entrepreneurial fund-raiser or a service-providing member of the supporting industry. Indeed, I have been for several decades an active individual angel investor, and am now a professional fund manager for others. As few would dispute, the manifold social and economic benefits of crowdfunding are dependent on the willingness and ability of individuals to write the all-important checks. However, most of the public discussion of crowdfunding focuses on the benefits to entrepreneurs and society as a whole. This book represents a major step in filling this gap, by providing a primer to the newly enfranchised crowdfunding investor on both early-stage entrepreneurial finance in general, and by explaining practically how recent legal and regulatory changes allow everyone—not just the wealthy few—to participate in this attractive and beneficial asset class. The book is well written and enjoyably readable, and has background and other information of interest even for the experienced and already involved participant.

The benefits of crowdfunding, in all its multiple forms, are essentially fourfold. Indeed, two are implied by the name of the significant recent enabling legislation, the aptly named JOBS Act. Employment as well as other economic benefits result when projects and enterprises are better able to obtain the necessary start-up and growth funding. Crowdfunding has already proven its foundational promise of being able to provide important additional financial resources to the high growth and often high tech enterprises that are of greatest interest to professional investors and public markets, and that make such an important contribution to any nation's economic advancement and well-being. Crowdfunding also provides new and valuable mechanisms for helping support the Main Street, lifestyle businesses that employ large numbers of citizens and form the essential fabric of everyday life in our communities. Such businesses previously had only the financial resources of their owners and of community banks to call upon, and were often strapped for sufficient funding.

The third major benefit of crowdfunding, and a major reason for my personal support of the movement, is that it broadens and democratizes access to an asset class previously accessible primarily to a minority of wealthy and well-connected individuals and institutions. The majority of this book is directed at illuminating JOBS Act Title III crowdfunding, including its relationships to and distinctions from other forms of securities-based crowdfunding. For the inexperienced but financially motivated investor, numerous issues and aspects are common to all forms of securities-based crowdfunding, and are well-introduced and explained in this book. Title III of the JOBS Act, and securities-based crowdfunding in general, provide an historic opportunity to expand the community of angel investors (those who write checks with their own funds to support and participate in early and growth-stage businesses) from a small subset of the wealthy elite to virtually everyone.

The last major benefit of the crowdfunding movement, which must be mentioned for completeness but which will not be discussed extensively here, is that it provides a new, and potentially disruptive in a good sense, alternative mechanism for civic decision-making and practical progress. Thus, sufficient groups of citizen donors can now come together and collectively enable and support projects and activities that cannot gain the required consensus from our all-too-frequent politically deadlocked current government. This aspect flows equally from all forms of crowdfunding, including the securities-based and specifically the equity forms to which this book is devoted.

As this book rightly and frequently points out, both the foundational JOBS Act legislation and its lengthy rule-making implementation are presently incomplete, imperfect in many eyes, and will almost certainly be further amended and improved. Given these uncertainties, what might the future hold for equity and other forms of securities-based crowdfunding, and what issues merit further attention and effort?

The fact remains that most knowledgeable and experienced early-stage investors firmly expect that the great majority of individuals participating in equity-based crowdfunding will lose money overall. This does not deny the likelihood that a minority can and will achieve net positive returns (if they are diligent, disciplined, and follow the recommendations contained in this book and elsewhere), but like their wealthier individual accredited angel colleagues, most equity crowdfunding investors can only be realistically expected to sustain overall loss from their participation in this endeavor. Indeed, the frequent public pronouncements by politicians and some industry leaders to the contrary represent for some a form of misguidance bordering on systemic fraud. This misrepresentation is far more worrisome in practice than the occasional possibility of issuer fraud (as opposed to failure) that has been given such public scrutiny but has in fact been almost totally absent in the more advanced crowdfunding experiences of several other countries for many years now.

What can be done to maximize and make positive the financial outcome for a greater fraction of individual crowdfunding investors? Numerous pearls of wisdom are contained in this book, and are inescapably critical for generating reliable financial success from any form of early-stage equity investing including crowdfunding. Among the most important of these are the essential importance of knowing and operating according to one's own priorities and goals, budgeting for and building towards a portfolio of at least 10–20 early-stage investments, and engaging in, having access to, or at least following others' extensive due diligence on every potential investment as conducted by investors and beyond the legal minimums provided by issuers and intermediaries, who necessarily have motivations different from those of the investor.

Even faithfully following all of this well-founded guidance, however, the deck remains stacked against the financial success of most small-scale equity crowdfunding investors for several reasons. As discussed at length in this book, early-stage investing is inescapably a risk-filled endeavor in which most ventures and commitments do not succeed. This is true even for all investors including angels and venture capitalists. Furthermore, wealthier private investors and investors in public securities can invest through the offices of, and thus benefit from, the consistent diligence and substantial experience of interest-aligned and full-time professionals. They can also thereby aggregate larger sums and thus obtain greater voice in their invested companies.

Finally, and learned only through hard experience and not acknowledged in most public forums, everything leading up to and including writing the initial check does not constitute the full story leading to success in early-stage investing, whether of the equity crowdfunding or traditional angel sorts. That first check is not the end itself, but really only the end of the beginning. As companies grow and prosper, more and larger sums of money are usually required to enable a company to reach the promised lands of independent success, private acquisition or public offering, and the final returns to earlier investors often depend critically on what takes place in these later rounds of fund-raising. These additional and later increments of financial support typically come from professional investors and pooled funds, and the norm rather than the exception is that later and larger money throws its weight around in self-interest and because it can, often to the detriment of earlier investors (the so-called Golden Rule of investing, namely, that [s]he who has the gold makes the rules).

It is by no means certain that successfully growing firms that earlier raised financial support through equity crowdfunding will choose or even be able to garner future and larger rounds through further Title III equity crowdfunding, that initial Title III investors will be allowed to participate again due to the financial limitations built into equity crowdfunding for investors' protection, or lastly, that smaller crowdfunding investors would in general have the greater financial resources necessary to take part even if allowed to do so. Concretely, in the more than 50 private investments that this investor has made personally, each and every company invested in has come back for additional funding, and later funders of the more successful companies have often (legally or otherwise, and in any case requiring often difficult negotiation or even opposition) abused the interests of their earlier co-investors. The ability of equity crowdfunding investors to aggregate as well as employ professional diligence and experience (as discussed above), and potentially partner with larger investors from the get-go, will be critical to their achieving financial success comparable to those of traditional angel and venture investors; these mechanisms are not yet either allowed legally or developed practically, however.

To close, *Equity Crowdfunding for Investors* performs an invaluable service by introducing the broad endeavor of early-stage investing in general and crowdfunding specifically, and giving much practical guidance on how to understand and approach participating as an investor in securities-based and particularly equity crowdfunding. It is also "a good read," deserving the attention of anyone interested in understanding an important and growing phenomenon in our modern economic and social world. I remain a committed supporter of crowdfunding despite its multiple uncertainties and complexities, firmly believing that success with this rewarding asset class lies within the reach of anyone willing to devote the diligence and effort required, and I am pleased that the opportunity is becoming available to all. Some participants can, do, and will continue to make lots of money with these investments. The authors deserve our recognition and gratitude for the significant contribution of this book.

Charles Sidman, MBA, PhD
February 19, 2015
Managing Partner, ECS Capital Partners LLC
Founding Member, Angel Capital Association
Past President, Crowdfunding Professional Association

# Preface: The New Angel Investors

**D**o you ever wish you could have invested in Apple Computer when it was still operating out of Steve Jobs's parents' garage? Or bought a piece of Facebook when its headquarters were in Mark Zuckerberg's college dorm room?

Few opportunities in life can generate personal wealth as profoundly as being a founder or early investor in a startup that achieves grand success.

Mike Markkula was the first angel investor in Apple. He met the founding Steves—Jobs and Wozniak—in late 1976, after they developed the Apple II prototype and just before they moved their headquarters from the garage in Los Altos, California, to an office in Cupertino. Markkula, who had recently retired from Intel at age 32, helped Jobs and Wozniak write their business plan, and then invested $80,000 in the company in return for one-third of the equity (he also loaned Apple $170,000). That transaction valued the company at far less than $1 million. When Apple went public three years later, the company's value soared to $1.778 billion, and Markkula's share was worth about $200 million. That's way more than a 2,000-times increase in his original investment in the company.

Reid Hoffman was one of Facebook's first two outside investors. As an entrepreneur himself, Hoffman had been a founding board member of PayPal and then founded LinkedIn in 2003. He staked $37,500 on Facebook in 2005, when the social network had just moved out of a Harvard dormitory to its new headquarters in Silicon Valley, and was valued at $5 million. When Facebook filed its initial public offering (IPO) seven years later, and the company's value topped $100 billion, Hoffman's piece of it was worth something like $75 million, giving him roughly a 2,000-times gain over his initial stake.

These are two high-profile examples of spectacularly successful angel investments. The overwhelming majority of angel investments are not so successful; some of them are moderately to very successful, and—this is the sad part—most of them are losses. As you know, the possibility of meteoric growth in the value of startups is accompanied by commensurate risk of sluggish growth or outright failure. That's why successful angel investors typically buy equity stakes in several startups and, by doing so, diversify the risk and increase the chances of a hitting one out of the park.

The potential rewards of angel investing are not just financial, though. There are also strategic benefits, which may include:

- Close association with talented developers and inventors, brilliant entrepreneurs, and well-connected directors of the companies.
- Participation in company management or governance based on professional expertise, possibly as a board member, paid consultant, or strategic partner.
- An up-close, insider look at innovative business models, new products, cutting-edge technology, and proprietary research.
- The opportunity to invest in future rounds of later-stage angel, venture, and pre-IPO financing.

In the process of seeking financial returns and strategic benefits, angel investors can also derive social rewards: boosting community development (especially when the investors and issuers represent the same metropolitan area or region), creating new jobs, supporting favorite products and brands, and helping good people make their dreams come true. The rewards and benefits from successful ventures reach far indeed.

In 2012, a peak year for angel investment, more than 268,000 angels funded roughly 67,000 seed-stage, startup, early-stage, and growing small businesses in the United States. The total amount invested in those deals was almost $23 billion. That does not include venture capital investments, which involve funds (or pools of capital), rather than individuals, typically investing at later stages of business development (but still pre-IPO).

The most popular sectors among individual angel investors in 2012 were software and healthcare. Trailing these two leading sectors, in order of popularity, were retail, biotech, industrial/energy, and media.[1]

That gives you an idea of the volume of angel activity in America—before the rules changed.

## THE OLD RULES

Before the legalization of equity crowdfunding, for the vast majority of Americans, investing in fast-growing startups was either highly impractical or illegal.

---

[1] Jeffrey Sohl, "The Angel Investor Market in 2012," Center for Venture Research, University of New Hampshire, April 25, 2013. Among angel clubs (comprising accredited investors only), the sectors that attracted the most capital in 2012, ranked by the Angel Capital Association, were: healthcare, Internet, software, mobile/telecom, business products/services, energy/utilities, computers, consumer products/services, electronics, industrial, environmental services/equipment, media, and financial services.

Based on legislation enacted in 1933—as long as most of us can remember—angel investing was largely closed to all but (1) the wealthiest people in America and (2) founders of private companies[2] seeking capital and their family and friends, known as the "three Fs." The legal basis for those restrictions began with the Securities Act of 1933 and was further shaped by the Securities and Exchange Commission (SEC) and federal courts. In Chapter 2 we will explain just enough of that regulatory framework to help you understand the new equity crowdfunding rules, but here is the nutshell version:

- Issuers of private company stock, whether in startups or existing businesses, could offer shares to an unlimited number of "accredited investors," which includes individuals with a net worth of at least $1 million or annual income of $200,000 ($300,000 for married couples). Those issuers could also sell shares to as many as 35 nonaccredited investors per round of financing, as long as those nonaccredited investors were smart enough to understand the risks of buying private securities *and* had a personal relationship with the founders or their close advisers.
- Private issuers and their registered intermediaries (broker-dealers, for example) could offer shares only to people with whom they had "substantial" prior relationships, with a few exceptions. They could not engage in "general solicitation," which means they could not advertise an investment offering to the general public.

For Americans who did not have such wealth or relationships with issuers (or their intermediaries), the door to angel investment was locked tight and the curtains were drawn. The doors to other kinds of private securities, too, were barred (and still are) for most average Americans, including venture capital, private equity, hedge funds, and other "alternative" investments. So don't blame yourself for not being remotely aware that Apple shares were available for purchase in 1977 or that Facebook was looking for early investors in 2005, when they were startups.[3]

---

[2]Private company securities are those not registered with the Securities and Exchange Commission and not listed on a public stock exchange.

[3]We don't mean to imply that if you had known about Apple's and Facebook's early investment opportunities then, you would have been able to invest in them. At that stage, the companies wanted only strategic investors, i.e., people who had expertise to help the companies develop, market, and distribute their products, populate their boards of directors, and attract future rounds of venture capital.

## THE GAME CHANGER

The rules changed radically in 2012 when Congress unlocked that door to angel investing and lifted the ban on general solicitation. The Jumpstart Our Business Startups (JOBS) Act, signed by President Barack Obama on April 5, 2012, aimed to give small companies a boost by making it easier for them to raise capital. Title III of the JOBS Act created an exemption to the registration requirements of the Securities Act of 1933 to allow startups and growing businesses to sell equity to *all* investors, not just accredited ones, through online crowdfunding portals. This "crowdfunding exemption" was codified as Section 4(a)(6) of the Securities Act. The concept of registration and exemption can be confusing, so we will clear it up in Chapter 2.

In 2015, the Securities and Exchange Commission, alongside the Financial Industry Regulatory Authority, are expected to issue rules for the operation of equity crowdfunding portals, swinging the door to online angel investing wide open. The SEC and FINRA will continue to regulate equity crowdfunding, adjusting the rules and attempting to police the system against any fraud.

The new Section 4(a)(6) of the Securities Act limits the amount of capital that a company can raise via equity crowdfunding to $1 million per year,[4] and it limits the amount of money that nonaccredited investors can invest based on their net worth or income, to make sure nobody goes broke via crowdfunding. (We will describe these limits in detail in Chapter 3.) But it does not limit the number of investors to whom a company can sell shares via a funding portal. Whereas traditional angel deals typically required investors to put up tens or hundreds of thousands of dollars apiece just to walk in the door, equity crowdfunding investors may be able to buy shares for as little as $1,000 and perhaps less. So companies that issue shares on crowdfunding portals or through broker-dealers, based on Section 4(a)(6), can expect to receive many smaller investments from a much larger number of investors. This essentially turns the traditional angel deal on its head: from a small group of large-dollar-amount investors to a big group—a crowd—of small-dollar-amount investors.

If 268,000 angel investors funded startups and early-stage companies in 2012, when such deals were effectively restricted to a tiny segment of the population, now that those restrictions have been lifted there is no telling how many more investors will participate in the angel capital market. We can be a nation of angel investors, boosting opportunities for entrepreneurs

---

[4]Some members of the House of Representatives have proposed increasing the capital-raise limit to as much as $5 million.

to raise capital, hire employees, and pay taxes—not just in the metropolitan areas and high-tech corridors where angel capital tends to cluster, but everywhere.

## ENTER AT YOUR OWN RISK

Although the door to angel investing, at least the online version, is now open to all investors, not everyone is prepared to walk through it. Investors who have never done an angel deal, even those who consider themselves sophisticated when it comes to investing in publicly listed stocks and bonds, need to get familiar with a new universe of securities investing. Seed and early-stage investments include substantial risks as well as the possibility of exciting returns and benefits. You need to understand how angel investments can affect your overall portfolio in terms of diversification, asset allocation, liquidity, and long-term financial objectives. That will be covered in Chapter 8.

For all investors, including accredited investors who have actually done angel capital deals but don't understand the nature of crowdfunding, we will delve into the evolution of crowdfunding, from donation- and rewards-based crowdfunding to lending- and equity-based crowdfunding. This brief history offers lessons about the risks, rewards, occurrence of fraud, and wisdom of the crowd (or madness of it, depending on the context).

Ultimately, for those of you who have carefully weighed the pros and cons and believe that you (and/or your community) will benefit from investing in startups and growing private companies, we present four chapters on how to invest, including guidance on the following topics:

- Budgeting for angel investments, including the need for "dry powder" reserves.
- Setting realistic expectations for returns, liquidity, and management participation.
- Deciding what kind of industry, company, and development stage (seed, startup, growth, or later) to invest in.
- Identifying your primary motivation for angel investing: financial gain or community development.
- Selecting the appropriate crowdfunding portal(s) or broker-dealer(s) among dozens or hundreds in the marketplace.
- Conducting (and/or relying on the crowd or lead investors to conduct) due diligence, such as researching the company founders and reviewing their financial projections.
- Understanding the deal terms, especially what sort of securities you are buying, and what your rights and obligations are as a shareholder.

- Monitoring the companies you invest in and managing your crowdfunding portfolio.
- Understanding the likely time, place, and manner of your exit from your investment (where angel investors "cash out"), including secondary markets, management buybacks, mergers and acquisitions, IPOs, and other exit strategies.

## IPOS, EXITS, AND SECONDARY MARKETS

Speaking of IPOs, naturally you hope that the startups in which you invest will grow and eventually go public, as did Apple and Facebook, so you can earn spectacular returns, as did Markkula and Hoffman. One of the aims of the JOBS Act (Title I), after all, was to make it easier for fast-growing companies to go public (an important part of the new law but one which is not a focus of this book). Keep in mind, though, that an IPO—while conceivable—is probably the *least* likely exit for your angel investment. Only a fraction of 1 percent of angel investments end in IPOs,[5] although some successful investor groups—such as the oldest angel group in the western United States, the Band of Angels in Menlo Park, California—achieve "IPO hit rates" of more than 3 percent of their portfolio companies.[6]

Still, you can earn a return on your investment through other exit strategies, including management buybacks, acquisitions, and resale on new kinds of secondary markets. We expect that the emergence of equity crowdfunding will spawn new, online secondary markets and/or public stock exchanges for crowdfunded equity—that is, Internet-based marketplaces where crowdfunding investors can sell their shares (after a mandatory one-year holding period). Secondary markets that launch after this book is published, as well as many other useful resources for crowdfunding investors, will be listed on our website, www.wiley.com/equitycf.

Exit strategy is relevant only if the startup you invest in survives and grows. Many do not. Some of them simply fail to gain traction in the marketplace and wind up in dissolution or bankruptcy. Some of them stay small even if they succeed, in which case there may be no practical exit for angel investors (depending on the terms of the deal).

---

[5] Scott A. Shane, *Fools Gold? The Truth behind Angel Investing in America*, Oxford University Press, New York, 2009, pp. 11 and 158.
[6] Specifically, out of 269 companies in which the Band of Angels invested between 1994 and 2013, 10 have gone public, for an IPO hit rate of 3.7 percent. Data provided by Ian Sobieski, PhD (in aerospace), managing director, Band of Angels (www.bandangels.com), December 10, 2013.

## FINANCIAL, STRATEGIC, AND SOCIAL BENEFITS

We began this preface by highlighting the potential benefits of traditional angel investing, including financial (return on investment) and strategic (rubbing shoulders with brilliant entrepreneurs, bringing your professional expertise to the project, getting an insider look at innovations, etc.).

With respect to financial benefits, we predict that equity crowdfunding will be similar to traditional angel investing—at least after the funding portals[7] launch and work out their technological and operational kinks, and this new industry matures somewhat. Assuming you diversify your angel portfolio with a number of investments over a period of years, you will have a chance to achieve good overall returns. Your ultimate financial goal, to be realistic, should not be to earn triple-digit returns (if that happens, consider it a very pleasant surprise), but to beat the familiar market indexes such as the Dow and S&P. You may conceivably hit a grand-slam home run, but some or even most of your investments will probably be strikeouts.

The most successful angel investors have learned how to pick enough winners, and limit their losses from the losers, to earn a good overall return on their angel portfolios. Still, the most authoritative sources of data on angel investing indicate that, although *in the aggregate* angel investors may achieve good returns, the majority of *individual* angel investors actually lose money.[8]

You may wonder why, if most angel investors lose money, they keep making such investments. Some successful (or not so successful) entrepreneurs become angel investors because "it's a way to stay in the startup world without having to work 80 hours a week," explains Ian Sobieski, PhD, managing director of the Band of Angels, who also taught entrepreneurial finance at the University of California at Berkeley. "Many angels are retired CEOs or heads of industry who invest because they want to help startups grow and mentor younger executives. They are often motivated by the energy of a young company. But for most angels, the simplest answer is, it's fun."

With respect to strategic benefits, equity crowdfunding is a radically new environment, with nontraditional relations between founders and investors. Remember that it involves much larger numbers of smaller investors. Beyond

---

[7]When we refer to "funding portals," we intend to include online offering platforms of broker-dealers who intermediate equity crowdfunding deals.

[8]Most surveys and studies of angel investment returns use self-reported data from investor groups and individual angels, and thus are not necessarily reliable. It is likely that some investors and investment groups exaggerate their returns based on both practical and ego-related motives.

their earliest handful of investors, which tend to be the three Fs and close business associates, issuers cannot be selective about who they accept as investors based on their expertise or strategic value to the company. Even if you believe you bring consummate strategic value to the deal, you'll be investing alongside hundreds or maybe thousands of other "small" investors, many of whom believe they too bring valuable expertise to the deal. So don't assume that the strategic benefits of an equity crowdfunding deal will be as compelling as in a traditional angel deal.

Now for the good news. In place of those kinds of strategic benefits, equity crowdfunding investors will enjoy social benefits that are unique to this new financial ecosystem, the infrastructure of which has a strong social networking component. In addition to the social benefits of traditional angel investing (community development, job creation, supporting good people and ideas), the social benefits unique to equity crowdfunding include the opportunity to:

- Connect and build relationships with entrepreneurs and fellow investors who share your passion for a particular product, brand, team of founders, community, or sector (such as games, movies, fashion, 3D printing, or sustainable energy, to name a few).
- Collaborate with other investors to analyze an issuer's business plan and financial projections, research and evaluate the competence of its executives, verify its claimed customer base, and estimate scalability (room for growth), to judge whether the company has a good chance for success.
- Leverage the wisdom of the crowd to conduct due diligence—for example, ferret out evidence of fraud or incompetence, detect any misstatement or omission in disclosures, and (postfunding) monitor spending of proceeds from the investment round. (Chapter 6 will explore the concept of the wisdom of crowds.)
- Participate in online platforms where equity crowdfunding investors are rated by their peers, where you can optionally rate and be rated, and where you can follow the highest-rated investors to see what they are investing in across many funding portals (which you can rate as well).[9]

To some readers, especially Millennials and others who are accustomed to social networking and rewards-based crowdfunding, the social benefits of equity crowdfunding can be summed up in one word: fun.

---

[9]Be careful not to view highly rated investors, who are not paid fees for their opinions and advice, as true investment advisers. People who give advice to investors and earn fees for it must comply with strict regulations, including the Investment Advisers Act of 1940.

If the risks don't scare you, and you want to consider investing via equity crowdfunding, please approach it with the following guidelines, for starters:

- Allocate no more than 5 to 10 percent of your investable capital to "alternative" private investments such as startup and early-stage deals.
- Because of the highly illiquid nature of angel investments in general, don't invest more money than you can afford to lose access to for several years.
- Give yourself time—say, a year or two—to make small angel investments, learn the fundamentals, maybe make mistakes, and acquire investment skills before you commit substantial money to angel investing.

The following chapters will help you learn the fundamentals, navigate the portals, comply with the rules, make smart decisions, minimize mistakes, and become a skilled equity crowdfunding investor.

## REGULATIONS WILL EVOLVE

Equity crowdfunding is a new branch of the highly regulated private capital markets. Just as the existing branches have evolved over the decades, with revision and fine-tuning of the laws and rules that govern them, so will this new branch evolve, especially in the next five years or so.

As this book goes to press, we expect the SEC to issue final rules to implement Title III in 2015, and then equity crowdfunding portals can launch and all investors will be able to participate in Title III equity offerings. It is possible that Congress will pass new legislation to improve some provisions of Title III in 2015 or soon thereafter.

Throughout the following chapters, we will point out where it is likely that the laws and rules might change. We will post updates on this book's website (www.wiley.com/equitycf) and in "refreshed" editions of the book and other Wiley publications.

# Definitions of Key Terms

**V**arious terms are being used by different people in reference to equity crowdfunding and related platforms, portals, and rules. The variety of terms can get confusing. Because this is a brand-new industry, governed by fairly complex laws and regulations, it will take a few years before everyone settles on a single nomenclature. To avoid confusion, here are the terms we use predominantly in this book:

**Crowdfunding platforms**   Websites that host crowdfunding campaigns. These include donation, rewards, and Title III securities (debt and equity) crowdfunding sites that are open to participation by everyone (the crowd). They do not include Regulation D securities offering platforms because those are open only to accredited investors, not the crowd. (Some people, nevertheless, might refer to Reg D offering platforms as crowdfunding platforms—we think this nomenclature creates confusion.)

**Equity crowdfunding**   The offering and sale of equity-based private securities to all investors (including nonaccredited ones), authorized by Title III of the JOBS Act. Equity means ownership, and an investor who purchases equity shares becomes a part owner in the company that issues those shares. Such offerings can be made only through registered intermediaries, whether broker-dealers or funding portals.

**Funding portals**   One of the two kinds of intermediaries (the other kind being broker-dealer platforms) authorized by Title III of the JOBS Act to host offerings of private equity-based securities via crowdfunding.

**Regulation D offering platforms**   Websites that host offerings of Regulation D (or Reg D) securities, open only to accredited investors. These platforms, which may feature both Rule 506(b) and Rule 506(c) offerings, look like crowdfunding portals in some respects, but they are *not* open to all investors (the crowd).

**Title III**   One of the seven titles in the Jumpstart Our Business Startups (JOBS) Act of 2012. Title III authorizes equity crowdfunding and allows participation by all investors, both accredited and nonaccredited. Title III adds the "crowdfunding exemption" to the list of offerings that are exempt from SEC registration, as set forth in Section 4 of the Securities Act of 1933.

**Title III equity offerings**    This means the same thing as equity crowdfunding offerings, but we sometimes refer to Title III in order to (1) remind readers of the legal basis for equity crowdfunding and (2) distinguish between equity crowdfunding (for all investors) and Regulation D offerings (for accredited investors only).

# Acknowledgments

The authors thank Sara Hanks, securities lawyer and CEO of Crowd-Check, for her help in reviewing each chapter and making suggestions for improving the book's accuracy and usefulness.

Thanks to Harriet Kohn and Paulina Freedman for their love and inspiration.—David M. Freedman

Total and unqualified thanks to my stunningly beautiful, near perfect wife, Christine, and the perfect God who created her.—Matthew R. Nutting

# About the Authors

David M. Freedman has worked as a financial and legal journalist since 1978 (www.freedman-chicago.com). He has served on the editorial staff of *The Value Examiner* (published by the National Association of Certified Valuators and Analysts) since 2005. He is coauthor of the 1987 book *Death of an American* (Crossroad/Continuum), about the *Singer v. Wadman* civil rights lawsuit in Salt Lake City. He is also the author of *Box-Making Basics* (Taunton Press), a bestselling woodworking book.

Matthew R. Nutting practices corporate law with the firm Coleman & Horowitt (www.ch-law.com) in Fresno, California, where he advises entrepreneurs, early-stage companies, and investors on all facets of business law, including a special emphasis in rewards-based and securities-based crowdfunding. He is a director of the National Crowdfunding Association (www.nlcfa.org), was its National Legal Affairs Director, and cofounder of CrowdPassage (www.crowdpassage.com).

# CHAPTER 1

# The Foundations of Online Crowdfunding

## A History of Rewards-, Donation-, and Debt-Based Crowdfunding Platforms

The emergence of online crowdfunding platforms over the past decade, like the birth of e-commerce in the 1990s, has generated a lot of excitement among entrepreneurs, Web developers, consumers, and investors (and their lawyers) eager to exploit new opportunities. Crowdfunding also threatens to disrupt some existing financial institutions and professions, as e-commerce disrupted the retail landscape two decades ago.

In fact, some exuberant pioneers and early participants have predicted that crowdfunding will spark a revolution in private capital markets, if not the *redefinition of Wall Street*.[1] At this early stage, nobody can say definitively whether their exuberance is misplaced.

It perplexes those pioneers, therefore, that so many people still have not even heard of crowdfunding, or have heard of it but barely understand how it works, or don't realize that there are big differences between the various kinds of crowdfunding.

So we begin with a broad definition. Crowdfunding is a method of collecting many small contributions, by means of an online funding platform, to finance or capitalize a popular enterprise. It is a new, high-tech version of a centuries-old practice. As crowdfunding is so new, there is much confusion in the marketplace about it—for example, many people still think of Kickstarter as the epitome of crowdfunding. Kickstarter may be the prime example of rewards-based crowdfunding (which is the most popular kind today), but there are a few other distinct kinds of crowdfunding, including donation- and securities-based crowdfunding; the latter includes both debt-based and equity-based offering platforms. We will help you distinguish

---

[1] A December 17, 2013, conference in New York City, cosponsored by Thomson Reuters, was called "Crowdfinance 2013: Redefining Wall Street."

between them and, especially, learn what makes equity crowdfunding different from its ancestors.

A classic example of old-fashioned (pre-Internet) crowdfunding is
Joseph Pulitzer's campaign to finance the construction of a granite pedestal
for the Statue of Liberty in 1885. France had donated the statue, designed
by sculptor Frederic Auguste Bartholdi, to the United States to celebrate the
friendship between the two countries and their mutual respect for republi-
can ideals. After France shipped the statue to America in June 1885, it sat
unassembled in a warehouse for a year while the pedestal was being built
here. Construction of the pedestal had been delayed because the American
Committee of the Statue of Liberty ran out of money for the project.

The cost to build the pedestal and place the statue upon it was estimated
at $300,000, but the American Committee could raise just over half of that.
The State of New York refused to help fund it, as did the U.S. Congress.

The cities of Baltimore, Boston, San Francisco, and Philadelphia offered
to finance construction of the pedestal if the statue would be relocated.
Pulitzer, the Hungarian-born publisher of the *New York World* newspaper,
dearly wanted the statue to remain in his city, so he used the power of the
press to urge New Yorkers to help fund the project. He wrote in the *World*,
with a fair measure of accuracy, that construction of the statue itself had been
paid for by many small donations from "the masses of the French people—by
the working men, the tradesmen, the shop girls, the artisans—by all, irrespec-
tive of class or condition." He made a dramatic appeal in his newspaper to
the masses on this side of the Atlantic:

> *Let us not wait for the millionaires to give us this money. It is not a
> gift from the millionaires of France to the millionaires of America,
> but a gift of the whole people of France to the whole people of
> America.*[2]

Fund-raising activities sponsored by Pulitzer included boxing matches,
art exhibitions, theater productions, and the sale of small statuettes of liberty
for $1 (6 inches tall) and $5 (12 inches tall). The largest donors received
commemorative gold coins.

Within five months, the *World* collected $102,000 in donations (roughly
$2.3 million in today's dollars), from 125,000 people, all of which it for-
warded to the American Committee, and the pedestal project was revived.
Most of the donations were in amounts of $1 or less.

---

[2]Joseph Pulitzer, *New York World*, March 16, 1885, as reported by the National
Park Service, U.S. Department of the Interior, at www.nps.gov/stli/historyculture/
joseph-pulitzer.htm, accessed October 2013.

As a reward to donors, the *World* published their names, regardless of the dollar amount (which had the fortunate result of increasing the paper's circulation).

The Statue of Liberty was assembled, mounted, and dedicated to America on October 28, 1886, in a ceremony presided over by President Grover Cleveland—who, ironically, as governor of New York, a year earlier had vetoed a plan to fund the pedestal project.

## THE INTERNET DOESN'T CHANGE EVERYTHING

That was the nineteenth-century version of crowdfunding, although the word didn't yet exist in the English language. The twenty-first-century version relies on the power of the Internet, of course—specifically, e-commerce and social networks merged into online funding platforms and portals.

Although the technology is vastly different, in many ways Pulitzer's version of crowdfunding is strikingly similar to today's version. Both versions involve issuing emotional appeals via the most advanced mass dissemination tools of the time to crowds of ordinary (rather than just wealthy) supporters, most of whom contribute small amounts and receive rewards commensurate with their level of contribution. For some of those contributors, simply the satisfaction of helping a worthy project succeed is a significant benefit.

## BUT THE INTERNET CHANGES SOME THINGS

You have probably heard of Joseph Pulitzer, more likely because of the Pulitzer Prize than his 1885 civic crowdfunding project. You have probably not heard of Brian Camelio, one of the pioneers of modern crowdfunding. A Boston musician and computer programmer, Camelio attended a West African dance show in 2000 and was amazed (and inspired) when people in the audience got up out of their seats, ran up to the stage, and literally threw money at the dancers.

It occurred to Camelio that this method of funding artists provided a solution to the growing problem of piracy in the music industry. That is, once a digital version of a recording is published on the Internet, it's too easy for pirates to download it illegally, depriving the composer, recording artist, and/or producer of revenue that they deserve. Throwing money at a performing artist on stage certainly solves the problem on a very small scale, but what about the thousands of recording artists who haven't yet performed in public?

Camelio developed a website where fans of a musician can figuratively throw money at the artist, in effect prepurchasing the recording (or other reward), before their digital recording was released. He named the site Artist-Share. Launched in 2003, ArtistShare's first crowdfunding project (which the ArtistShare team called "fan-funding" then) was Maria Schneider's jazz album *Concert in the Garden*. Through the funding platform, Schneider's fans could contribute money in specified amounts to help her compose and produce the album. Fans who contributed $9.95, for example, got to be among the first customers to download the album *legally* upon its release in 2004. Fans who contributed $250 or more (in addition to receiving an album download) were listed, in the booklet that accompanied the album, as Bronze Participants who "helped to make this recording possible." One fan, who contributed $10,000, was (as specified in the ArtistShare campaign) listed as an executive producer and invited to dine with the artist at a New York restaurant; another, who contributed $18,000, went bird-watching with Schneider in Central Park, among other rewards.

Schneider's ArtistShare campaign raised about $130,000, although neither Schneider nor Camelio is willing to disclose the number of contributors.[3] That funding enabled the artist to compose the music, pay her musicians, rent a large recording studio, and produce and market the album (it was sold exclusively through the ArtistShare website), which won a 2005 Grammy Award for best large jazz ensemble album.

ArtistShare still supports many musicians and composers in various genres, and also a small number of photographers and filmmakers, each of whom must submit an application and be selected before they can appear on the platform—in other words, the site is curated. The site enables artists to "share" their creative process with fans through innovative content management tools. Artists typically offer, in exchange for funding, such rewards as advance copies of CDs, "VIP access" to performances (e.g., front-row seats or backstage passes), private concerts, attendance at rehearsals and recording sessions, getting your picture taken with the artist, being named as a producer, and other perks, in addition to the basic (legal) digital download. When Schneider won another Grammy in 2008, for her work on the *Sky Blue* album, one of her biggest ArtistShare contributors was named executive producer and attended the Grammy Award ceremony with her.

When Schneider embarked on her groundbreaking crowdfunding campaign, before the fan-funding concept had been tested, much less proven, "a lot of other musicians and people in the recording industry told me I was crazy to abandon the traditional model of production and distribution," she says. The key to her success on ArtistShare was her devoted fan base, on which she knew she could rely. The funding platform allows connection and

---

[3] Based on e-mail correspondence with Maria Schneider and the ArtistShare publicity team, October 2013.

communication between artist and fans that the traditional business model could not. The success of crowdfunding for Schneider went beyond dollars to "long-term relationships with my fans," she says.

In all ArtistShare campaigns, the artists keep 85 percent of the funds generated and retain full ownership of their copyrights and master tapes—a significant departure from the traditional music industry. The funding platform keeps 15 percent. The platform also earns revenue on sales of music-related merchandise.

By the end of 2013, ArtistShare had funded music projects that resulted in four more Grammy Awards in addition to Schneider's two.

## REWARDS CROWDFUNDING BLASTS OFF

ArtistShare is an example of what we call rewards-based crowdfunding. U.S.-based Indiegogo, launched in 2008, and Kickstarter, launched a year later, are now the biggest rewards-based crowdfunding sites in the world, in terms of visitor traffic.[4] In addition to the arts (including fine art, comics, dance, design, fashion, film and video, music, photography, creative writing, theater), these sites host funding campaigns for social causes (animals, community, education, environment, health, politics, religion) and entrepreneurs and small businesses (food, sports, gaming, publishing, technology).

From its launch in 2009 to September 2014, Kickstarter hosted more than 180,000 funding campaigns, of which about 40 percent were successful. The 70,923 campaigns that succeeded raised a total of $1.335 billion from more than 7.1 million backers. That's about 100 backers for each successful campaign. About 27 percent of the campaigns raised more than $10,000, and about 2 percent raised more than $100,000. The business category with the most successfully funded projects on Kickstarter is—no surprise—music, followed closely by film/video, followed at a distance by art, publishing, theater, games, and nine other categories.[5] Kickstarter charges a fee of 5 percent of the funds collected in a fully funded campaign.

Not all projects are funded, of course. In an all-or-nothing funding model, roughly 44 percent are fully funded based on their stated goals, while the majority walk away with nothing. All-or-nothing means that if a project does not reach its stated funding goal within a stated campaign period, the campaign fails and the funders' credit cards are not charged—and the platform earns nothing. (Indiegogo allows both all-or-nothing and

---

[4] "Top 10 Crowdfunding Websites by Traffic," GoFundMe, October 16, 2013. Ranking by Alexa.com.
[5] Source: www.kickstarter.com/help/stats?ref=footer.

keep-it-all campaigns. In the latter, the project may keep all the funds it raises even if the goal is not reached.)

Rewards for funders of Kickstarter projects, like those on ArtistShare and most other crowdfunding sites, are usually tiered according to the size of the contribution. The Chipolo campaign is a good example, although the reward schemes vary so widely that it's hard to say what's typical.

The Chipolo is a small, colorful, battery-powered Bluetooth chip that you can fasten to valuable belongings such as mobile phones, laptops, backpacks, cameras, car keys, or even a pet collar, so that you can locate them if lost. The Slovenian-American inventors call it a "virtual leash." The chip connects wirelessly to a smartphone via the Chipolo app (for iPhone and Android), which you can use to locate the item with a beep within 60 meters, or on a GPS-based map anywhere. In fact, anyone with the app, not just the owner of the item, can use it (with the owner's consent) to find the lost item on behalf of its owner—making it a "crowd*finding*" device. The Chipolo team established a goal of raising $15,000 in 25 days on Kickstarter, starting October 21, 2013, so they could manufacture and market a pilot production run. The team promised to reward backers as follows (not a complete list):[6]

- Those who contributed $19 or more would receive a first-run Chipolo (estimated retail price $35), free shipping worldwide, with a projected delivery date in December 2013. This slot was limited to 200 backers, and indeed 200 people pledged $19 or more within two days.
- Those who pledged $34 or more would receive a Chipolo chip and T-shirt.
- Those who pledged $99 or more would receive four Chipolos in their choice of colors, with their names imprinted on them.
- Those who pledged $2,999 or more would receive nine Chipolos with their names imprinted and nine Chipolo T-shirts, personally delivered by one of the Chipolo team members to any major city in the world.

It is important to note that more than 20 backers pledged amounts less than $19, which means they did not receive a tangible reward—they simply wanted to support the Chipolo team and its product. To run a successful crowdfunding campaign, said another entrepreneur who did just that, "You don't want to merely sell people a product, you want to sell them a dream."[7]

---

[6] http://www.kickstarter.com/projects/1015015457/chipolo-bluetooth-item-finder -for-iphone-and-andro?ref=live, accessed October 23, 2013.
[7] Quoting Jake Bronstein of Brooklyn, owner of Flint and Tinder, which manufacturers "premium men's underwear" made in the USA. Bronstein's April-May 2012 Kickstarter campaign raised $291,493 from 5,578 backers, based on a goal of $30,000. (From e-mail correspondence with the authors on October 24, 2013.)

A week after the Chipolo Kickstarter campaign began, the pledges already amounted to $100,000, which is more than six times their goal ("6x" in the vernacular of venture capital)—although nobody had yet signed up for personalized delivery. Backers suggested additional applications for the chip, some of which the team incorporated into the design.

Campaigners whose contributions exceed their goals get to keep it all (minus Kickstarter's 5 percent), under the assumption that they will use those funds to keep the promises they made to their contributors.

One of the most outrageously successful, and subsequently famous, Kickstarter campaigns thus far was the Pebble watch. A group of entrepreneurs in Palo Alto, California, created a digital, customizable "smart watch" that runs downloadable sports and fitness apps and connects wirelessly to an iPhone or Android smartphone. The innovative high-tech features of this product are too numerous to mention here. The team sought $100,000 during the funding period spanning April and May 2012. With a pledge of $99 or more, backers could preorder the Pebble, the retail price of which was estimated at $150. Pledges of $220 or more were rewarded with two Pebble watches, and so on. The campaign raised a whopping $10,266,845 from 68,929 backers (average pledge $149).[8]

The most successful Kickstarter campaign to date has been the Coolest Cooler, which raised $13,285,000 from 62,000 backers in 2014. The company's funding goal was $50,000. Notably, that company failed in its previous Kickstarter campaign.

Significantly, all rewards-based crowdfunding campaigners retain their intellectual property (IP) rights: patents, trademarks, copyrights. In other words, Kickstarter (based in New York City) is not a producer or publisher or marketer but a sophisticated intermediary that connects campaigners with backers and enables backers to communicate among themselves in order to assess the merits and prospects of the campaign.

New rewards-based crowdfunding sites are emerging that focus on a narrow product category or niche market. Experiment (originally Micro-ryza), for example, is a crowdfunding site for hard-science research projects; funders are rewarded with "insight behind the science." Teespring is a Kickstarter-inspired site for designers of custom T-shirts.

An entrepreneur who wants to raise money does not have to use an established platform like ArtistShare, Kickstarter, or GoFundMe to mount a crowdfunding campaign. Anyone with a WordPress-based website, in fact, can use a crowdfunding plug-in to host a campaign on his or her own

---

[8] This project wasn't an unalloyed success. The company had fulfillment problems, and then some of the big tech companies copied its idea.

website. (Self-hosting will not work in the equity crowdfunding world, as we will see.)

Backers assume risks. Even when projects are fully funded, there is no guarantee that the entrepreneurs will fulfill their promises to backers, or do so on time (at least two studies found that most projects miss their delivery deadlines[9]). In that sense, contributing money to a project is risky, but the promised reward is perceived as sufficient to justify the risk. One Seattle company, ZionEyez (which later changed its name to Zeyez), raised $343,400 from more than 2,100 backers in June and July 2011 to produce eyeglasses with built-in high-definition video cameras. The company ran into production problems and as yet has neither shipped a product to backers nor offered them refunds.[10] Kickstarter does not mediate or intervene when funded companies fail to keep their promises.

## Wisdom and Madness of the Crowd

You might expect that giving hundreds of thousands of dollars to a bunch of startups in exchange for promises of products that haven't yet been marketed would result in a high occurrence of fraud. The fraud rate appears to be quite low, however. Ethan Mollick, assistant professor of management

---

[9]The latest study was Ethan R. Mollick, PhD, "The Dynamics of Crowdfunding: An Exploratory Study," *Journal of Business Venturing*, 2013. Mollick reported that "over 75 percent deliver products later than expected." His study was based on a dataset of over 48,500 Kickstarter projects with a combined funding of over $237 million. Available at http://papers.ssrn.com/sol3/papers.cfm?abstract_id= 2088298&http://papers.ssrn.com/sol3/papers.cfm?abstract_id=2088298. The other study relied on here was Julianne Pepitone, "Why 84% of Kickstarter's Top Projects Shipped Late," CNNMoney.com, December 18, 2012, http://money.cnn.com/2012 /12/18/technology/innovation/kickstarter-ship-delay/. This CNNMoney study focused on the 50 highest-funded Kickstarter campaigns, primarily in the technology and video game categories, with projected delivery dates of November 2012 or earlier. Only eight of those 50 projects hit their delivery deadlines.

[10]Mark Gibbs, "The Truth about Kickstarter and ZionEyez," *Forbes*, August 20, 2012. Also Blair Hanley Frank, "Eyez: One of Kickstarter's Biggest Busts Is Trying to Come Back from the Dead," GeekWire.com, July 12, 2013. See also the ZionEyez Kickstarter page: www.kickstarter.com/projects/zioneyez/eyeztm-by-zioneyez-hd -video-recording-glasses-for. ZionEyez or Zeyez is apparently under new leadership, including Matt Krumholz, vice chairman. The authors attempted unsuccessfully to contact Krumholz and the company through its website (www.zioneyez.com), via his LinkedIn profile, and by other means.

at the Wharton School, University of Pennsylvania, concluded in a 2013 study of 48,500 Kickstarter projects that "less than 1 percent of the funds in crowdfunding projects in technology and product design go to projects that seem to have little intention of delivering their results."[11] Mollick believes that the low rate of fraud (at least this particular type of fraud) is a result of "the influence of the community," by which he means the ability of backers and prospective backers to interact with each other, and with the campaigner, via comments and responses on the crowdfunding campaign's Web page. In other words, the continuous presence of the crowd and its highly social nature serve as a kind of screen or deterrent against possible abuses. The reason for the low rate of fraud on Kickstarter, for example,

> *is the persistent community built around Kickstarter projects, which allow many individuals (with verifiable real-world identities) to weigh in on projects, discussing the merits and probability of success of each project.*[12]

Such discussions are similar to those that "take place on other social media sites, blogs, and forums [as well as] Wikipedia and open-source software development," writes Mollick, whose main areas of study at Wharton are innovation and early-stage entrepreneurship. "These communities play several important roles in improving offerings, preventing fraud, and making crowdfunding successful. In the case of Kickstarter, communities have successfully detected fraudulent projects." The kind of fraud that Mollick addresses in his 2013 study is what we colloquially call "take the money and run." To be sure, there are other kinds of fraud in the context of crowdfunding that Professor Mollick does not address in his 2013 study. For example, Sara Hanks, CEO of CrowdCheck (a due diligence service provider in the Washington, D.C., area), points out that intentional or negligent misstatement in a rewards-based crowdfunding campaign could form the basis for liability, and there have been a number of campaigns where such misstatements have been alleged. But Mollick clearly believes in the wisdom of crowds, in the context of both rewards-based and equity-based crowdfunding. Unfortunately, Charles Mackay wrote his book *Extraordinary Popular Delusions and the Madness of Crowds* 270 years before Kickstarter.

---

[11] Mollick, op. cit.
[12] Letter from Ethan Mollick to Vladimir I. Ivanov, financial economist, Office of Corporate Finance, U.S. Securities and Exchange Commission, December 2012.

## OCULUS RIFT HIGHLIGHTS THE DIFFERENCE BETWEEN REWARDS AND EQUITY CROWDFUNDING

The distinction between rewards- and equity-based crowdfunding zoomed into widespread consciousness in March 2014, when Facebook acquired Oculus VR for more than $2 billion. Oculus had two years earlier run a successful Kickstarter campaign, where it raised more than $2.4 million.

On March 26, 2014, the *Huffington Post* posted an article with the intentionally naive title "I Backed Oculus Rift on Kickstarter and All I Got Was This Lousy T-Shirt."

Oculus VR, based in Long Beach, California, is an "immersive virtual reality technology" developer. Its very first product was Oculus Rift, a virtual reality headset for 3D gaming, which looks like big, industrial-strength goggles that wrap around the eyes and ears. The company launched its Kickstarter campaign in the summer of 2012 with a relatively modest (in hindsight) goal of raising $250,000. Backers who pledged $25 or more would receive as a reward an Oculus VR T-shirt. Those who pledged $275 or more would receive an unassembled Oculus Rift prototype kit. Several steps up the pledge ladder, backers who pledged $5,000 or more got 10 kits (and a T-shirt, poster, and a few other things) plus a full-day visit to the Oculus lab. Seven backers went for it.

Oculus blew through its goal and raised $2,437,429 from 9,522 backers in about a month. The campaign closed on September 1, 2012. Backers eventually received their promised rewards. A consumer version of the Rift could be available in the spring of 2015. Everyone was happy.

Then venture capital firm Spark Partners and hedge fund Matrix Partners each invested $19 million in Oculus. Facebook finally bought Oculus for $300 million in cash, $1.6 billion in Facebook stock, and another few hundred million in incentives (subject to Oculus meeting certain milestones). When that happened, the value of those equity investments by Spark and Matrix grew to about $380 million each, a 20x gain in less than a year.

The Kickstarter backers had not bought equity in Oculus, but some of them posted crabby and even angry messages on the Oculus Rift Kickstarter page (and elsewhere). One backer, for example, wrote: "You selling out to Facebook is a disgrace. It damages not only your reputation, but the whole of crowdfunding. I cannot put into words how betrayed I feel." The gist of most of the complaints was that the early backers deserved better rewards because they helped Oculus shareholders strike it rich.

Mo Koyman, a partner at Spark Capital, responded to the ruckus by explaining: "Just because people say 'Well I want equity in this company' doesn't mean it's available. I don't think the Kickstarter backers were backing it because they wanted a financial win. . . . They wanted to try it, wanted to experience it, wanted to see it. They got exactly what they bargained for."[*]

Business media outlets took the opportunity to explain that Kickstarter is not an equity-based platform, and the law did not allow average investors (the crowd) to buy equity on any kind of platform in the United States at that time, so backers (who received the rewards they expected) had no right to expect capital gains from their contributions. Bloomberg posted an article on the same day as the *Huffington Post* story, in which it distinguished between rewards-based Kickstarter and equity-based CircleUp. Bloomberg said that CircleUp "is among crowdfunding sites focused on letting individuals buy stock in startups," and quoted CircleUp's CEO Rory Eakin, in a plug for equity-based crowdfunding: "Imagine if those early [Kickstarter] supporters were equity investors . . . "

[*] Originally quoted by Adrianne Jeffries, "If You Back a Kickstarter Project That Sells for $2 Billion, Do You Deserve to Get Rich?" The Verge, March 28, 2014.
Source: Serena Saitto, "Oculus Deal Said to Deliver 20-Fold Return to Spark, Matrix," Bloomberg News, March 26, 2014. On that same day, CircleUp announced that it had raised $14 million in venture capital from Canaan Partners and Google's venture arm.

## Rewards as a Gateway to Equity

As the Oculus Rift campaign on Kickstarter demonstrated (see sidebar), rewards-based and equity-based crowdfunding are two very different animals in terms of what you can expect in return for the funds you provide to startups. You can't buy equity in companies listed on Kickstarter, and, beyond the specific reward you sign up for, you can't share in the upside if the startup you fund gets acquired by Facebook for billions of dollars.

Even if your aim is to be an equity crowdfunding investor, by first exploring a few rewards-based crowdfunding platforms you can learn a lot about the crowdfunding infrastructure and vernacular, the social media aspect of crowdfunding, and the collaborative nature of the crowd. It is a valuable orientation that will not cost you much. We recommend that you at least browse through the projects seeking backers, read the updated funding stats and comments posted by other visitors, and then register on the portal that you like most and spend a few tens or hundreds of dollars to experience the process. Perhaps acquire some new music or gadgets while you're at it, and maybe have more fun than you expected. See how it feels to be a member of a crowd. You can find various lists of crowdfunding sites (including "top 10" lists compiled by *Forbes, Entrepreneur,* GoFundMe, and others) by searching for "crowdfunding sites" on a search engine.[13]

We strongly recommend that before you risk thousands of dollars investing via equity-based crowdfunding, you should become familiar with the crowdfunding concept and process in a relatively risk-free environment like the rewards-based version. Rewards-based crowdfunding platforms like Kickstarter can be good training, from a navigation and social point of view, for equity-based crowdfunding portals. We will help you learn the investing aspects of equity crowdfunding in later chapters.

## DEBT AND DONATION CROWDFUNDING

Before we introduce the equity-based version, it is worth looking at two more types of large-scale crowdfunding platforms that preceded equity-based crowdfunding in the United States: debt-based and donation-based.

Debt-based (or what in the United Kingdom is called "lending-based") crowdfunding began at the nonprofit level in 2005, when Kiva Microfunds was launched by Matt Flannery, a software programmer in San Francisco, and Jessica Jackley, who had worked for a microfinance institution in Africa. Kiva is now the fourth-biggest crowdfunding site in the world in terms of traffic, as measured by Alexa (a website information, analytics, and ranking service).

Flannery and Jackley, a married couple, call their business model "person-to-person microfinance." The Kiva website features individuals in the "developing world," some of them impoverished, who apply for

---

[13]Most of the lists that rank crowdfunding sites do so from the point of view of entrepreneurs and business owners, not investors. An example is *Forbes*'s "Top 10 Crowdfunding Sites for Fundraising," by Chance Barnett, May 8, 2013, www.forbes .com/sites/chancebarnett/2013/05/08/top-10-crowdfunding-sites-for-fundraising/.

unsecured loans to build or grow small businesses, ranging from amounts as small as $25. In the beginning, Kiva featured only overseas borrowers, especially in Africa and Latin America. In 2009 it broadened its scope to include borrowers in U.S. and Canadian communities that are underserved by banks and traditional lenders, and in 2012 it introduced student loans (in a partnership with Strathmore University in Kenya). Kiva also serves borrowers in the Middle East, Southeast Asia, and India.

Kiva is not an investment platform. People who register as lenders on Kiva can get back their principal, but no interest. The borrowers do pay interest on their loans, but those interest payments flow to the local and regional microfinance institutions that administer the loans in the various countries.

People who lend money through the Kiva website get to "meet" their borrowers through online profiles, photos, and updates. A majority of lenders end up considering it a donation. When their principal is returned—which happens 98 percent of the time—a majority of lenders keep the funds in the Kiva system, loaning them out again and again. For that reason, lending money via Kiva or a similar nonprofit debt-based crowdfunding platform is not considered investing. (Debt-based investing is where the lender seeks a return in the form of principal plus interest.)

By the end of 2014, Kiva had provided microloans totaling $668 million to more than 1,546,000 borrowers in 85 countries, funded by around 1.26 million lenders on the Kiva platform, and facilitated globally by 290 microlending institutions (which Kiva calls "field partners"). The average loan size to borrowers is $417, and the average amount that lenders contribute is a modest $9.90. The repayment rate, based on a total of 834,274 loans, is 98.8 percent.[14] The largest loan Kiva ever made was $100,000 for an agricultural project in ruralHaiti, in 2014.

Kiva itself generates revenue ($17,394,130 in 2012, according to its annual report that year) not by billing its field partners who collect interest on loans, but from grants, corporate sponsors, foundations, and individual donors on the Kiva website. Opting not to take any bit of the interest on loans earned by field partners gave Kiva freedom from regulation by the U.S. Securities and Exchange Commission (SEC), as it is not considered an investment company.

While Kiva is not an investment platform, its success does help us understand the power of crowdfunding to reach the charitable and other interests of the public at large. In effect, sites like Kickstarter and Kiva proved the concept that crowds of people will fund projects and enterprises they believe in.

---

[14]Kiva statistics are updated at www.kiva.org/about/stats.

## Lending to Your Peers

Debt-based crowdfunding emerged as a for-profit investment vehicle in 2006 in the United States, and a year earlier in the United Kingdom. The debt-based version of crowdfunding (also known as peer-to-peer lending, or P2P) lets individual borrowers apply for unsecured loans (not backed by collateral) and, if accepted by the platform, borrow money from "the crowd," then pay it back with interest. Unlike the nonprofit Kiva model, the for-profit P2P platform generates revenue by taking a percentage of the loan amounts (a one-time charge) from the borrower and a loan servicing fee (either a fixed annual fee or a one-time percentage of the loan amount) from investors. The application process is free for borrowers. Investors earn the interest on each loan (or package of similar loans), assuming the borrowers make timely payments.

From the borrower's point of view, getting a P2P loan can be simpler, quicker, and cheaper than borrowing from a bank. It is cheaper (that is, fixed interest rates are generally lower) because most of the P2P platform's services (application review and verification, credit check, loan disbursement, payment processing, collection, compliance and reporting, etc.) are automated. This results in lower overhead.

Only a small percentage of applications are approved. For example, Lending Club (launched in 2007 in San Francisco by Renaud Laplanche), the largest P2P platform in the world in terms of issued loan volume and revenue, has an approval rate of about 10 percent.[15]

Interest rates are still high enough, though, to generate strong returns for investors (assuming sufficient diversification)—potentially better returns than traditional money markets and bonds, with less volatility than stocks—and a reliable monthly cash flow of interest and principal payments throughout the term of the loan. In October 2013, Lending Club was charging borrowers a rate of 24.44 percent for its riskiest loans, sliding down to 7.65 percent for its least risky ones.

From the investor's point of view, although the minimum investment can be as low as $25,[16] P2P platforms are more complex than rewards-based platforms because they involve securities regulated by the SEC. You'll find a lot more fine print and footnotes on P2P platforms, and you'll come across terms you might not have heard of, such as "prime consumer notes." Unlike the Kickstarter experience, you'll need to spend quite a bit of time learning

---

[15]Data from May 9, 2013.

[16]Prosper, the second-largest P2P platform, recommends, however, that you should invest "a minimum of $10,000 to create a well-diversified portfolio of at least 400 loans" to diversify the risk, according to Ron Suber, head of global institutional sales.

how the P2P system works, what the possible risks and returns are for each particular lending opportunity, and what kinds of secondary markets exist[17] before you commit your money to a single borrower or a package of loans. Note that P2P investors do not have to be accredited, which will be thoroughly explained in Chapter 2.

Most P2P platforms lend only to individuals, not to businesses, although the funds can be used by the borrower to pay small-business expenses. We are starting to see the emergence of small-business lending platforms, which will proliferate if P2P default rates stay reasonably low. Lending Club, for example, launched a small-business lending platform in 2014.

Each borrower whose application is approved on a P2P platform receives a credit-risk score and interest rate set uniquely by that platform, acting as an intermediary between borrower and investor. Higher risks must yield higher rates to stay attractive, of course. Investors can select individual creditworthy borrowers based on their risk/rate profiles, in addition to other characteristics such as reason for the loan (debt consolidation, home improvement, major purchase, car finance, healthcare expense, small-business expense, vacation, etc.). Alternatively, investors may select a package of dozens, hundreds, or even thousands of loans in the same risk/rate tranche, which allows diversification among many borrowers. In all cases, the risk for investors is that one or more borrowers will default, so that some or all of the investor's capital may be lost.

After the 2008–2009 recession, when banks tightened up consumer credit and borrowers were more willing to consider alternative financing options, P2P lending took off. As of June 2014, Lending Club alone had serviced more than 379,000 loans for over $5 billion, with an average loan size of $14,000 for personal loans. The platform has paid investors $494 million in interest since its launch in 2007. Its default rates have varied from about 1.5 percent for the least risky borrowers to 10 percent for the riskiest.

By far the most common purpose for borrowing money via Lending Club was refinancing existing loans and paying off credit card balances (those two categories account for 83 percent of all loans), followed by home improvement (about 6 percent), business (2 percent), major purchases, car financing, medical expenses, and others.

Given its historical rates of interest and default, Lending Club projects returns to investors of about 5.6 percent for prime consumer notes in the least risky tranches and 9.2 percent in the riskier tranches. So, for example, according to the Lending Club marketing pitch, "if you invested $100,000

---

[17]The largest U.S. P2P platforms, Lending Club and Prosper, formed partnerships with Folio Investing to create a secondary market for their notes.

in 36-month, grade C notes [Lending Club's ratings range from grades A through G] providing an aggregate 9.5 percent net annualized return, you would receive approximately $3,200 each month in cash payments,"[18] which you can withdraw or reinvest.

The growing popularity of P2P, especially since 2009, started attracting institutional investors such as insurance companies and pension funds, which accelerated growth further. In fact, because institutional investors are not really peers, some finance professionals are starting to refer to P2P as "marketplace lending."

Some P2P platforms, including Lending Club and Prosper (the second-largest P2P platform, also launched in 2006 from San Francisco) pay referral fees to financial advisers who direct investors to those platforms. As a sign of commercial validation, in 2013 Google invested $125 million in Lending Club. Finally, Lending Club went public in December of 2014, raising $1 billion and nailing down a valuation of almost $9 billion.

Although we urge you to consider debt-based crowdfunding as a means to diversify your investment portfolio, we are focusing narrowly on equity-based crowdfund investing in this book.

## Donation Crowdfunding

Large charitable organizations began collecting donations online long before Web-based crowdfunding emerged. But by 2010, new donation-based crowdfunding sites allowed small organizations and individuals to solicit donations from the crowd. Examples include local organizations set up for disaster relief and emergency fund-raising, or for a Little League team's travel expenses to a championship tournament, or for a high school choir's trip abroad. This online fund-raising strategy is also used by individuals who need to raise money from family and friends (and friends of friends) for "personal causes" such as covering medical and veterinary expenses, paying college tuition, or for "life events" like buying someone a graduation or anniversary gift.

GoFundMe, launched in 2010, is a pioneer in donation-based crowdfunding. As of October 2014, the GoFundMe platform had enabled its "users" to raise $500 million in 1 million campaigns, from 7 million donors. The platform takes 5 percent of each donation. Users also pay a processing fee on each transaction to WePay (a third-party payment service provider), amounting to at least 2.9 percent plus 30 cents in the United States. In 2014 GoFundMe was the second-most-visited crowdfunding site in the world

---

[18]LendingClub.com, October 2013, https://www.lendingclub.com/public/steady-returns.action.

(behind Kickstarter; Indiegogo was ranked third), according to Alexa rankings.

Whereas Kickstarter accepts only U.S.-based projects, GoFundMe (located in San Diego, California) operates in Australia, the United Kingdom, and the European Union, as well as the United States and Canada. Also unlike Kickstarter, GoFundMe lets users embed their donation pages on their own websites and blogs and still track donations and manage performance from the GoFundMe dashboard.

Here is an example of the power of a GoFundMe campaign. When teenager Farrah Soudani was critically injured in the Aurora, Colorado, movie theater massacre in November 2012, her family, friends, and social networking connections donated $171,525 in 15 months, via 6,088 donations, on the GoFundMe platform—still short of the $200,000 goal—to help pay her medical expenses. Farrah and her unemployed mother had no health insurance at the time.

## EMERGENCE OF EQUITY CROWDFUNDING

By the time Congress passed the JOBS Act in 2012, and the slow process of implementing equity crowdfunding began to roll in the United States, funding platform technology was maturing, and crowdfunding business models had been tested and proven. Many entrepreneurs and small-business owners, starved for capital in a slow-growth, postrecession economy, were eager to exploit crowdfunding as a way to raise equity as well as debt financing. (You'll find a definition and comprehensive description of equity crowdfunding, with an explanation of its rewards and risks for investors, in Chapter 2.)

Many individual investors, starved for yield, welcomed equity crowdfunding as a way to gain access to venture and angel capital deals. But the equity crowdfunding industry faced (and still faces) two obstacles to its popular acceptance. First, because of securities regulations dating back to 1933, investing in U.S. startups and small, private businesses was restricted largely to accredited investors—the high-net-worth and high-income elite. So tens of millions of nonaccredited investors had no familiarity or comfort with the idea of investing in small, nonpublic companies. Second, although rewards-based crowdfunding was well known to everyone in the recording industry and to many high-tech entrepreneurs, many, if not most, investors—and their financial advisers—had not heard of crowdfunding, and fewer still knew anything about *equity* crowdfunding.

Thanks to (1) the JOBS Act of 2012, which opened equity crowdfunding to nonaccredited investors and (2) the regulations for equity crowdfunding to be issued by the SEC and FINRA in 2015 or soon after, equity crowdfunding is about to become a lot less obscure.

# CHAPTER 2

# Equity Offering Platforms (under Regulation D)

## For Accredited Investors Only

The success of rewards-based crowdfunding platforms like Kickstarter (which we described in Chapter 1) proved that large numbers of people would happily fund artists, startups, and small enterprises that they believed in, even when the promised reward was modest and/or had not yet been produced. It was only natural that intermediaries in the angel capital world would exploit and adapt the rewards-based crowdfunding platform infrastructure, harnessing the power of website technology, social media, and e-commerce to accomplish the following objectives:

- Unite startups and growing companies with angel investors.
- Announce equity offerings and disclose deal terms.
- Enable investors to collaborate on due diligence.
- Facilitate investment transactions.

From the issuer's point of view, equity offering platforms present a streamlined process compared with the old, "off-platform" angel capital funding model. Off-platform, it typically takes 8 to 12 months for an entrepreneur to find angels who are interested in an offering and negotiate a deal. Today on equity offering platforms it typically takes two to eight weeks from the time an issuer lists its offer to closing a deal with investors, and in some cases less than a week or even a day. Further, equity offering platforms attract strategic investors to deals from across the country, whereas in the past it was frequently a matter of promoting a deal through a network of personal and professional relationships that spanned a metropolitan area or narrow region of the country. These platforms aggregate angel investors in a way that had not been possible before.

It's not just the ability to aggregate a larger number of potential investors from a wider area that makes funding platforms powerful tools for issuers of equity shares. Another advantage is that these platforms

**TABLE 2.1** Websites That Facilitate Equity Investment in Private Companies

| Regulation D offering platforms<br>*Short version: Reg D platforms* | Title III equity crowdfunding portals<br>*Short version: Title III portals* |
|---|---|
| Authorized by Regulation D under the Securities Act of 1933. | Authorized by Title III of the Jumpstart Our Business Startups (JOBS) Act of 2012. |
| First U.S. platforms launched 2011. | First U.S. portals may launch 2015. |
| For accredited investors only.<br>No investment limit for investors. | For all investors, including nonaccredited.<br>Investment limit based on net worth, income. |
| For issuers, no limit to amount raised. | Amount raised limited to $1 million per year. |

make it cost-effective for issuers to engage with investors who can afford to invest only small amounts. Off-platform offerings often involve face-to-face meetings with many potential investors, individually and occasionally in groups, which is time-consuming and expensive. Funding platforms automate much of that process, typically lowering the minimum investment for angel investors by a factor of 5 or 10.

From the investor's point of view, instead of making a lot of inquiries via phone calls and e-mails, meeting with broker-dealers, and joining angel investor clubs to find suitable private offerings, it is now possible to find deals by browsing one or more offering platforms (or visiting deal aggregators such as CrowdWatch and others). Smart investors might still make phone calls, attend meetings, and join clubs, but they can complement and accelerate the search online, where there are no travel and entertainment expenses.

In the United States, on the national level, equity offering platforms developed along two separate tracks: Regulation D and Title III. (See Table 2.1.) We will give you an orientation to Regulation D platforms first, not only because they are several years older than Title III crowdfunding portals, but also because, from a technical point of view, most Title III portals derived directly from Reg D platform infrastructure.

## DEFINITIONS

As we write this in early 2015, many financial advisers, not to mention average investors, still have not heard of equity offering platforms or equity crowdfunding. We can't assume readers of this book know exactly what *equity* means, in fact, so we will define that first. *Equity* has various meanings in law, but in finance it means ownership. When you make an equity investment in a company, you purchase ownership shares of, or equity in, the company. When the company issues, offers, and sells shares of stock, it is raising funds by means of equity financing.

The success of an equity investment in a company depends *primarily* on the company's profitability. More accurately, it depends on (1) the investing public's expectations of the company's future profitability and (2) the perceived value of the company to another company that might acquire it. If the company earns a profit consistently, its board of directors may approve distribution of dividends (i.e., a share of the profits) to its shareholders (equity owners), and the value of the company, and therefore its stock shares, will probably rise. For a broader perspective, see the sidebar "The Difference between Equity and Debt Financing."

---

## THE DIFFERENCE BETWEEN EQUITY AND DEBT FINANCING

To really understand equity financing, it is useful to compare it with its counterpart, debt financing. When a company borrows money, whether from an institution or from an individual, that is debt financing. The instrument might be called a bond, note, loan, or indenture, but they all mean about the same thing—they are loans that must be repaid. The company is obligated to repay the principal (amount borrowed) plus interest to the lender over a specified term. If the company is profitable and the business grows during the term of the loan, the company still owes the lender the same principal and interest, which—thanks to the company's growth—now seems relatively modest. If the company operates at a loss, however, and is barely solvent at any point during the loan term, it still owes the lender the same principal and interest, which now seems like a huge burden. On the other side of the table, whether or not the borrower is profitable, the lender earns the expected return on its loan, assuming no default; the lender does not otherwise benefit from the company's strong growth (i.e., it does not share the upside) or suffer from its lack of growth (the downside).

Notes are negotiable, meaning they can be transferred or resold, like bonds, at a premium or at a discount, depending on the borrower's perceived ability to pay.

Equity is a different arrangement altogether. When a company raises money by selling stock, the investor buys a stake in the company's success. If the company is profitable and grows, its stock will rise in value, and at some point the investor can sell it for a gain. A shareholder may also benefit from any distributions, such as dividends, that the company pays. If the company fails to earn a profit, its stock will probably lose value and the investor's return can be negative or even a total loss. So the equity investor shares in the upside or the downside, whichever it may be.

From the company's point of view, there are trade-offs: Debt financing involves keeping control (ownership) and upside, while being obligated to repay the loan in full plus interest no matter what—profit or no profit. (If it files for bankruptcy protection, it may owe only a percentage of its debt, but that's a complicated subject.) With equity financing, the company gives up some ownership and it must share its profits—in the form of dividends and/or capital gains—with investors at some point, but if the company is not profitable it has no obligation to share any revenue with investors. A capital gain is the increase in the value of company stock from the time you buy it to the time you sell it.

Mark Cuban, billionaire entrepreneur and *Shark Tank* shark, famously offered this advice to entrepreneurs: "If you're starting a business and you take out a loan, you're a moron. Because there are so many uncertainties involved with starting a business, yet the one certainty . . . is paying back your loan."* On the other hand, if the company fails, in most cases it is not obligated to repay equity investors. (We do not necessarily endorse Cuban's approach to finance, but many companies do take that approach.)

From the investor's point of view, debt financing provides a reasonably assured cash flow for the lender, whether the company is profitable or not. Equity financing provides a share of the profit to the investor *only if* the company earns a profit. For the investor, equity investing is generally considered riskier than debt investing because the equity investor can suffer a total loss, and any income or gains depend on the company's profitability (and even if the company does earn a profit, the value of its stock can fall).

The biggest benefit of equity investing is that when the company is *very* profitable, there is no limit to how high its stock value can soar. The biggest risk is that the company could conceivably stop operating and liquidate its assets, in which case some creditors may get paid but equity investors suffer a total loss.

Note also that startups and early-stage companies experience greater swings in both failures and grand successes than later-stage companies. For this reason the differences between the flat but steady return of debt financing and the variable up or down in equity are pronounced. This is one of the keys to understanding equity crowdfunding.

*Mark Cuban, interviewed on CGI America, Clinton Global Initiative, June 14, 2013.

For a realistic perspective on equity investing, there are two more elements to consider besides the company's profitability, growth, and stock value: liquidity and liability.

## Liquidity

If an asset is relatively easy to sell in exchange for cash, it is liquid. When you buy stock in a public company—one that is listed on a public stock exchange like the New York Stock Exchange (NYSE)—it is fairly simple to sell the shares anytime you want. That is, you can go to the stock exchange (or instruct your broker to do so) and offer your shares for sale, and almost certainly someone will buy them at or near the "running" price per share, as reported in the financial news media. In other words, public stock is *relatively* liquid—more liquid than real estate, for example, but not as liquid as cash, of course.

When you buy stock in a private company—a startup or growing small business not listed on a public stock exchange—then it is not so certain that you'll be able to sell those shares exactly when you would like to. The financial media do not routinely post private stock prices. In later chapters we will explain more about *secondary markets* for private shares, along with various "liquidity events" when investors can "cash out" of their private-company investments. As a preview, we'll just say here that although the market for small private-company shares (especially in response to the legalization of equity crowdfunding) is growing and evolving, equity in private companies is still quite illiquid.

Another obstacle to liquidating your shares is the legal or company-issued limitations. Title III of the Jumpstart Our Business Startups (JOBS) Act of 2012 imposes a 12-month minimum holding period, for example.

Also, companies can require some shareholders to sign agreements that restrict their ability to sell shares to anyone besides other shareholders of the same company. Such agreements are often in the company's formation documents, so each investor ought to carefully understand what limitations may apply prior to making an investment.

Of course, if the company you invest in ultimately goes public (i.e., it grows big enough to be listed on a public stock exchange), your liquidity worries are over. As we mentioned in the preface to this book, that happens rarely, although the JOBS Act may improve those chances, as we'll explain in Chapter 3. Another liquidity event is when a public company acquires the smaller entity and buys it in a stock-for-stock transaction, known as a *merger*. In that case, as a shareholder of the acquired company, you would end up inheriting public stock in exchange for shares held in the predecessor entity.

### Liability

As an equity investor—part owner—in a company, you are entitled to share in its success, whatever those benefits might be (e.g., dividends and capital gains). What about its liabilities? If the company is a defendant in a civil lawsuit, for example, are you obligated to show up in court and pay your share of any judgments? The short answer is usually no, as long as (1) the entity is properly established in compliance with state and local laws; (2) the entity is one where investor assets are protected from business risks, such as a corporation or limited liability company; and (3) you don't personally guarantee an obligation of the company. The terms of your equity investment will spell out the limits on investor liability, as we'll discuss in Chapter 11.

## REGULATION D BASICS

To understand how Reg D platforms work, and how investors can use them to their advantage, it helps to back up a few steps and learn the basics of Regulation D itself. Don't be concerned if this is all new to you. By the end of this chapter you will be well versed in the essentials.

Under U.S. securities law, predominantly the Securities Act of 1933, any company that wants to offer securities to investors, whether debt-based or equity-based securities, must either (1) register an offering with the SEC or (2) comply with the conditions for an exemption from SEC registration. Registration is *very* expensive and time-consuming (whether or not the offering is successful), so small and midsize companies usually attempt to rely on one of the several exemptions that the SEC and the courts have established over the years.

How expensive is registration? "The costs depend on the complexity of the business, the ability of the company's management team to provide support to outside attorneys and auditors, and the dollar size of the offering," explains Samuel S. Guzik, a securities lawyer with offices in Los Angeles and New York City. "For a [relatively small] company conducting an initial public offering, these fees alone will generally range from $200,000 on the low end to well over $1 million. These costs can drop significantly for a company that is already public, often as low as $25,000 to $75,000, since the company will have already developed comprehensive SEC disclosure documents, including audited financial statements, and typically will have internal financial controls in place." For a larger company, legal and accounting fees can amount to several million.

The SEC website (at http://www.sec.gov/info/smallbus/qasbsec.htm #noreg) summarizes the most commonly used exemptions for small businesses, including:

- Regulation D.
- Private placements under Section 4(a)(2) of the Securities Act.
- Intrastate offerings under Section 3(a)(11) of the Securities Act.
- The crowdfunding exemption (created by Title III of the JOBS Act) under new Section 4(a)(6) of the Securities Act.

Investors can be assured that all securities offerings and transactions, whether registered or exempt from registration, are subject to various antifraud provisions of federal securities laws. For example, any information that issuers provide to investors must be free of false or misleading statements. We will discuss fraud prevention further in Chapter 12.

In addition to federal securities laws and regulations, some types of offerings must comply with state securities laws and regulations (known as *blue sky laws*) in each state where their securities are offered and sold.

Regulation D is a set of rules adopted by the SEC in 1982 to clarify the conditions of certain exemptions from registration under the Securities Act of 1933. Reg D actually contains three different exemptions for private offerings: Rules 504, 505, and 506. Of the three, Rule 506 is by far the most popular; it accounts for 99 percent of the capital raised in Reg D offerings and 94 percent of the number of successful raises.[1] Those include offerings on Reg D platforms.

---

[1] Vladimir Ivanov and Scott Bauguess, "Capital Raising in the U.S.: An Analysis of Unregistered Offerings Using the Regulation D Exemption, 2009–2012" (updated July 2012), Division of Economic and Risk Analysis, U.S. Securities and Exchange Commission, p. 3.

In 2012, capital raised under Regulation D offerings amounted to more than $900 billion. Of that amount, 80 percent was raised by pooled investment funds and 20 percent by operating businesses. The median raise was about $1.5 million (the average was much higher, $30 million, because a small number of very big "outlier" deals skewed the average). For perspective, $1.2 trillion was raised in registered offerings in 2012.

## Regulation D Offering Platforms

The first equity offering platforms emerged in the United States in 2011, using Web technology adapted from rewards-based crowdfunding platforms. These are not true Title III equity crowdfunding portals, as we'll explain in Chapter 3, but they do give us insight into equity crowdfunding infrastructure.

Equity offering platforms were originally governed by Rule 506 of Regulation D (as opposed to Title III of the JOBS Act for equity crowdfunding). They became commonly known as Reg D platforms.

Among the most prominent and successful of the pioneering Reg D platforms are MicroVentures, launched in 2011 (focusing on technology companies), and CircleUp, launched in 2012 (focusing on consumer products and retail). We will give you in-depth profiles of those two platforms later in this chapter.

Off-platform, Rule 506 allowed an unlimited number of accredited investors and up to 35 nonaccredited investors in each private securities deal. In the preface to this book, we defined an individual accredited investor as an adult who has a net worth of $1 million (excluding the value of his or her primary residence), or annual income of at least $200,000 ($300,000 for a married couple).

To simplify compliance (because Regulation D mandates significant disclosure when nonaccredited investors are involved), Reg D offering platforms chose to allow only accredited investors to register on their platforms and participate in the equity offerings. On Reg D platforms, Rule 506 allowed investors to "self-certify" their accredited status, usually by checking a single box on the platform's registration form.

Significantly, Rule 506 offerings are exempt from compliance with state securities laws (blue sky laws), making Rule 506 ideal for online offerings, which potentially reach investors in all 50 states. Otherwise, a company would need to comply with the laws of each state where a prospective investor was domiciled, making it impractical.

Rule 506 does not limit the size of an offering in terms of dollars. Rule 506 deals typically involve small businesses making offers of less than $2 million, but the offering amounts vary from much less than $1 million to well over $50 million. Nor does Rule 506 limit the amount a single investor can invest in each deal. (As Table 2.1 shows, a major distinction between Reg D and Title III offerings is that Title III limits the amount raised in a year to $1 million and also limits the amount each investor can invest.)

Before September 2013, general solicitation was banned for all private securities offerings, including those under Reg D. Issuers could make direct offers only to people with whom they had substantial personal or business relationships, or to investors they knew to be accredited; they could not advertise their offers to the public.

General solicitation includes advertising to the general public the price, equity percentage, terms, and other details of an offer of securities through the media, seminars, meetings, social networks, and so on.

For equity offering platforms, *general solicitation* means announcing or advertising the offering outside of the platform where the offering is listed. From a legal point of view, any communication that might indiscriminately foster interest in a company's offering could be considered general solicitation.

### Deregulating General Solicitation

Based on Title II of the JOBS Act of 2012, the SEC split Rule 506 into two parts (see Table 2.2):

- Rule 506(b) is the "traditional" part, still allowing up to 35 nonaccredited investors, prohibiting general solicitation, and letting accredited investors self-certify.
- Rule 506(c) is the "new" part. It lifts the ban on general solicitation and limits an offering to accredited investors only. It also requires Reg D platforms to "take reasonable steps" to verify each investor's accredited status. For example, an offering platform can require investors to submit tax returns or bank statements or a confirmation letter from a lawyer, banker, or financial adviser.

Lifting the ban on general solicitation lets issuers reach a much wider universe of potential investors and helps to accelerate the capital formation process. But the SEC worried that lifting the ban would also result in many unsophisticated investors receiving solicitations and not understanding the risks of Reg D offerings. So the commission closed the door to nonaccredited investors and tightened the certification and verification process for accredited investors. (Congress reopened the door to nonaccredited investors under Title III.)

Companies that decide to offer securities through a Reg D platform must choose whether they want to use Rule 506(b) or Rule 506(c).

**TABLE 2.2**   Comparing Rules 506(b) and 506(c) of Regulation D*

| | "Traditional" Rule 506(b) | "New" Rule 506(c) |
|---|---|---|
| Raise limit for issuers ($) | No limit | No limit |
| Investor status | Unlimited number of accreditited investors, self-certification allowed on Reg D platform: up to 35 nonaccredited investors | Accredited investors only; Reg D platform must take reasonable steps to verify AI status |
| Investment limit ($) | No limit | No limit |
| General solicitation | Prohibited | Permitted |
| Blue sky law compliance | Exempt | Exempt |
| Red D platform example | Micro Ventures | CircleUp |

*This table summarizes important provisions of the two rules from the investor's point of view. It is not meant to include all provisions or to be comprehensive.

If they choose the 506(b) exemption, whereby general solicitation is not permitted, they can alert individuals who they know are accredited investors, and with whom they have existing relationships, that they are offering securities on their platforms. The companies can give those individuals the offering platform's URL, but they cannot disclose offering details such as the amount being raised, share price, terms, principals' backgrounds, financials, and risk disclosures. The prospective investors must go to the platform and register before they can see details of the offer and make a purchase.

Issuers that choose Rule 506(c) can publicly announce and advertise many details of the offer to the public (including amount being raised, share price, equity percentage, etc.) and refer investors to the platform where they can find more information and disclosures and make the purchase. But again, they can only invite accredited investors to purchase securities.

Some Reg D platforms make a choice between Rule 506(b) and 506(c) offerings and operate under one rule exclusively—rejecting issuers that make offerings under the "wrong" rule. Other Reg D platforms use a hybrid model that lets issuers choose whether to use 506(b) or 506(c).

A Reg D platform that operates strictly under the Rule 506(b) exemption may present generic descriptions (without identifying information such as name or location) of issuing companies on its home page and other pages that are visible to the public, but must post the offering details behind a "gate" that is accessible only to accredited investors who register (and self-certify) on the site.

People in the private finance industry started referring to 506(b) offerings as "quiet deals" because they cannot generally solicit. (No, they don't refer to 506(c) offerings as "loud deals.")

Title II went into effect on September 23, 2013, and some (not all) Reg D platforms permitted their issuers to engage in general solicitation if they chose to make 506(c) offerings. (See the example in the sidebar at the end of this chapter.) CircleUp immediately began featuring 506(c) offerings; MicroVentures did not. One disadvantage of opening up a Reg D platform to 506(c) offerings is that investors might be spooked by the need to submit documentation or engage their professional advisers to verify their accredited status. Platforms that stuck with the 506(b) "quiet deal" structure could still let their investors "one-click certify."

By September 23, 2014, one year after Title II went into effect, well over 500 companies had raised more than $215 million in equity capital in 506(c) offerings, according to Crowdnetic, which tracked results on 13 equity offering platforms in the United States. The sectors that dominated that activity were services and technology (especially social media, e-commerce, and mobile apps). The securities in Title II offerings were predominantly equity (72 percent), followed by convertible debt (20 percent) and straight debt (8 percent).[2]

### Distinguishing Reg D and Title III

When Congress passed the JOBS Act in 2012, a new kind of equity offering platform was born, based on Title III of the act. Title III allows all investors to participate, including unlimited numbers of nonaccredited investors—"the crowd." This was a profound shift. Suddenly all Americans, not just the wealthiest 7 percent, could invest in startups over the Internet. In fact, a single Title III equity crowdfunding deal might involve hundreds or thousands of nonaccredited investors.

The language of Title III explicitly referred to "crowdfunding portals," rather than the then-prevalent industry term "offering platforms."

Reg D professionals made an effort to distance their upscale ecosystem (open to wealthier investors only) from the new Title III ecosystem that would be open to all investors. Reg D pros urged people *not* to refer to their websites as crowdfunding, which makes sense because Reg D platforms are not open to "the crowd." Many people in the industry observed that the

---

[2] "Crowdnetic's Quarterly PIPR (Private Issuers Publicly Raising) Data Analysis for the Period Ending September 30, 2014," Crowdnetic Corporation; also SeedInvest.

word *crowdfunding* referred only to Title III, and not to Reg D. This was not social class struggle—it was simply a means of defining two different investment classes, operating under different regulatory frameworks.

To avoid confusion, in this book we will distinguish between:

1. Regulation D offering platforms, or simply Reg D platforms (which we focus on in this chapter).
2. Title III equity crowdfunding portals, or simply Title III portals (which we focus on in Chapter 3).

Note: The intermediaries that conduct Title III equity crowdfunding include (1) portals that are not registered broker-dealers and (2) platforms operated by broker-dealers. We will explain this distinction further in Chapter 3.

To complicate matters a bit further, when Title III portals finally launch, probably in 2015 or 2016, after the SEC and FINRA issue final rules for their operation, some Reg D platforms will set up sibling Title III portals, creating hybrid D/III platforms/portals. The rules allow parallel offerings through both systems, but we will keep them separate for the moment to avoid a head full of hubbub.

## Reg D Offering Platform Categories

Many Regulation D offering platforms choose to focus narrowly on a particular industry, stage of development, and/or other criteria. They can fall into a number of categories, depending on:

- What kinds of issuers they list (for example, they may focus on certain industries such as technology, consumer products, renewable energy, clothing and fashion).
- What stages of development they focus on (seed stage, startups, growth stage, later-stage, etc.).
- Whether they (1) permit general solicitation of offerings, and therefore must verify each investor's accredited status; (2) prohibit general solicitation and allow investors to self-certify; or (3) use a combination of the two.
- Whether they allow investors to invest directly in companies or through pools of capital known as nominated agents, special-purpose vehicles (SPVs), or other fundlike entities.
- Whether or not they qualify as or operate through registered broker-dealers.

Regarding the last item: The SEC and FINRA hold broker-dealers to a stricter standard of due diligence than other intermediaries. This distinction is very important, especially for investors who have little experience conducting their own due diligence.

Being a broker permits the platform to trade securities on behalf of its customers, and being a dealer allows the platform to trade on its own account.

Acting as an intermediary, a broker-dealer must take reasonable steps to ensure that the information and disclosures that issuers post on its platform are materially accurate and complete. If the broker-dealer fails to take those steps it will face disciplinary action (including fines and civil enforcement action) by the SEC and FINRA.[3] That means the platform's staff has to examine *carefully and in depth* an applicant's financial disclosures, perform criminal background checks on its executives, and so on. The broker-dealer is obligated to take reasonable steps to screen out dishonest issuers and fraudulent offerings.

Registered broker-dealers are subject not only to the general antifraud and antimanipulation provisions of federal securities laws and regulations, but to additional due diligence and anti–money laundering rules, and other requirements specific to broker-dealers.

Two fairly new requirements are the Know Your Customer Rule (FINRA 2090) and the Suitability Rule (FINRA 2111). Together, they require broker-dealers to collect sufficient information about each investor to determine that investor's risk profile and whether particular investments are suitable. To accomplish that, the broker-dealer operating an offering platform should review applicant companies' business plans in order to screen out offerings that it believes are generally unsuitable for its registered investors.

A Reg D platform that is not itself a broker-dealer may establish a contractual relationship with an outside broker-dealer, which allows it to perform activities that would otherwise require it to become a registered broker. This relationship subjects the platform to the same strict standard of due diligence with which broker-dealers must comply. An example of this kind of Reg D platform is Miami-based EarlyShares (when it offers securities through its relationship with a registered broker).

Reg D offering platforms that are not registered broker-dealers and not affiliated with an outside broker-dealer may still accept applications from issuers and list their offerings on their platforms. These platforms generally operate in one of two ways:

- They can operate much like a venture capital (VC) fund, where individual investors may invest in a portfolio of issuers through a venture fund

---

[3]See the SEC's "Guide to Broker-Dealer Registration" (2008) at http://www.sec.gov/divisions/marketreg/bdguide.htm.

or invest in a single issuer alongside other investors in a single-entity fund. If this Reg D platform is not a broker-dealer, you should not assume that it is as selective as, or conducts due diligence on its offerings with the same rigor as, a broker-dealer. An example is FundersClub.

- They can operate as a passive bulletin board, which (as the name suggests) accepts all or most issuers without conducting due diligence and without considering suitability. In this situation, the platform serves as a matchmaker, and investors and/or issuers carry the burden of engaging outside broker-dealers or other service providers that can facilitate the transaction and issue the securities. Example: EquityNet.

Most platforms that are broker-dealers, or are affiliated with one, are happy to disclose that information, usually in the website's footer (the text at the bottom of the home page) or on the "About Us" page. Some platforms that are not broker-dealers provide a disclaimer to that effect in the footer or on the "About Us" page, or maybe in the FAQs. If that information is not readily available, you can (1) contact the platform's staff and ask about their broker-dealer status and/or (2) visit FINRA's BrokerCheck page (http://www.finra.org/Investors/ToolsCalculators/BrokerCheck/) and conduct a search to see if the platform is registered as a broker-dealer.

If you are considering registering as an investor on a non-broker-dealer platform, ask the principals exactly what kind of selection process and due diligence they conduct before they accept an issuer. Some platforms conduct it in-house, and some use third-party services such as CrowdCheck. (Some actually emphasize that they do not conduct formal due diligence, leaving that up to the investors.) If the platform does claim to conduct due diligence, make sure the principals have relevant experience in the securities industry so that their due diligence is meaningful.

Keep in mind that you (along with the crowd) still need to conduct your own due diligence before you invest, even if the platform is a broker-dealer. We will explain more about this in Chapter 12.

In certain circumstances, investor-facing staff of a Reg D platform who are registered representatives affiliated with a registered broker-dealer may advise their investors regarding investment suitability—that is, which offerings would be most suitable for a particular investor's portfolio. Intermediaries and advisers who are not registered representatives are generally prohibited from giving such advice directly to investors; they must function more like a conduit, helping issuers and investors connect, inform, and communicate.

To demonstrate how Reg D platforms work, we will profile two of them: MicroVentures, which focuses primarily on high-tech entrepreneurial companies and prohibits general solicitation under Rule 506(b), and

CircleUp, whose issuers are consumer-product and retail companies and which permits general solicitation under Rule 506(c). Both of these are registered broker-dealers. Although we believe both are among the most reputable platforms with the highest professional standards, we do not necessarily endorse or recommend either one for any particular investor. The platform where you choose to invest should depend on your personal financial objectives and confidence in the platform's principals and staff.

## PROFILE: MICROVENTURES

Based in Austin and San Francisco, MicroVentures is one of the earliest equity offering platforms to launch in the United States. It is also the very first to see one of its issuers achieve an exit via acquisition, providing an attractive return for investors.

Founded in 2009 and launched online in early 2011, MicroVentures focuses primarily (but not exclusively) on "high-growth" technology startups with some revenue, or at least "executing on their business plan," according to founder Bill Clark. The platform's offerings also include an occasional later-stage company, perhaps in a secondary offering round. The platform operates mostly under Rule 506(b), thus in most cases does not permit general solicitation. Investors must be accredited to register on the site and may self-certify their accredited status. Still, the platform has a "high touch" policy with respect to its investors: The staff speaks by phone with each investor who registers on the platform before allowing him or her to gain access to confidential disclosures or make an investment.

MicroVentures is a registered broker-dealer, and the principals—as well as investor-facing employees—are registered brokers with Series 7 licenses. This permits them to advise investors about most kinds of securities, including private placements as well as publicly traded stocks and bonds (but not real estate or insurance). By the way, the Series 7 exam is by far the longest and most difficult of the various securities license series.

The platform's principal is Clark, the founder and president, who has a degree in finance from Michigan State University and 11 years of experience in credit risk management and financial services.

MicroVentures earns a 10 percent fee on all successful raises, half of that from the issuer and half from the investors. It also earns 10 percent of any capital gains (after returning 100 percent of invested funds to investors), known as *carried interest,* or "carry," if and when the crowdfunded issuer experiences a liquidity event such as an acquisition or IPO. Compare that with a venture capital fund, which typically takes a 20 percent carry and 2 percent management fee per year—which would amount to a 20 percent management fee over 10 years, a common fund life span. Clark says the platform's goal is to increase the flow of deals and therefore the volume of success fees, so that the platform can reduce or eliminate the carry.

## Done Deals

As of September 2014, MicroVentures has completed 80 equity raises on its platform, amounting to about $50 million of capital. (That figure does not include capital raised by the same issuers off-platform in the same period—from angel investors or venture capital funds, for example.) Only three of those 80 raises were 506(c) offerings. The typical raise, according to Clark, is around $250,000, although there have been a few outliers over $1 million (such as 3D printing startup Structured Polymers, which raised $1.2 million in 2013 through MicroVentures). The lowest raises have come in around $100,000. About 80 percent of the raises were primary—that is, the first such raise for an issuer on the platform—and the other 20 percent were secondary.

The minimum investment is $5,000, and there is no maximum. Such a low minimum allows a mere millionaire to diversify by investing in several risky, relatively illiquid Reg D deals and still keep his or her total Reg D investments under 5 percent of a $1 million investment portfolio.

The maximum time to fund a deal, from the first day of listing to the closing transaction, is 6 weeks, but the average time is 3.5 weeks. Clark says that a recent real estate deal closed in three days.

As of September 2014, MicroVentures has about 9,000 accredited investors registered on the platform, roughly 15 percent of whom are actively investing, while the rest are still browsing and studying. Clark attributes this impressive rate of activism to the platform's high-touch investor relations. He estimates that most of those investors have also registered on at least one other Reg D offering platform.

MicroVentures cautions its investors to expect that their investment may be illiquid for five to seven years before a liquidity event or exit, assuming the issuer survives that long.

## Deal Flow

Deals start flowing on the platform in two ways. First, a high-growth tech startup can go to the Funding Request page of the MicroVentures website, fill out a formal application, and upload its "pitch deck." The pitch deck, or condensed business plan, is typically a PowerPoint presentation that includes the "elevator pitch" (a quick problem/opportunity overview), team and board member profiles, marketing strategy, competitors, business model, revenue streams financial projections, exit strategy, capital needed, and so on.

The second way that MicroVentures generates deal flow is more active. From their phone conversations and other communications with their registered investors, the staff gets a feel for what segments of the tech industry investors are most interested in—at a particular time it might be cloud services, telemedicine, and mobile devices. Staff members regularly visit high-tech incubators, accelerators, and entrepreneur "demo days" (where startups pitch ideas to a roomful of angel investors). These events are effectively used to scout out promising startups that could fill investors' needs, and invite them to apply on the Funding Request page of the platform.

That is how the early stages of deal flow begin. The staff still has to review all funding requests, and promises to do so within a week of each request being submitted. This is the first round of review, an abbreviated version of the due diligence process, which includes examining the company's fundamental "metrics," management team, and any early investors that may be involved. MicroVentures responds only to those that they judge to be potentially "successful on our platform," which turns out to be fewer than 2 percent of all requests. Those 2 percent that pass the first round of review are invited to appear in the Proposed Companies section of the platform.

The Proposed Companies section, informally called "the bullpen," shows the following information about each issuer: company name and logo, industry (Internet tech, digital media, software, green tech, gaming, etc., and occasionally consumer products), stage of development (usually startup/seed but occasionally growth or later-stage), a one-sentence description of the business, and the number of registered investors who have indicated an interest in investing in the company (but not a commitment to do so), pending the next, more comprehensive phase of due diligence. About one in four of the proposed companies makes it to the final phase of acceptance and undergoes the broker-dealer level of due diligence. That involves examining the company's business plan, break-even analysis, "burn rate," use of proceeds, risk factors, management resumes, litigation status, a site visit or validation, list of assets, existing liabilities, and so on. (Again, we want to emphasize that investors should not necessarily rely solely on the platform's due diligence process, even if they trust the expertise of the platform's staff. Investors may need to do further research on each offer.)

Clark believes that the wisdom derived from the crowd of registered investors is "at least as smart" as Silicon Valley venture capitalists when it comes to screening good candidates for offerings.

Ultimately, about one-half of 1 percent of companies that request funding end up listed in the Current Offerings section of the platform. Some people refer to that percentage as the platform's "curation rate," meaning the percentage of applicants that are accepted. Most Reg D platforms have curation rates below 5 percent.

In the Current Offerings section, each listing shows the company's name and logo, industry, stage of development, one-sentence description, the date on which the offer was listed, the minimum investment (ranging from $5,000 in most cases to $15,000 or more for later-stage companies), and the amount raised so far. That is the information available to investors who have gone through the initial registration process. To gain access to the complete offering information, investors must go through a secondary registration phase, which includes a phone conversation with a MicroVentures staff member.

Complete offering information usually begins with a short promotional video and/or a "slide deck" produced by the issuer. Following those are names of the founders, notable seed and angel investors if any, terms of the deal (e.g., $x$ in convertible debt at $y\%$ interest), and a statement written by a MicroVentures executive about why it selected the company. This is usually followed by descriptions of the business model, products or services, intended use of proceeds raised on the platform, performance charts, financial forecasts, industry and market analysis, competitive landscape, executive team, press coverage, and more. Investors can download the private placement memorandum, or PPM (the document, usually several dozen pages long, used to execute and close the deal), in PDF format on the condition that they keep it confidential and not distribute it to anyone else. If any investor violates that agreement, he or she will lose access to the platform. (We'll explain more about PPMs in Chapter 11.)

Because MicroVentures operates largely under Rule 506(b) of Regulation D, visitors to the platform who are not registered (accredited) investors will not see any specific offering information. As general solicitation is not permitted with 506(b) offerings, the platform can make offers only to those investors who are registered on the platform and thereby known by MicroVentures to be accredited.

Reg D platforms that operate under Rule 506(c), on the other hand, can show basic offering details to all who visit the platform, whether accredited investors or not. But then only registered, accredited investors may go "behind the gate" to see deeper details about each offering. Furthermore, Rule 506(c) allows websites such as the *Wall Street Journal*'s MarketWatch[4] to aggregate offering data from various 506(c) platforms into a centralized

---

[4]See the "Private Issuers Publicly Raising" page of MarketWatch's "Investing" section at http://www.marketwatch.com/investing/crowdnetic?page=dashboard. This data is supplied and updated by Crowdnetic, a New York City–based provider of technology and market data to the securities crowdfunding and peer-to-peer lending industry.

marketplace for investors in 506(c) offerings. Such offering data aggregation sites may not include offers from 506(b) platforms like MicroVentures.

The inability to solicit more widely than its own platform creates a competitive disadvantage, in some respects, for a 506(b) platform, because 506(c) offerings have higher visibility. On the other hand, some investors are unwilling to submit to the "reasonable steps" that 506(c) platforms must take to verify their accredited status.

At any point while considering a particular offer, registered investors can "chat" with other similarly interested investors through the forum-like social networking features of the platform. Also, investors may ask the issuer questions and receive answers, and the Q&A is visible to the other investors in that forum. The chat becomes, in essence, a collaborative due diligence process.

## Closing the Deal

Finally we come to the moment when the investor decides to commit $5,000 or more to a deal. Again MicroVentures offers a high-touch experience where a broker can walk the investor through the process, or the investor can choose to proceed through the transaction without help. When the investor completes that transaction on the platform, the money is held in escrow until other investors have made commitments and the deal closes. Then the money is transferred to the issuer and equity is granted in return. If the deal does not close for any reason, the money is refunded and no fees are taken out.

One of the features that distinguish MicroVentures from CircleUp (profiled next) and many other Reg D platforms is that for each equity deal, MicroVentures pools investors' money into a single entity, a limited liability company (LLC), which then executes the private placement memorandum. For example, investors A, B, and C commit to investing in issuer X Corp. MicroVentures forms an LLC for the sole purpose of pooling money from A, B, and C, and the LLC invests in X Corp. In this arrangement, each investor buys membership units in the LLC rather than investing directly in the issuer. That way, the issuer adds only one entity to its capitalization table—a spreadsheet that lists all the company's investors, showing when each one invested, the amount of each investment, and how much equity each investor holds, among other data.

Most companies prefer to keep the cap table as simple as possible, especially because they are obligated to respond to pertinent questions and comments from, as well as provide regular reports to, each and every investor. Small companies that do not have full-time investor relations staff may prefer to avoid having to respond to inquiries from many investors so they can focus on building the business and earning a profit.

More important, selling shares to a pooled investor entity can minimize the level of control that each individual investor has over corporate governance. Thus, the LLC creates a buffer between the company and its investors. (Looking ahead to Chapter 3, pooled funds cannot be used for investments on Title III crowdfunding portals at this point. Rather, investors will invest directly in issuers that raise capital on Title III portals, even if there are hundreds or thousands of investors on a single deal. Proposed new legislation in Congress, however, could revise Title III to allow funding portals to pool investor funds into single-entity investment vehicles.)

The disadvantage for investors of a pooled-funds, single entity making the investment is that those investors who want to communicate with company executives may have to do so through MicroVentures, which manages the LLC. Also, a single-entity pool is limited to 99 investors.

It is important to distinguish the fundlike LLC entity from a traditional venture capital fund. VC funds are blind pools where individual investors do not select portfolio companies in which to invest. (An exception is a VC pledge fund, in which investors can opt out of investing in a particular portfolio company—but investors still cannot select portfolio companies in which to invest.) Each MicroVentures LLC, by contrast, invests in only one issuer, and the investors who buy LLC units have selected that particular issuer in which to invest.

Because investors can expect to hold their LLC units for five to seven years before a liquidity event, it is still too soon to evaluate returns on Reg D platform investments, with one prominent exception. The very first issuer that MicroVentures listed in 2011 was Arizona-based Republic Project, a developer of cloud-based digital content management systems for advertisers. Republic Project raised $100,000 in its 2011 primary round on the MicroVentures platform, and another $250,000 in a secondary round. In November 2013, Republic Project was acquired by Digital Generation, a publicly traded company. The acquisition price is confidential. Primary-round investors would see a larger return than second-round investors, and the exact return on investment (ROI) "depends on a two-year earn-out," Clark explains. "Our first payout is to be delivered in Q1 2015. That said, all reports have been positive since the acquisition."

## PROFILE: CIRCLEUP

While MicroVentures specializes in offerings by tech startups, sometimes with little revenue, CircleUp focuses on consumer product and retail companies that have roughly $1 million to $10 million in trailing (over the past 12 months) revenue. The platform also features some pre-revenue companies in this sector, which they label "CircleUp Seeds." CircleUp candidates are usually "entering a high-growth stage" with an established brand and distribution networks in place. Other distinguishing features of CircleUp include:

- Its use of Rule 506(c), which allows general solicitation for some offerings—which means you might see them advertised elsewhere besides the CircleUp platform, but you still have to register on CircleUp to view disclosures and invest in them.
- Its policy of allowing investors to invest directly in listed issuers rather than in pooled-capital entities like the LLCs used by MicroVentures.
- Its strategic partnership with leading consumer product companies such as Procter & Gamble and General Mills, which host incubator days to assist entrepreneurs during and after their raise on CircleUp. They also have the ability to invest in some of the platform's offerings in order to stay current with industry innovations, and open the possibility of later acquisitions, which translate to exit options for investors.

When they launched CircleUp in San Francisco in April 2012, founders Ryan Caldbeck and Rory Eakin decided to focus on consumer and retail companies because it was an industry "largely ignored by the traditional venture capital community," Caldbeck told *Accredited Investor Markets* in April 2013. They don't attract the same attention from VCs and private equity that technology companies do, even though they have fast growth potential. Private equity firms typically will not invest in a consumer company until it reaches $15 million in revenue. Eakin points out that only 4 percent of total venture capital funding went to consumer products in 2011, while the sector accounted for 15 to 20 percent of GDP.[5]

The appeal for investors in consumer and retail segments is different from the appeal of glamorous high-tech startups that might be the next Apple or LinkedIn. For one thing, a prospective investor can request samples of most of the products featured on the platform and "experience" the products before investing in them. Some of them are already on the shelves of local grocery or pet stores. Investors may be interested in an issuer because they "identify with the company and its products" as much as because they're impressed by the financial statements. An emotional connection to the underlying product is a core aspect of consumer investing.

"Imagine 40 parents investing in a baby food company, or 25 pet owners investing in a pet business. Now they are talking about the business not just because they love the product, but because they are equity investors," says

---

[5]National Venture Capital Association; Bureau of Economic Analysis, U.S. Department of Commerce.

Caldbeck. "Growth-stage consumer companies are unlikely to grow into $10 billion businesses—they would get acquired far in advance of that—but they can do very well and produce solid returns for investors. The average company on CircleUp is growing at more than 70 percent a year."[6]

CircleUp's website points to Kauffman Foundation data showing that angel investments in consumer companies, when properly diversified, generate an average return of 3.6 times invested capital over 4.4 years.[7] That doesn't necessarily beat the returns you might expect from investing in high-tech startups, but investing in established consumer brands could be considered less risky.

Caldbeck and Eakin both have Stanford MBAs. Caldbeck, the CEO, was previously a director at Encore Consumer Capital, a private equity firm that focuses on consumer products and retail. Eakin, the COO, was formerly the director of investments at Humanity United and a consultant at the Boston Consulting Group. Both hold Series 24 and 82 securities licenses, the latter covering primary offering of private placements (not secondary-market trading). Megan Roeske, an investor executive at CircleUp, holds the broader Series 7 securities license. (Roeske is a former senior vice president at EnTrust Capital.) CircleUp staff do not offer individual investment advice to the investors who register on their platform, although their broker-dealer status entitles them to do so.

CircleUp earns a fee on each successful raise, which is paid by the issuer, not by investors. Those fees vary depending on the amount raised. The platform does not earn carried interest (a portion of the capital gains after a liquidity event or exit). So, although the potential gains are not as spectacular for consumer and retail as they may be for high-tech, the costs of investing are generally lower.

In 2013 CircleUp itself raised $9 million in seed and first-round funding led by mega-angels Google Ventures and Union Square Ventures.

## Done Deals

As of October 2014, CircleUp has supported 50 capital raises, totaling more than $50 million. The largest deal to date was a $3 million equity raise by

---

[6] Alicia Purdy, "A Few Minutes with Ryan Caldbeck, CEO, CircleUp," Accredited Investor Markets, April 29, 2013. Available at http://www.accreditedinvestor markets.com/a-few-minutes-with-ryan-caldbeck-ceo-circleup/.

[7] Angel Investor Performance Project, E.M. Kauffman Foundation, https://circleup .com/blog/2012/06/06/returns-in-angel-investing-and-what-it-means-for-crowdfunding/.

Sustain, makers of fair trade condoms, in 2014. In the largest deal of 2013, SmartyPants Vitamins raised $2.5 million in a convertible note offering.

The average raise period is less than eight weeks, although one company, Rhythm Kale Chips, closed a $700,000 round in two weeks. Compare that with a typical raise period for angel-round funding of three or four months offline in the consumer and retail industries.

Each issuer sets its own minimum investment level. Some offerings require a minimum of $1,000, and the high end tends to be around $25,000. At the low end, "small" investors are better able to diversify their private equity portfolios. Offline, in the angel investment world, minimums tend to be $25,000 to $50,000.

Many of CircleUp's registered investors are strategic investors located throughout the country, which means they have experience, often at the executive level, in consumer products and retail. Often they are retired, and they want to "stay in the game" by not only investing their money but also offering their expertise to growing businesses. One or two of them may end up on the boards of directors, or serve as paid consultants, for the companies they invest in through the platform. These are the kinds of investors that issuers covet.

CircleUp's investor-facing executives speak with many of the investors by phone to verify their identities, learn about their expertise, and gauge their interest in specific sectors of the industry. From such conversations, executives learn, for example, that roughly half of investors have invested in early-stage private companies before. Occasionally these investors include their financial advisers and/or lawyers in the conversation. Some are novices in the private capital markets who are plunging into it for the "fun factor."

According to Roeske, many of CircleUp's active investors participate in multiple deals. There are some who invest the minimum amount in all the issuers listed on the platform. A minority of them make only one investment.

CircleUp provides investors, free of charge, research reports, retail metrics, survey results, and analysis (for which the platform pays subscription fees) from consulting firms such as Chicago-based Spins LLC, a consultant to "natural products" retailers and manufacturers.

## Deal Flow

Companies can apply to list their offers on the CircleUp platform via an online application, which includes the basic information about the product and executives, along with revenue history, gross margins, and growth rates. The CircleUp team narrows down the applicants and conducts due diligence on those that show potential. Caldbeck wrote the following on the MarketWatch website in November 2013:

> *Besides company metrics, we scrutinize the exit prospects of CircleUp applicants. Large consumer products firms increasingly don't want to spend the time or capital to innovate; it's easier to buy a proven brand than to spend millions of dollars and several years trying to launch a product whose time might have passed once it gets to market. For example, if we see a coconut water product, it's unlikely to make it onto CircleUp because retail beverage giants Coca-Cola and PepsiCo have already made their coconut water plays. We look for companies selling products that are both differentiated from competitors and complementary to the relevant strategic buyers.*[8]

The CircleUp team also scrutinizes valuations. "The number one reason why we will not accept an otherwise qualified company . . . is that the entrepreneur seeks a valuation that is out of line with comparable transactions," Caldbeck explains. "Entry valuation goes a long way toward determining an investor's return, so it's critical that investors are not paying 10x revenue if a strategic buyer will pay only 3x down the road."

Less than 5 percent of the applications are finally approved, most of them Subchapter C corporations. Although the CircleUp team conducts due diligence in the curation process, "we encourage all investors to do their own [due diligence]—not just on our site but off-platform as well—rather than relying on the work of other investors," says Caldbeck. This is good advice for many reasons, one of which is that due diligence should also go to the suitability and economic needs of individual investors, which vary from person to person.

In late January 2014, CircleUp's "investment opportunities" page showed 48 companies raising capital, by far the largest sector being food (26), the second-largest beverages (9), and the rest falling into personal care, household products, e-commerce, apparel, sporting goods, and others. All visitors to the website see all 48 offerings. Only 10 of those, however, were identified by company name, short description, and a photo of the product; those were the issuers using Rule 506(c), which permits general solicitation. The other 38 were identified only by a generic description that included the sector (food, personal care, household products, etc.), launch date, trailing

---

[8]Ryan Caldbeck, "All Crowdfunding Capitalist Should Ask this Question," MarketWatch.com, November 19, 2013, http://www.marketwatch.com/story/all-crowdfunding-capitalists-should-ask-this-question-2013-11-19.

revenue, and in some cases distribution channels; these are 506(b) offerings. Only registered accredited investors can go beyond the gate to see more offering details.

The CircleUp platform facilitates forum-like communications between and among prospective investors, committed investors, and issuers, including scheduled conference calls during which prospective investors may ask questions.

A prospective investor gains access to the issuer's deep-dive offering documents, typically including PPM, cap table, and other disclosures, only with individual permission from the issuer.

Investors outside the United States may be able to invest in an offering listed in CircleUp, but may not do so online—he or she would have to complete the process off-platform and provide more personal information, such as a photo ID or passport and a W-8 form.

## Closing the Deal

CircleUp is an all-or-nothing platform—like Kickstarter in the rewards-based wing of crowdfunding—meaning that if the issuer does not reach its stated funding goal, it gets nothing and investors' money held in escrow is refunded. If the funding goal is exceeded, the issuer keeps the entire amount and everyone is happy—for now. Investors make deals directly with issuers by means of subscription agreements, and depending on the offering they may receive preferred stock, common stock, or convertible debt (notes that can be converted to equity when the company passes certain financial milestones).

When the funding round closes, investors and issuer can still use the CircleUp forum-like social network to communicate, but only those investors who participated in the offering can continue to view the issuer's CircleUp page.

Although MicroVentures and CircleUp do not allow nonaccredited investors to participate in Reg D offerings, those equity offering platforms—being precursors to Title III equity crowdfunding, which does allow nonaccredited investors to participate—provide valuable lessons about the operation of the platforms, their niche focuses, collaborative due diligence, and other aspects of the investment process.

## SUSPENSE BUILDS AROUND TITLE III

By the end of 2014, several Regulation D platforms in the United States were consistently bringing issuers and accredited investors together and facilitating equity deals. Some platforms focused narrowly on specific industries aside from tech and consumer (AgFunder and Healthfundr, for example). Several Reg D platforms (including EarlyShares) as well as rewards-based Indiegogo tentatively planned to add Title III equity crowdfunding offerings as soon as the final rules are issued by the SEC and FINRA, perhaps in 2015.

Meanwhile in other countries, most notably Australia and the United Kingdom, equity crowdfunding platforms welcomed all investors, with minimal or no restrictions based on net worth or income. And some U.S. states, starting with Georgia, Wisconsin, and Michigan, began allowing intrastate equity crowdfunding with the participation of nonaccredited investors.

By early 2015, a lot of equity crowdfunding platform operators and developers, entrepreneurs, investors, and their advisers in the United States waited, and waited some more, for the SEC and FINRA to issue final rules so that the Title III portals could be launched and interstate equity crowdfunding could be open to tens of millions of nonaccredited investors. In the media, financial pundits alternately predicted (1) that Title III crowdfunding, populated mostly by unsophisticated investors, would herald a glorious democratic revolution in the private capital markets or (2) an inglorious train wreck.

## GENERAL SOLICITATION UNDER RULE 506(C)

An example of a 506(c) equity offering is Fasslane LLC, a hypothetical designer and retailer of competition swimwear and gear, based in Providence, Rhode Island.*

In January 2014, Fasslane was accepted by EquityThrust, a hypothetical Reg D offering platform, to list its offering of membership units (equity) in the LLC to investors on the platform. Fasslane elected to use Rule 506(c) of Regulation D, which permits general solicitation of its offering. That means Fasslane could announce its offering not only on the EquityThrust platform but also on its own website, in the news media, on social networking sites, and in other public forums. Although *anyone* might see those public announcements, only accredited investors could register on the EquityThrust platform, gain access to confidential details and disclosures, and invest in Fasslane.

If Fasslane had chosen to make the offering under Rule 506(b), it would not have been permitted to advertise generally. It would have been able to announce and describe its offering only on the EquityThrust platform (which is accessible only by accredited investors) and directly to investors with whom the issuer already had relationships.

Less than half of the offerings on the EquityThrust platform used Rule 506(c) in January 2014. Most elected to make 506(b) offerings, also known as "quiet deals."

The Fasslane offering appeared on the EquityThrust home page in January through March 2014. Figure 2.1 is a simulation of the banner that appeared, among other offerings, on EquityThrust's home page. Clicking on this image took users (whether they were registered on the

**FIGURE 2.1**   This banner appeared, among other issuers' banners, on the EquityThrust home page in January 2014. Because the offering is filed under Rule 506(c), the company name and logo can be visible to everyone. Viewers who clicked on this image went to Fasslane's Offering Overview page, still on the EquityThrust platform. To see confidential disclosures and offering terms, you would have to register on the portal and verify your accredited investor status by submitting tax returns, bank statements, or a statement from your professional adviser, for example

platform or not) to Fasslane's Offering Overview page with a richer description of the company, including:

Funding goal ($450,000), amount raised so far ($215,000 or 48% on February 25)

History, mission, key employee profiles, location

Market description, size (in total sales), and growth rate

Product photos

Funding type: equity

A short promotional video

External links: Fasslane website, social media pages, news media coverage

"Get product samples" button

Accredited investors had to register on the platform to gain access to the company's business plan, financials, risk disclosures, and deal terms.

By contrast, issuers that chose to make "quiet" offerings under Rule 506(b) were identified on EquityThrust's home page only by a generic description of the company's product and economic sector, not by name (see Figure 2.2). To find more information, you would have to register on the platform, self-certifying your accredited investor status with one click.

In addition to its listing on EquityThrust, Fasslane announced its offering on its own website by placing a 1.5-inch by 3-inch banner in the footer, which appears at the bottom of every page of the Fasslane site (see Figure 2.3). The banner displayed the EquityThrust logo prominently, with the message "Now funding on EquityThrust . . . learn more." Clicking on that banner took users to a full-page announcement, still on the Fasslane website. From the bottom of the announcement, users could click on prominent hypertext link to the Offering Overview on the EquityThrust platform.

Fasslane also distributed the full-page announcement, in the form of a press release, to local business news media, to trade journals in the swimming pool and spa industry, and to regional angel investor groups.

Why would any issuer opt to use Rule 506(b) and forgo the chance to advertise widely? One reason is that Rule 506(b) allows accredited investors to self-certify their accredited status when they register on the platform. Rule 506(c), on the other hand, requires investors (in most cases) to comply with the platform's request to verify their accredited status by, for example, providing documents such as tax returns or bank statements, or letters from a professional adviser.** Some issuers worry that the 506(c) verification requirement might scare away investors due to privacy concerns. Another reason some smaller companies forgo the chance to advertise widely is that they simply do not have the marketing budget to do so.

## Food Company
**Consumer product LLC**

Equity

2013 Revenue: $1.65 million

Founders experience: consumer packaged goods, sales and marketing

Retail outlets: Whole Foods, Costco

**FIGURE 2.2** This banner represents a hypothetical 506(b) offering on EquityThrust's home page. It does not identify the company by name, but it does indicate the issuer's sector, trailing revenue, founders' experience, and retail outlets where the product is sold. To see more information about this offering, starting with the company's name, you would have to register on EquityThrust as an accredited investor. You would be able to self-certify your accredited status

**FIGURE 2.3** As Rule 506(c) permitted Fasslane to advertise the offering on its own website, the company placed this banner in the footer, which appears on most pages of its site. Clicking on the image took viewers to a full-page announcement, still on the Fasslane website, with some of the offering information and a hyperlink to the Offering Overview page of the EquityThrust platform, where investors could register to see more information

*Both the company, Fasslane, and the platform, EquityThrust, are fictitious, created for illustrative purposes. Any resemblance to a real entity is unintentional.

**Under the principles set out by the SEC, it would be possible for some platforms not to require additional verification steps regarding accredited investors' status at all if, for example, the minimum investment amount was at least $1 million.

# CHAPTER 3

# Equity Crowdfunding

## For All Investors (Under Title III of the JOBS Act)

**S**teve Wozniak designed the Apple II computer in 1976. He recently pointed out that if you had asked people in 1976 if they would like to have a home computer, most would have responded, "What's a home computer?"

Today if you ask most people if they would like to invest in startups and small businesses through equity crowdfunding, they would respond in much the same way: "What's equity crowdfunding?"

Are we implying that in a decade or two most people will know what equity crowdfunding is and might even want to buy some early-stage equity? Yes. Everyone who has an investment portfolio will seriously consider diversifying by investing hundreds or thousands of dollars in startups and early-stage companies via equity crowdfunding.

Since 1976, personal computers have dramatically improved and expanded with respect to power, user-friendliness, and functionality. Wozniak himself could not have fully envisioned how home computers would change most aspects of commerce and society. We want to be careful not to paint a grandiose portrait of equity crowdfunding, but to extend our analogy, equity crowdfunding will likewise improve and expand, and change private capital markets, in ways that we can't yet envision, even if it gets off to a slow (maybe rocky) start.

To understand equity-based crowdfunding, it helps to understand some of the basics of Regulation D offerings, which we looked at in Chapter 2—especially the concept of exemption from SEC registration. A private company that wants to offer stock to investors must either (1) register the offering with the SEC and "go public" or (2) comply with the conditions of an exemption from registration. Because registration is profoundly expensive, most private companies choose to make offerings under exemptions such as Regulation D, the intrastate exemption, or—starting in 2015 or soon thereafter—the new Title III crowdfunding exemption. (We discuss the intrastate exemption further in Chapter 4.)

One other idea we want to review from Chapter 2 is the distinction between Regulation D equity offering platforms and Title III equity crowdfunding portals. (See Table 3.1.) Some people mistakenly lump Reg D offering platforms and Title III crowdfunding portals together and call them all equity crowdfunding. It is true that both Reg D and Title III involve equity investing. But people should not consider Reg D offering platforms to be crowdfunding, because they are effectively open only to accredited investors, not to "the crowd." In this book we do refer to Title III *crowdfunding portals*, because (1) they are open to *all* investors—to the crowd and (2) Congress described them as "funding portals" in Title III of the JOBS Act of 2012. To keep it simple, we'll stick to *equity crowdfunding*.

**TABLE 3.1**   Funding Platform Highlights

| Year | World | USA | | | |
|------|-------|-----|---|---|---|
| | Equity Crowdfunding | Regulation D, Rule 506 | Title III Equity Crowdfunding | Intrastate Equity Crowdfunding | Non-Equity Crowdfunding |
| 2003 | | | | | ArtistShare |
| 2004 | | | | | |
| 2005 | | | | | Kiva |
| 2006 | ASSOB (Australia) | | | | Lending Club |
| 2007 | | | | | |
| 2008 | | | | | Indiegogo |
| 2009 | | | | | Kickstarter |
| 2010 | | | | | GoFundMe |
| 2011 | | MicroVentures | | *Georgia* | |
| 2012 | Seedrs (UK) | CircleUp | *JOBS Act signed* | | |
| 2013 | CrowdCube (UK) | *General solicitation* | | *Michigan, Wisconsin* | |
| 2014 | | | | | |
| 2015 | | | *SEC/FINRA rules expected* | | |

**Legend:**
Items in Roman type are websites (platforms, portals)
Items in italics are legislative/regulatory events

## PAVING NEW ROADS TO CAPITAL MARKETS

As we explained in the preface to this book, the purpose of the JOBS Act was to make it easier and less costly for entrepreneurs, startups, and small businesses (issuers) to raise capital from investors and lenders. Capital is needed to fuel growth, and thereby to boost the economy and create new jobs. The act accomplishes that objective mainly by loosening some of the "most onerous" restrictions on the ability of small companies to raise capital in the private securities markets.[1] Despite its name, the Jumpstart Our Business Startups Act benefits not only private startups that want to grow but also "the overwhelming majority of companies going public."[2] The provisions of the JOBS Act that benefit larger and more established companies are not the focus of this book, but the point is simply to understand that the act is broader than creating equity crowdfunding. The other provisions are summarized later in this chapter.

The JOBS Act enhances the flow of capital in both directions: While it helps growing companies reach out to more investors, it also helps investors find more growing companies in which to invest. It does that partly by allowing equity crowdfunding portals to publicly showcase multiple private offerings, the likes of which were previously hidden, in effect, from tens of millions of average investors.

The JOBS Act was enacted in March 2012 with strong bipartisan support in both the House of Representatives (390–23) and the Senate (73–26). The act combines seven substantive parts, Title I through Title VII. The first six of these were derived from six separate pieces of legislation. For example, what started as the Crowdfunding Act, debated in both the House of Representatives and the Senate in 2011, was later folded into the JOBS Act as Title III.

Titles I through VI each pave a different road to raising capital for startups and small businesses in the U.S. financial markets:

- **Title I** has been nicknamed the "IPO on-ramp." It creates a class of businesses known as emerging growth companies (EGCs), defined as those with less than $1 billion of revenue, to be indexed for inflation. Title I reduces regulatory burdens and costs associated with going public for EGCs and creates a "transitional on-ramp" that "phases in certain

---

[1] "Client Alert—JOBS Act of 2012," Friday Eldredge & Clark, LLP, April 6, 2012.
[2] Elizabeth J. Chandler and Patrick S. Murphy, "Jumpstart Our Business Startups Act Signed into Law," April 10, 2012, white paper published by Milwaukee-based law firm Godfrey & Kahn, April 2012, http://www.gklaw.com/news.cfm?action=pub_detail&publication_id=1176.

SEC compliance measures over a period of [years] following an initial public offering."[3] (One of the advantages of going public is the ability to sell shares through a public stock exchange.) Title I is the only part of the JOBS Act that applies specifically to EGCs.

- **Title II** lifts the ban on general solicitation and advertising for private offerings under Rule 506 of Regulation D. The benefit of general solicitation is that issuers can announce their offers to a much wider pool of potential investors (but still must sell shares only to accredited investors). See Chapter 2 for a summary of how general solicitation has affected Reg D offering platforms. Title II also permits general solicitation for the sale of some restricted securities to "qualified institutional buyers" under Rule 144A.

- **Title III** legalizes the offering of up to $1 million in securities (equity and debt) by private startups and small businesses to all investors (including nonaccredited investors) through two kinds of intermediaries: broker-dealers or the newly created class of regulated entities called funding portals. We will cover this in more detail later in this chapter. Title II does not apply to Title III crowdfunding; that is, issuers may not generally solicit or advertise their Title III offerings.

- **Title IV** increases the amount of securities that can be issued in a 12-month period by a private company under Regulation A, from $5 million to $50 million. This has become known as Regulation A(2) or A+.

- **Title V** increases the maximum allowable number of shareholders in a private company from 500 to 2,000 (up to 500 of whom may be nonaccredited investors). Beyond that threshold, a company must register the applicable class of shares with the SEC under the Securities Act of 1934, which is a process as onerous as making an IPO registered under the Securities Act of 1933.[4]

- **Title VI** helps banks and bank holding companies stay private longer (or go private) by increasing the maximum allowable shareholder of record threshold from 500 to 2,000.

---

[3]"The JOBS Act (Jumpstart Our Business Startups Act)—What Does It Mean for Entrepreneurs"? *Cooley Alert!,* April 2012, Cooley LLP, http://www.cooley .com/66282.

[4]For purposes of the 2,000-shareholder threshold, shareholders who received securities pursuant to an employee stock ownership plan (ESOP) or other employee compensation plan and crowdfunding investors will not be counted as shareholders of record.

- **Title VII** directs the SEC to "provide online information and conduct outreach to inform small and medium-sized businesses, women-owned businesses, veteran-owned businesses, and minority-owned businesses of the changes made by this Act."

Congress specified that Title I would go into effect immediately. Titles II through VI would go into effect only after the SEC issued rules that would implement these parts of the law (although part of Title V is self-executing). In the case of Title III, that did not happen for more than three years.

## A DEEPER DIVE INTO TITLE III

Title III is the only part of the JOBS Act—and indeed the only piece of legislation since before the Securities Act of 1933—that unequivocally opened the floodgate for masses of nonaccredited investors to participate in the private equity markets.

The idea for "crowdsourced securities offerings" arose in the United States at least as far back as 2007.[5] After the dot-com bust in 2000, venture capital investment fell off dramatically. (Part of that fall-off, to be sure, was related to the lower cost of starting up Web-based enterprises after the introduction of powerful open-source software and Web 2.0 development tools.) There was a perception that startups did not have adequate access to available capital, particularly through online capital raising, and that small investors did not have access to early-stage investment opportunities.[6]

Based on the success of Kickstarter and Indiegogo, the idea for legalizing equity crowdfunding gained momentum in 2009 among a handful of entrepreneurs and lawyers. Paul Spinrad, a projects editor for *MAKE* magazine, may have been the first to post the idea on a public forum, namely the blog BoingBoing.[7] He was joined by a lawyer named Jenny Kassan, director of a community-supported entrepreneurship program at the Sustainable

---

[5]A version of equity crowdfunding emerged in Australia in 2006. See Jay Parkhill, "The World Isn't Ready for Crowdsourced Securities Offerings," the Startup Toolbox blog, April 26, 2007, http://blog.jparkhill.com/2007/04/26/the-world-isnt-ready-for-crowdsourced-securities-offerings/.

[6]Brian Korn (securities lawyer), "Equity Crowdfunding Legal Landscape: What's Allowed and What's Not," November 15, 2013, Pepper Hamilton, LLP, New York, NY.

[7]See Paul Spinrad, "How Crowdfunding and the JOBS Act Got Started," Crowdsourcing.org, September 19, 2012, http://www.crowdsourcing.org/editorial/how-crowdfunding-and-the-jobs-act-got-started-told-by-the-guy-behind-the-big-idea/19288.

Economies Law Center, and Danae Ringelmann, founder of Indiegogo, who developed the idea further.

Subsequently, a trio of entrepreneurs and graduates of the Thunderbird School of Global Management in Arizona—Sherwood Neiss, Jason Best, and Zak Cassady-Dorion—decided to codify the idea and take it to Congress. They had been leaders in companies that had raised millions of dollars from traditional angel investors and venture capital firms, and had built successful businesses. "We were frustrated that, at the depths of the financial crisis, you could give away money on rewards-based crowdfunding sites, and you could lend money to entrepreneurs in the developing world on sites like Kiva.org, but most people were not allowed to invest in businesses that they used every day, or in entrepreneurs whom they believed in," says Best. The trio gathered around a kitchen table one night and wrote the first draft of what they called the Startup Exemption Crowdfunding Framework.[8] This 10-point framework became the basis of the Crowdfunding Act and then Title III of the JOBS Act. They self-funded their campaign to lobby the White House, the House of Representatives, the Senate, and the SEC for its adoption into law, working closely with Karen Kerrigan, CEO of the Small Business & Entrepreneurship Council, the lobbying group for small business in Washington, D.C. Other organizations lobbied independently for an equity crowdfunding law, including the American Sustainable Business Council and the Cambridge Innovation Center.

We skip ahead to April 2012, when President Barack Obama signed the JOBS Act into law. The decisive stroke of Title III was that it amended the Securities Act of 1933 by adding a new paragraph to Section 4(a) of the act, designated as new Section 4(a)(6). Lawyers and regulators may refer to equity crowdfunding as "Section 4(a)(6) crowdfunding," but (partly because that's hard to remember) most people call it "Title III crowdfunding" or simply "equity crowdfunding."

Here is a summary of the most important provisions of Title III as it relates first to issuers, then to investors, and finally to intermediaries (the latter includes Web-based funding portals and broker-dealers).

## Title III Provisions for Issuers

To offer equity on a crowdfunding portal (or through a broker-dealer operating an online offering platform under Title III[9]), the issuer must be a private

---

[8]See the original Startup Exemption Crowdfunding Framework at www.startup exemption.com. Neiss, Best, and Cassady-Dorion are also the authors of *Crowdfund Investing for Dummies*, John Wiley & Sons, 2013. The *Dummies* book is written primarily for entrepreneurs.

[9]When we refer to equity crowdfunding portals, we intend to include Title III offering platforms operated by broker-dealers, unless otherwise stated. Most likely,

company based in the United States. Some categories of issuers are prohibited from using the new equity crowdfunding exemption. For example, investment companies, including mutual funds and private equity funds, may not raise capital via crowdfunding portals. In addition:

- Issuers may raise up to $1 million in any 12-month period through equity crowdfunding portals that are registered with the SEC. (Some legislators, notably Rep. Patrick McHenry of North Carolina, have proposed increasing the raise limit to $5 million.) Issuers may not raise capital on platforms that are not registered with the SEC, nor can they do so on their own websites. All deal flow must go through a registered intermediary, either a funding portal or a broker-dealer.
- Each issuer must provide accurate information concerning the following:
  - Its name, legal status, physical address, and website URL.
  - Names of officers, directors, and shareholders owning 20 percent or more of total equity.
  - Description of the business, business plan, capital structure (how the company finances its overall operations and growth, which may include long-term debt, specific short-term debt, common equity, and preferred equity).
  - Offering amount, deadline for raising that amount, and intended use of the proceeds raised from crowdfunding investors.
  - Price of the securities offered via crowdfunding, or method used to determine the price (in the latter case, an investor would have a right to rescind a commitment to purchase after the price is actually determined).
- Each issuer must provide an accurate description of the terms and risks of its offering, including the following (which we will explain further in Chapter 11, on deal terms, and Chapter 12, on due diligence):
  - Class of securities currently offered and previously issued (and the differences between them), and how the rights of existing shareholders will affect the rights of new crowdfunding investors/shareholders.
  - Holdings of 20 percent security holders.
  - How new crowdfunding equity is valued, and how that value may be affected by future rounds of capital investment and other corporate actions.

---

broker-dealer platforms will closely resemble crowdfunding portals, but there are some key differences. A broker-dealer license is more difficult and costly to receive, but the license holder is permitted to offer investment advice. Funding portals for Title III offerings are easier to register but must not advise investors on potential investments.

- Risks associated with minority ownership (including lack of control and discounted valuation), future corporate actions, and related-party transactions.
- Issuers seeking to raise $100,000 or less must provide tax returns (if any) and financial statements, certified by the company principal executive officer, typically the president or CEO. For those seeking between $100,000 and $500,000 in capital, the financials must be *reviewed* by an independent accountant (tax returns are not required). Issuers seeking $500,000 to $1 million must have the financial statements *audited* by a certified public accountant. (If Congress increases the raise limit to $5 million, the audit requirement may kick in at $3 million.) Note that an audit may cost the issuer in the neighborhood of $15,000 to $25,000, a key point that we will discuss further. (We will discuss the differences between reviews and audits in Chapter 12.)
- Issuers may sell shares to an unlimited number of investors in a deal, within the $1 million raise limit.
- Issuers are limited as to what they may say off-platform about the offering other than to direct prospective investors to the intermediary that is hosting their offering. All prospective investors must be funneled into the funding portal where their offerings are listed.
- Issuers must file their offerings with the SEC on a newly created Form C and make that information available to investors at least 21 days before any sales can be made on a funding portal. Filings include information about officers, directors, and 20 percent shareholders; offering share price; target offering amount (raise) and deadline to reach the target; whether the company will accept investments above the target amount; financial statements; related-party transactions; and other information.
- After a successful funding round is complete, issuers may have to file annual reports with the SEC, and share them with investors as well.
- Issuers may participate in equity crowdfunding offerings and Reg D offerings at the same time; these would be known as *parallel offerings*. Thus, it is possible to seek $1 million from everyday investors through a Title III offering *and* to seek an unlimited amount of capital from accredited investors through a Reg D offering.
- Under both federal and state law, issuers (including company officers, directors, sellers, and promoters of the offering) will be held liable for any fraudulent or intentionally misleading statements or material omissions made in connection with their offerings. If an issuer fails to "exercise reasonable care" and knowingly makes untrue or misleading statements, it must reimburse investors for their purchase of securities, plus interest.

## Title III Provisions for Investors

The ability of everyday people to invest small amounts of money in private companies represents a monumental shift in the private capital markets. The traditional rules that locked most nonaccredited investors out of the markets aimed to protect presumably unsophisticated investors from the riskiest kinds of investments. With Title III, Congress attempted to balance the new freedom to invest, on the one hand, with requirements and restrictions designed to protect "new" angel investors, on the other hand. Such requirements include greater offering disclosure (as previously listed), and such restrictions include limits on the amount people can invest (and possibly lose). The amount of money that an investor can plow into equity crowdfunding deals *each year* depends on the investor's net worth and/or income, detailed here. Congress's intent was to help prevent catastrophic losses being incurred by unsophisticated investors in high-risk securities.

- Individuals with annual income and net worth of less than $100,000 may invest the greater of $2,000 or 5 percent of their income or 5 percent of their net worth. For example, someone who earns $80,000 a year could invest up to $4,000 in a year. In any case, *anyone* can invest at least $2,000 in equity crowdfunding each year.
- Individuals with income or net worth of $100,000 or more can invest up to 10 percent of their income or net worth (whichever is greater), but not more than $100,000, per year.
- Investors may self-certify that they are not exceeding their investment limits. In other words, they do not have to submit tax returns or other documentation to prove it.
- When registering on a funding portal, investors must demonstrate that they understand the risks of private equity investments. Presumably they can do that by studying the educational content on each portal and filling out a quiz-like form.
- Investors must hold shares for at least one year after purchasing them via equity crowdfunding, with some exceptions (for example, they may sell shares back to the issuer or to an accredited investor).
- Investors in crowdfunded securities may file a lawsuit against an issuer for rescission of funds if the issuer is liable for material misstatements or omissions in connection with the offering.[10]

## Title III Provisions for Intermediaries

As we explained earlier, companies cannot directly offer crowdfunding investments to the public. All equity crowdfunding offers must be funneled

---

[10]Under Section 12(a)(2) of the Securities Act of 1933.

through an intermediary, which can be either a funding portal or a broker-dealer (not a passive bulletin board, which we defined in Chapter 2). In addition:

- Funding portals that are not broker-dealers must register with the SEC and a registered national securities association, of which FINRA is currently the only one.
- Funding portals that are not broker-dealers may not offer investment advice or make recommendations to, or solicit investments from, individual investors. In this way, these portals are purely conduits between issuers and "the crowd," with some educational content added (see next item).
- Intermediaries must provide "investor education" content on their portals that helps investors understand, among other things, the risks of investing in private equity, including loss and illiquidity. They must ensure that investors review that material and affirm that they understand the risks, presumably by filling out a questionnaire. The SEC will soon clarify how portals must go about demonstrating investors' understanding.
- The rules that apply to funding portals are different from those that apply to broker-dealers, but in general they both may establish objective criteria for accepting and rejecting issuers that apply to their portals (i.e., they may curate their offerings based on, for example, industry or geographic location). Broker-dealers may curate based on subjective criteria as well. The SEC has not yet clarified to what extent, if any, funding portals may use subjective criteria.
- An intermediary may not pool investors' funds into a single investing entity (as MicroVentures does for Reg D investments). In other words, each individual investor will invest directly in the company that offers shares.
- Intermediaries must conduct background checks on officers, directors, and 20 percent equity holders of each issuer, as a means to reduce the risk of fraud. Intermediaries must disqualify an issuer if one of its officers, directors, or "participants" (such as promoters) in the offering is a "bad actor," as defined by the SEC (a convicted felon, person subject to a finance-related injunction or restraining order, person subject to SEC disciplinary action, etc.).
- An intermediary *may* potentially be liable in an offering where there is a fraudulent or inaccurate statement made by an issuer. This is another provision that should be clarified by the SEC when it issues final rules. We will discuss this item further in Chapter 7.
- Intermediaries (including funding portals, their directors, officers, or partners) may not have a financial interest in an issuer using their

services and may not compensate any third parties (including promoters, finders, or lead generators) for identifying potential investors.

- Intermediaries may not receive, manage, or hold investor funds. All intermediaries must use a third-party escrow service for that purpose and release the funds to the issuer only when the offering is successful. The money is returned to investors if a campaign is not fully funded.
- Intermediaries must make reasonable efforts to ensure that issuers comply with offering limits and do not receive funds from investors until their target offering amount is achieved, ensure that the personal information collected from investors is kept private and secure, and make an effort to ensure (it is not yet clear how they will do this) that investors do not exceed their limits based on income and/or net worth. SEC commissioner Luis A. Aguilar referred to this as the intermediaries' "gatekeeping role."
- The JOBS Act did not address how funding portals can charge fees from issuers and/or investors based on crowdfunding transactions. The new law is clear, however, that funding portals are not permitted to take an equity stake from companies whose offerings they list.

## Broker-Dealers and Due Diligence

As we pointed out in Chapter 2, platforms that are broker-dealers are held to a stricter due diligence standard than other intermediaries. They must take reasonable steps to ensure that the information and disclosures that issuers post on its platform are materially accurate and complete. They must collect sufficient information about each investor to determine that client's risk profile and whether particular investments are suitable. Broker-dealers are subject not only to the general antifraud and antimanipulation provisions of federal securities laws and regulations, but to additional antifraud, anti–money laundering, and other requirements specific to broker-dealers.

Most equity crowdfunding platforms that are broker-dealers, or are affiliated with one, disclose that information in the website's footer or on the "About Us" page. Some portals that are not broker-dealers provide a disclaimer to that effect in the footer or on the "About Us" page, or maybe in the FAQs. If that information is not available, you should (1) contact the platform's staff and ask about their broker-dealer status and/or (2) visit FINRA's BrokerCheck page (http://www.finra.org/Investors/ToolsCalculators/Broker Check/) and conduct a search to see if the platform is registered as a broker-dealer.

If you consider registering as an investor on a non-broker-dealer funding portal, ask the principals exactly what kind of screening and selection process they conduct before they accept an issuer. Some portals use outside services, such as CrowdCheck (based in northern Virginia) to conduct background checks. (Some actually emphasize that they do not conduct formal due diligence, leaving that up to the investors.) If the platform does claim to conduct due diligence, make sure the principals have relevant experience in the securities industry so that their due diligence is meaningful.

Keep in mind that you (in collaboration with the crowd) may need to conduct your own due diligence before you invest, even if the platform is a broker-dealer. We will explain more about this in Chapter 12.

## Experts and Pundits Analyze Title III

In the midst of a slow economic recovery, with stubborn unemployment rates still on the minds of Americans, the JOBS Act as a whole wasn't much of a blip on most people's radar. Within the entrepreneurial and financial communities, however, it was a huge and obvious BLIP. The lifting of the ban on general solicitation (in Title II) made the earliest and biggest splash among prospective Reg D issuers and advisers. The SEC issued final rules governing general solicitation in July 2013, and the rules went into effect 60 days later, making general solicitation legal on Reg D platforms that relied on Rule 506(c). Experts and pundits anticipated a surge of interest in alternative investments (including private equity, venture capital, and angel investing) among the several million accredited investors who had not previously been solicited because they just did not have the "right" connections.

Title III was perhaps the most controversial part of the JOBS Act, because it opened the riskiest area of alternative investing to tens of millions of investors who, because they were not wealthy, were presumed to be less sophisticated—certainly they were less experienced. And because they are not wealthy, their capacity to endure a lost investment is presumably small.

Dara Albright, the provocative editor of *NowStreet Wire* and former chief strategy officer of Crowdnetics, wrote, "One day when historians look back on this era, history will show that it was crowdfinance that saved America by democratizing its markets and leading it into a new era of economic prosperity."

A more moderate optimist, and one with whom we agree, was Duncan Niederauer, CEO of NYSE Euronext (a merger of the New York Stock Exchange and Euronext NV). Niederauer predicted that equity crowdfunding, if properly done, "will become the future of how most small businesses are going to be financed."[11]

Mary Jo White, the SEC chair since April 2013, said that thanks to the JOBS Act, " . . . we are at the start of what promises to be a period of

---

[11] "The New Thundering Herd," *The Economist,* June 16, 2012, p. 71.

transformative change in capital formation."[12] What makes this statement interesting is that previous SEC chairs were believed to be averse, or at best indifferent, to the idea of equity crowdfunding.

Several experts predicted that Title III crowdfunding would make the early-stage financial markets more "transparent," an annoying buzzword that in this case means that equity crowdfunding portals will let everyone observe private offerings, investor participation, and transaction terms that are otherwise cloaked in secrecy. Such transparency will help new private equity investors understand the process of early-stage capital formation. Indiegogo's Danae Ringelmann pointed out in a *Wall Street Journal* guest column:

> [S]ome people argue that unaccredited investors should be restricted to buying shares in large, publicly traded companies because invest-ing in small companies is too risky and complex for regular people. We won't really know if this is true until equity crowdfunding gets sufficient real-world testing. But my hopeful prediction is that equity crowdfunding will make investing less risky and complex for most people, improve the investing experience for both Wall Street and Main Street, and spur economic growth.[13]

We want to point out that if equity crowdfunding goes well for issuers and investors, a surging supply (of early-stage equity offerings) and demand (for investment opportunities in those offerings by newly enfranchised investors) will result in not only growth of private capital markets but also innovations that we can't anticipate yet. Innovation might include not only Web technology that better connects issuers to investors and facilitates transactions but also simplified deal terms and new business entities (like a *Subchapter CF corporation* or *crowdfund venture?*) structured specifically for equity crowdfunding transactions.

We believe there are large numbers of people who have great inven-tions being held up in boxes in garages because those people have not been able to find capital that they need to file patent applications and/or produce and market a product that would benefit consumers and industries. Title III will help those investors bring their innovations to the attention of massive numbers of new investors.

---

[12] Mary Jo White, SEC chairwoman, speech to the 41st Annual Securities Regula-tion Institute, Coronado, CA, January 27, 2014. Available at https://www.sec.gov/servlet/Satellite/News/Speech/Detail/Speech/1370540677500#.Uv1HLYUtpX2.

[13] "Danae Ringelmann, "Crowdfunding Unleashes a Different Segment of the Econ-omy," *The Wall Street Journal*, November 26, 2013.

## Supply-Side Pessimists

The pessimists weighed in, too. On the supply side, experts worried that the $1 million per year raise limit would confine crowdfunding issuers to the smallest, earliest-stage—therefore, probably the riskiest—companies. "This exemption is likely to be used primarily by early-stage issuers that do not yet have an operating history or, possibly, even financial statements," warned Columbia law professor John C. Coffee, Jr., in testimony before the Senate Committee on Banking, Housing and Urban Affairs.[14] "Such issuers are in effect flying on a 'wing and a prayer,' selling hope more than substance." (It is interesting to note that when the House passed the Crowdfunding Act in 2011, the raise limit was $2 million; the Senate insisted on lowering it to $1 million.)

Issuers that need to raise $500,000 to $1 million may believe that the cost of audited financial statements is too burdensome, even "brutal,"[15] and turn instead to a Reg D offering—or, for that matter, a rewards-based crowdfunding campaign—where there are no raise limits, and where audited financials are not required. As Ryan Caldbeck, the CEO of CircleUp, pointed out, "Very few private companies below $50 million in revenue have annual audits."[16]

Even for raises under $500,000, equity crowdfunding is not cheap. The SEC estimated that issuers seeking to raise up to $100,000 would spend roughly $13,000 to $18,000 to prepare and execute the offering (that doesn't include the fee paid to the portal), and issuers raising $100,000 to $500,000 would spend $25,000 to $55,000.[17] Joanna Schwartz, the CEO of EarlyShares, one of the pioneers in Reg D platforms, calculated the costs to be higher in some ranges.[18] However, once again, issuers and their advisers are working on creative ways to try to keep the total cost

---

[14] "Spurring Job Growth through Capital Formation While Protecting Investors," statement of Professor John C. Coffee, Jr., Columbia University Law School, December 1, 2011. This was before the Senate modified the House version of the JOBS Act.

[15] "Brutal" is the word used by Kim Wales to describe this requirement for raises over $500,000. Wales is the CEO of Wales Capital and an executive board member of the CrowdFund Intermediary Regulatory Advocates. Slava Rubin, CEO of Indiegogo, called the auditing requirement a "massive deal breaker."

[16] Interview with Caldbeck on CrowdFundBeat.com, February 13, 2014, https://www.youtube.com/watch?v=RUd1JPG_zSQ.

[17] "Crowdfunding: Proposed Rules," SEC, October 23, 2013, pp. 358–359, http://www.sec.gov/rules/proposed/2013/33-9470.pdf.

[18] Joanna Schwartz, CEO, EarlyShares.com, "Comments on the Proposed Rule: Crowdfunding," February 3, 2014, http://www.sec.gov/comments/s7-09-13/s70913-214.pdf.

under $10,000—for example, filing provisional patents (to avoid the higher costs of full patent applications), forming new entities instead of using established entities (to simplify any audit requirements), and the like. In this new regulatory environment, it is not clear how effective such strategies might be in reducing the prefunding financial burden on issuers, but there are various professional groups seeking this outcome.

Certain kinds of issuers—high-tech startups that would probably need future rounds of angel and VC funding, for example—might avoid equity crowdfunding because of the specter that raising capital from thousands of small investors would complicate their capitalization tables (detailed spreadsheets that list investors and their equity holdings). Complex cap tables *might* scare venture capitalists away from later-stage raises.

Realistically, we may not know how the Title III requirements and costs will affect deal flow for a year or two. We do know that if the costs remain high for issuers, then those who will be most disadvantaged will be lower-income entrepreneurs in the underserved communities that need economic development and new jobs the most. For that reason, the SEC indicated that it may consider adding an under-$50,000 raise category with simpler, less costly requirements. That doesn't sound like a lot of capital, but it might be just what an inventor needs to apply for a patent, produce CAD drawings, build a prototype, and license the invention to a big company.

## Demand-Side Pessimists

Pessimism thrived on the demand side, too. If institutional, private equity, and venture capital investors represented "smart money," the new crowd of nonaccredited investors were disrespectfully called "dumb money" by some skeptics, or, more respectfully, "new money." In other words, they feared that unsophisticated investors would not understand what they were getting into and would tend to be lured by slick marketing tactics to misallocate capital to poorly managed startups that were bound to fail, not only losing their savings but also depriving more deserving companies of growth capital. Moreover, some financial gurus say that new money tends to be eager and therefore overpay for equity, which could lead to a bubble—where "lots of new money flows into startups and other deals, only to dry up after losses or scandal trigger a backlash...."[19] To be sure, some of the folks who issued these warnings worked in investment brokerages and mergers and acquisition (M&A) advisory firms for which equity crowdfunding represented new competition. So their criticisms were self-serving, even if they

---

[19]Gary Phillips, president of Tech Coast Angels in San Diego, quoted in Dan McSwain, "Deregulation Focuses on Small Investors," *San Diego Union-Tribune,* September 21, 2013.

may have been valid. (We also want to point out, in response to their skepticism, that adding potentially tens of millions of investors broadens the capital pool beyond the formerly oligopolistic set of capital channels. Shattering that oligopoly with vast new sources of capital can benefit many worthy but overlooked startups and inventors.)

Another demand-side fear is that "new" investors might overreact to the inevitable losses they incur. Although equity crowdfunding portals are responsible for educating investors, still many novice angel investors will have a hard time shifting from their traditional mind-set: that the stock prices of public companies, in which they have invested for generations, might rise and fall a little, they may or may not beat inflation, but they rarely plummet. Equity crowdfunding is a different mind-set: When these novices invest in startups, some will most assuredly plummet to zero. The worry shared by several experts is that too many equity crowdfunding investors, new to the private capital market, will react unreasonably when they take a 100 percent loss due to poor management or become the victims of outright fraud, resulting in a "train wreck," said Brian Korn, a securities lawyer with Manatt, Phelps & Phillips in New York City. "One [bad] deal will be the poster child for why equity crowdfunding is too risky. If this happens enough, complaints will roll in to the SEC or legislators, which will probably prompt them to shut down or modify crowdfunding to reduce the risk."

Some in the securities industry worry that equity crowdfunding will become the "funding of last resort," used by companies that were rejected by traditional angel investors, venture capital firms, or Reg D offering platforms. We hasten to point out that angel groups, VCs, and Reg D platforms typically fund only a miniscule percentage of the applicants they review, and each year many thousands of worthy applicants trickle down through the capital channels unfunded. Many such "rejects" have gone on to be very successful, including Amazon.com. Jeff Bekiares, the COO of SparkMarket, an intrastate equity crowdfunding platform in Georgia, pointed out:

> The vast majority of potential campaigns [issuers] we speak to have been rejected by every traditional capital source. Having said that, that does not make them bad companies (or good, to be fair), it just means that they fall outside of the service area of these traditional sources. They are too young and don't have sufficient collateral to get a traditional loan, they are too small for VCs, they are too boring for angels.

Perhaps street-level members of "the crowd" will prove to be wise in their collective judgment of enterprise potential and will fund the gems that VCs in their mahogany boardrooms have missed.

The deepest cynics noted that the JOBS Act really did not have a direct impact on employment, only on capital formation, which may or may not lead to new jobs. "Slapping a catchy acronym like the JOBS Act on a piece of legislation makes it more difficult for politicians to oppose it," wrote Steven Rattner in the *New York Times*.[20] "Picking winners among the many young companies seeking money is a tough business, even for the most sophisticated investors. Indeed, most professionally run venture funds lose money. For individuals, it's pure folly. Buy a lottery ticket instead. Your chance of winning is likely to be higher." (Rattner, whose beat is economic policy, finance, and business, went on to say that Title II's legalizing of general solicitation is "less terrifying but still problematic." He finished his article by predicting, "The largest number of jobs likely to be created by the JOBS Act will be for lawyers needed to clean up the mess that it will create.")

So now there are voices saying the JOBS Act went too far in deregulating private securities law (and exposed inexperienced investors to too much risk), while other voices said that the act, by setting capital limits too low and compliance costs too high, "may have made matters worse through its heavy-handed regulatory action."[21] Like any novel area of law, the JOBS Act needs some tweaking.

The most common fear expressed in connection with Title III, however, was fraud. When the SEC issued its proposed rules for Title III in October 2013, Commissioner Aguilar warned that Title III crowdfunding "increases the risks of fraud, illiquidity, and self-dealing to relatively unsophisticated investors," and especially certain "vulnerable" communities:

> *The use of crowdfunding to reach potentially vulnerable segments of society is a particular concern. Many of the SEC's enforcement cases arise from 'affinity frauds' that exploit the trust and friendship that often exists among members of any ethnic, religious, or other community.*[22]

---

[20] Steven Rattner, "A Sneaky Way to Deregulate," *New York Times*, Opinionator Pages, March 3, 2013, http://opinionator.blogs.nytimes.com/2013/03/03/a-sneaky-way-to-deregulate/. Shortly thereafter, securities lawyer Samuel Guzik pointed out on his blog that Rattner had been charged by the SEC in 2010 with participating in a "pay-to-play scheme" whereby he allegedly received kickbacks to obtain investments from New York's largest pension fund. Rattner settled the SEC's charges by paying $6.2 million. See SEC Litigation Release No. 21748, November 18, 2010, http://www.sec.gov/litigation/litreleases/2010/lr21748.htm.

[21] Stuart R. Cohn, "The New Crowdfunding Registration Exemption: Good Idea, Bad Execution," *Florida Law Review*, Volume 64, Issue 5, p. 1434.

[22] Luis A. Aguilar, commissioner, U.S. Securities and Exchange Commission, "Harnessing the Internet to Promote Access to Capital for Small Businesses, While Protecting the Interests of Investors," October 23, 2013. See also "Investor Bulletin: Affinity Fraud," SEC Office of Investor Education and Advocacy, September 2012, www.sec.gov/investor/alerts/affinityfraud.pdf.

Supporters of crowdfunding acknowledge that some fraud will occur, as it does everywhere, including the public securities markets. But they point to the low instance of fraud in rewards-based crowdfunding in the United States, and especially in equity-based crowdfunding in Australia (since 2006) and the United Kingdom (since 2012), where unsophisticated investors may similarly participate. It is important to note that Australia and the United Kingdom have different securities regulations than the United States, and every country defines *fraud* a bit differently, so it is not an apples-to-apples comparison. But in general, equity crowdfunding has proceeded in those countries fairly successfully so far.

Of course, you can take steps to protect yourself against fraud in equity crowdfunding. We will discuss fraud prevention and detection in greater depth in Chapter 12.

## THE CAUTIOUS OUTLOOK

As a result of all these fears and uncertainties, after Title III crowdfunding portals launch, this new industry will be "flat" for a year or so, predicts Richard Swart, PhD, who leads a global crowdfunding research team at the Fung Institute, University of California at Berkeley. "Issuers are being advised by their lawyers to use extreme caution, because it's still so new. But after a year it will escalate very quickly."

Some equity crowdfunding professionals and their advisers believe it will take much longer for activity to escalate beyond a slow start, and it may take another act of Congress. "I am 99 percent certain that there will be a JOBS Act 2.0," says Kim Wales, CEO of Wales Capital in New York City and an executive board member of the CrowdFund Intermediary Regulatory Advocates (its acronym CFIRA is pronounced "Siffra"). Wales predicts that Congress will, among other revisions, increase the maximum amount that can be raised via crowdfunding from $1 million to possibly $5 million, which will attract more established companies (thus, less risky offerings) as well as more "smart money." If that happens, Wales says, "there will be a pivot point in the marketplace in five years, with major changes in the private equity financing system. Venture capital and private equity will evolve along with the maturing crowdfunding industry." But, she adds, "Everyone is cautious now."

Here is our outlook. Since the Declaration of Independence, all new, big ideas about government and commerce in America have been met with criticism, pessimism, and fear, along with optimism and hope. The American Revolution was a glorious success, the Articles of Confederation were an abject failure, the Constitution saved the new republic from near-disaster, and so it has gone for 238 years. We are a nation of pioneers, experimenting and sometimes failing, always recovering, and quite often succeeding spectacularly. Equity crowdfunding is a new, big idea, a wild frontier. No amount of legislation or regulation can guarantee that it will succeed or that there will not be fraud, or that some unsophisticated (and sophisticated) investors will not be wiped out.

There will be many crowdfunding investors who commit to an offering mainly because they have an emotional attraction—an affinity—to a product or brand or team of founders and want to support them, in the same way that you might buy a jacket with a team logo on it. These affinity investors might not even glance at the company's financial statements. They, along with the crowd that they invest with and have discussions with on their social networks, may turn out to be the company's most passionate brand advocates. If they earn a strong return on their investment, it will be a pleasant surprise. If the investment turns out to be a loss, oh well, maybe one of the other startups they invested in will be a home run. At the very least, they are members of the vanguard of "new" angel investors, participating in an experiment in democracy. This is *much* more fun and rewarding than dropping a bundle at the casino.

Donation, rewards, and debt crowdfunding have already become integral parts of our financial system, despite some disappointments and losses on both sides of the table. Donors, contributors, funders, and lenders of moderate income and net worth have realized benefits both tangible and intangible on crowdfunding platforms, and, in the case of debt crowdfunding, significant financial benefits. We believe equity crowdfunding will also become, maybe in a year or maybe in five years, just as integral to our financial system as its predecessors.

As a "new" investor in private securities, you can minimize the possibility of loss by exercising caution, taking it slow and educating yourself about private capital markets, diversifying your equity crowdfunding portfolio, and limiting your potential losses to 5 or 10 percent of your investment assets.

# CHAPTER 4

# Intrastate Equity Crowdfunding

## Nonaccredited Investors May Invest in Startups Located in Their Own State

For 36-plus months after the Jumpstart Our Business Startups (JOBS) Act was signed into law, U.S. entrepreneurs, intermediaries, and investors waited for the SEC to issue final rules for Title III equity crowdfunding. Crowdfunding portals could not be launched before the rules went into effect.

Meanwhile, some states decided to get their own jumpstart going. Relying on the intrastate exemption from SEC registration, at least 12 states—led by Kansas and Georgia—have enacted legislation or promulgated regulations that allow unlimited numbers of nonaccredited investors to participate in small private securities offerings (See Table 4.1). Several more states and the District of Columbia have introduced similar legislation or have begun the regulatory proposal process.

In October 2013, an intrastate funding portal in Georgia called Spark-Market became the first equity crowdfunding portal in the United States to facilitate the equity financing of a private company (Bohemian Guitars LLC) with participation by nonaccredited investors. The emergence of state-based platforms and what they mean overall for equity crowdfunding for investors are explored in this chapter.

## THE INTRASTATE EXEMPTION

In Chapters 2 and 3 we discussed various exemptions that private companies can use to avoid the costly process of registering securities offerings with the SEC. Rule 506 of Regulation D has been one of the most popular exemptions. Title III of the JOBS Act created the newest exemption, known as the crowdfunding exemption, inserted into the Securities Act of 1933 as Section 4(a)(6).

The purpose of the intrastate offering exemption, under Section 3(a)(11) of the Securities Act, is to "facilitate the financing of local business operations," according to the SEC. For an offering to qualify for the exemption,

**TABLE 4.1**   Intrastate Exemptions (as of November 30, 2014)

| State | Year Enacted | Annual Raise Limit ($) | Investment Limits? | Equity Crowdfunding Portals? |
|-------|--------------|------------------------|--------------------|------------------------------|
| Alabama | 2014 | 1 million | Yes | Allowed |
| Colorado | 2014 | 5 million | No | Allowed |
| Georgia | 2011 | 1 million | Yes | Allowed |
| Idaho | 2012* | 2 million | Yes | Not yet determined |
| Indiana | 2014 | 2 million | Yes | Required |
| Kansas | 2011 | 1 million | Yes | Allowed |
| Maine** | 2014 | 2 million | Yes | Allowed |
| Maryland | 2014 | 100,000 | Yes | Prohibited |
| Massachusetts | 2015 | 2 million | Yes | Allowed |
| Michigan | 2013 | 2 million | Yes | Allowed |
| Nebraska | 2013 | $250,000/2yr | No | Prohibited |
| Tennessee | 2015 | 1 million | Yes | Allowed |
| Texas | 2014 | 1 million | Yes | Required |
| Washington | 2014 | 1 million | Yes | Allowed |
| Wisconsin | 2013 | 2 million | Yes | Required |

**Legend:**
* Year of first administrative order.
** Based on Rule 504 of Regulation D, not Section 3(a)(11) of the Securities Act.

Sources: CrowdCheck, Anthony J. Zeoli (Ginsberg Jacobs), Nilene Evans (Morrison Foerster), and Georgia P. Quinn (Seyfarth Shaw). Check this book's website (wiley.com/equitycf) for updates on new intrastate exemption legislation and regulation.

the company making the offer must (1) be organized in the state where it is offering the securities, (2) carry out a significant amount of its business in that state, and (3) make the particular offer and sale of securities only to residents of that state.[1] The company is responsible for making sure securities offered under the intrastate exemption are not sold to any out-of-state residents. If that happens, the company could be in violation of federal

---

[1]Because these criteria are imprecise, Rule 147 under the Securities Act provides more specific "safe harbor" guidelines to help issuers determine whether they are in compliance with Section 3(a)(11). For example, what exactly does "organized in the state" mean? What exactly does "resident of the state" mean? Rule 147 lists numerous ways a company might comply with those requirements.

securities law. As long as the in-state issuers and intermediaries comply with Section 3(a)(11), they can avoid the (often) more complex federal securities laws in favor of the (usually) more relaxed state regulatory framework.

Section 3(a)(11) requires that securities sold through the intrastate exemption may not be resold to residents of other states within a certain time period, usually nine months. The law intends that intrastate-offered securities "come to rest" within the state.

Beyond that fundamental framework, the federal government is essentially backing away from regulation of intrastate offerings, except to protect investors from fraud. Even intrastate offerings are subject to the antifraud provisions of federal securities law, as well as the respective state antifraud laws. Issuers, therefore, still must ensure that investors are not misled by any oral or written communication concerning the company's operations or the terms and risks of the investment. Some states, like California, provide additional layers of protection for investors by, for example, considering whether or not an offering is fair before allowing it to be listed.[2]

Under the umbrella of Section 3(a)(11), each state has its own "blue sky" securities laws and regulations that govern intrastate securities offerings and sales within its borders. These laws vary from state to state.

Each state requires issuers to register their intrastate securities offerings with that state's securities commission, or else qualify for an exemption from state registration. In other words, there are two levels of registration: federal and state. All intrastate offerings qualify for the federal exemption from SEC registration, but then they must go through the process all over again at the state level: register with the state or qualify for a state exemption. Each state establishes its own exemptions for intrastate offerings. Registering securities offerings at the state level is not as mega-expensive as registering with the SEC at the national level, but it is still expensive. So small, private companies making an intrastate offering usually seek to qualify for a state exemption if they can.

It may appear at first glance that by creating their own intrastate securities laws and regulations, the states are just adding a layer of complexity onto an already complex federal securities regulatory framework. The main reason each state wants its own system, however, is to provide a less regulated—and usually less expensive—option for startups to raise capital within its borders, to spur economic development at the local and state level.

---

[2] Whenever there is a conflict between state and federal law, federal law is "preemptive." Under the Supremacy Clause of the U.S. Constitution, a state law must not frustrate the purposes of federal law.

(We should not ignore the fact that states earn revenue in various ways as a result of their securities regs.)

## THE SURGE OF INTRASTATE EXEMPTIONS

Before 2011, intrastate offerings were typically open to participation by large (or unlimited) numbers of accredited investors, plus limited numbers (usually between 35 and 75, depending on the state) of nonaccredited investors who had prior relationships with the issuers—we referred to them previously as the three Fs: founders, family, and friends. (We do not refer to these "connected" nonaccredited investors as "the crowd" because their ranks are extremely limited.) In this regard, these traditional intrastate offerings were similar to Regulation D offerings. Starting with Kansas in 2011, though, there has been a trend toward writing new state-level exemptions that allow unlimited numbers of nonaccredited investors to participate in small intrastate offerings. "Small" typically means up to $1 million or $2 million of capital. And starting with Wisconsin and Michigan in 2013, some states have begun to mimic the language of the Title III crowdfunding exemption at the state level. We can divide the intrastate exemptions into the following three categories:

- In some states, the intrastate securities exemption allows, but does not require, intrastate offerings to be listed on equity crowdfunding portals. These states include Alabama, Colorado, Georgia, Maine, Massachusetts, Michigan, Tennessee, and Washington.
- Some states established intrastate securities exemptions that *require* offerings to be made on crowdfunding portals, as does Title III at the national level. These states include Wisconsin, Indiana, and Texas. We can correctly refer to these as intrastate crowdfunding exemptions.
- In at least one state, Idaho, it is not yet clear whether equity crowdfunding (for nonaccredited investors) will be permitted under the existing intrastate securities exemptions.

Table 4.1 (earlier in this chapter) summarizes the intrastate securities exemptions to date. (You can find updated information—undoubtedly with more states—at this book's website: www.wiley.com/equitycf.) No two states' intrastate exemptions are exactly the same. For example, most of the states set a maximum capital raise of $1 million or $2 million, but at least one state (Colorado) sets a $5 million limit.

Also, the maximum investments that nonaccredited investors can make vary from state to state. (See the website for complete details.) Most of these investment limits are fixed dollar amounts per year or per offering. For example, Alabama and Indiana limit nonaccredited investors to a flat $5,000 per year, while at least four states (Georgia, Michigan, Tennessee, and Wisconsin) set the limit at $10,000 per offering (with no limit on the number of offerings per year). Washington is the only state at this point that sets a limit based on nonaccredited investors' income or net worth—specifically, the greater of $2,000 or 5 percent of income and/or net worth (similar to Title III at the national level).

## Can Funding Portals Receive Compensation?

There is a further distinction between (1) states that allow non-broker-dealers to operate intrastate equity crowdfunding portals and receive commissions (or other remuneration) from such operation and (2) states that require portals to be operated by broker-dealers in order to receive compensation. This gets confusing, because some of the state exemptions are unclear about this issue—and securities lawyers disagree about how to interpret those unclear exemptions. Undoubtedly in the next year or two we will get more definitive guidance on these laws and regulations, and we will update our website accordingly.

Why does the issue of portal compensation matter to investors? If only broker-dealer portals can earn compensation, it is unlikely that non-broker-dealers will launch portals. So what? Well, that leaves only broker-dealers that can operate the portals profitably, but they have very little incentive to do so in most states because intrastate offerings tend to be very small (typically in the five to low-six figures), and broker-dealers just can't make enough money off such small deals. So, especially in mostly rural states, the small size of equity offerings (and the small number of offerings) may simply slam the door to intrastate equity crowdfunding.

Kansas, for example, was the first state to enact an intrastate securities exemption, titled the Invest Kansas Exemption (IKE), in August 2011. This exemption allows Kansas-based for-profit companies to sell equity- and debt-based securities totaling up to $1 million per year without registering those offerings with the Kansas securities commissioner. The issuer needs only to file a one-page form with the securities commissioner's office, no filing fee, and no follow-up reporting. The issuer may not be, either before or as a result of the intrastate offering, an investment company such as a mutual fund.

Investors must be Kansas residents. If they are accredited investors, they may invest an unlimited amount. If they are nonaccredited, they are limited to $5,000 *per offering*, in any number of offerings each year. Contrast that with the Title III provision which limits low-income investors to $2,000 *per year*.

Kansas is one of the states where it is unclear if non-broker-dealer funding portals may earn commissions on equity crowdfunding offerings. The statute says: "A commission or other remuneration shall not be paid or given, directly or indirectly, for any person's participation in the offer or sale of securities for the issuer unless the person is registered as a broker-dealer or agent under the act."[3]

In fact, Lynn Hammes director of finance and administration at the Kansas Securities Commission, does not consider IKE a crowdfunding framework at all. "We look at IKE as a community offering," said Hammes in February 2014. "So far we've had eight issuers that have used or are using the exemption to raise capital. They are mostly rural groceries, restaurants and cafes, brew houses, a dairy.... One issuer said he needed $250,000 to open a restaurant. I don't know how much he actually raised, because they're not required to report back to us. But he did raise enough money from members of the community to open the restaurant." Hammes expects that broker-dealers will be reluctant to get involved in IKE offerings because the capital amounts tend to be so small.

### The Bohemian Guitar Success Story

While Kansas took a statutory approach to its intrastate exemption (i.e., its legislature passed a law), Georgia took a regulatory approach. On December 8, 2011, the Georgia State Securities Division promulgated a new regulation known as the Invest Georgia Exemption, or IGE. Like the Kansas law, Georgia's intrastate exemption allows an unlimited number of nonaccredited investors to participate in equity offerings of up to $1,000,000, and it allows issuers to use general solicitation. Issuers are not *required* to use registered intermediaries for IGE offerings, but they may do so.

The Georgia exemption lets nonaccredited investors invest $10,000 in each deal.

Unlike IKE, IGE is silent on the issue of commissions or remuneration for intermediaries. So, according to Georgia securities regulations, a crowdfunding portal—whether or not it is a registered broker-dealer—can earn fees for facilitating IGE equity deals, as long as it is based in that state.

Although IGE is not specifically dubbed a crowdfunding regulation (it does not mention crowdfunding, funding platforms, or portals), it does create a framework for intrastate equity crowdfunding portals to operate in Georgia. At least two of them have launched: SterlingFunder and SparkMarket.

**SterlingFunder.** Launched in early 2013, SterlingFunder rightfully claims to be "the first equity crowdfunding portal in the USA for both accredited

---

[3] 81-5-21 Invest Kansas Exemption, §(a)(5).

and non-accredited investors." The site hosts rewards-based campaigns as well as equity and debt securities offerings. The rewards campaigns are open to backers outside of Georgia, but the IGE-based securities offerings are open only to in-state residents. SterlingFunder also had one Reg D offering listed (for accredited investors only) in 2014, involving an issuer based in Connecticut. Of its 11 offerings listed in February 2014, seven were intrastate equity deals in a wide range of sectors: tech, medical, consumer products, entertainment, leisure, and so on. Only one issuer of those seven had actually received dollar commitments from investors by the end of February 2014.

**SparkMarket.** Launched in early October 2013, SparkMarket is truly a niche player. It hosts rewards and equity crowdfunding campaigns exclusively for Georgia-based companies. The equity arm of the platform is open only to in-state investors, but the rewards arm is open to backers across the country.

The SparkMarket website features a compelling appeal to investors, at the top of its "About" page: "We believe your investment dollars should do more for you than just generate a return—they should make your hometown better, too." This captures the community spirit of intrastate crowdfunding quite nicely.

SparkMarket made history in mid-October 2013 when its first listed offering, Bohemian Guitars, mounted a successful equity raise of over $100,000, the first one ever on an equity crowdfunding portal in the United States with participation from nonaccredited investors.

Bohemian Guitars was founded in the summer of 2012 by two brothers, Adam and Shaun Lee, in Marietta, Georgia. A year earlier they visited family in South Africa and returned home to Georgia with an oilcan guitar that they had bought in a township outside of Johannesburg. It was made from a used motor oil can as the body, along with carved wood neck, tuning pegs, steel strings, and an electric pickup. It had a distinctive, pleasantly twangy sound. Shaun started making his own version of the oilcan guitar and found that he could sell the funky instruments for $250 and up. Adam brought business management skills to the enterprise (Shaun won't allow him in the workshop), and the brothers started Bohemian Guitars LLC. To raise capital for production and marketing, they mounted a Kickstarter campaign on January 15, 2013, with a goal of $32,000. The campaign finished on February 22 with $54,233 raised from 297 backers. They started producing a few different models priced at $299 and selling them through their website and at music festivals and fairs.

Thanks partly to their exposure on Kickstarter, the national retailer Urban Outfitters placed a big order, and the Lee brothers needed to raise more capital for bigger production runs. They applied to community banks, national banks, angel investors, and venture capital firms, without success—notwithstanding their Kickstarter-based proof of concept. "The banks told us we needed to have at least a million in revenue before they could help us," says Adam Lee, now CEO. Finally they met Megan Johnson and Jeff Bekiares, the founders of SparkMarket, around the time they were preparing to launch SparkMarket. Bohemian Guitars became SparkMarket's first issuer when it launched in October 2013, using both rewards and equity channels. They set the equity raise target at $100,000, and achieved it in just over a week (during which Adam says he didn't sleep). By November 5, Bohemian Guitars had raised $126,000 on the equity side and $4,000 on the rewards side. Lee considers the rewards component "more of a tip jar for people who wanted to support us but couldn't afford the equity buy-in."

In the early days of the raise, the Lees had conversations, in person or by phone, with dozens of prospective investors. According to Adam Lee, it boiled down to six investors who participated in the equity offering, three of whom were accredited. The nonaccredited investors invested amounts ranging from the minimum level of $1,000 up to $8,000. "That's exactly how this process should work," says Bekiares, referring to the funneling of interested investors into the deal and the relative investment amounts among accredited and nonaccredited investors.

The Lee brothers are quick to point out that preparing their SparkMarket campaign involved hard work and expense. That included developing the offering documents and terms, working with a PR firm on publicity, educating the community about equity crowdfunding, and producing a video for the campaign. (Adam Lee advises entrepreneurs, "You don't want to produce a killer video, because then investors will think you've already got money.")

Now Bohemian Guitars carries a broader selection of models, starting at $299 (using oilcans and their custom-branded Bohemian Moonshine cans) and ranging up to $500 (using vintage oil, gas, and maple syrup cans). They are receiving international orders. The company also sells branded guitar picks and, of course, T-shirts. Kevin Harrington, the infomercial pioneer and *Shark Tank* shark, made an angel investment in the company after the SparkMarket raise ended. And in January 2014, the company began a "social action initiative," donating guitars to schools and community youth organizations.

SparkMarket earned fees for the Bohemian Guitars equity raise. The platform originally charged a $50 application fee but no longer does. Now it charges a $500 nonrefundable due diligence fee for applicants whose applications are not rejected off the bat, a posting fee based on the duration of the campaign, and a success fee (if the issuer achieves its stated goal) of 5 to 8 percent for both rewards and equity offerings.

## Deal Trickle, Not Flow

Since the Bohemian Guitar capital raise, the action on SparkMarket has been slow. At the end of February 2014 the platform featured no listed offerings, but by October it featured two Atlanta-based companies. Although Bekiares says SparkMarket has evaluated more than 100 potential offerings, it has approved only the aforementioned three to be listed so far.

At this point, screening out deals that don't seem to have a good chance for success on the platform (curation) has been a major limiting factor. Bekiares, a lawyer who formerly practiced in the areas of corporate, securities, and banking law, explains why he thinks deal flow will continue to be "limited" for some time to come:

> *The IGE concept is still so new that very few potential issuers understand it or have even heard about crowdfunding in general. In Georgia, awareness right now is very limited to the Atlanta beltway area. We receive very few inquiries from secondary or tertiary marketplaces in Georgia, even though our theory is that those marketplaces are better positioned to take advantage of these [equity crowdfunding] tools.*

Another factor restricting the flow of deals is that even those issuers who have learned about crowdfunding need time to plan a campaign. Based on conversations he has had with hundreds of potential issuers and their advisers, Bekiares told us:

> *The gap between companies that "want to crowdfund" and those who are "ready to crowdfund" is very wide, as we have discovered. The ecosystem of consultants who can cost-effectively (and just flat-out effectively) help companies to bridge this gap just simply isn't mature yet. It is going to take another couple of years for this to occur.*

In many ways Bekiares's outlook fits the interstate (Title III) version of equity crowdfunding as well as the intrastate version:

> *We hope to expand the number of deals aggressively (but responsibly) in the years to come. I expect most IGE deals to come from small but revenue-generating companies, mostly in the metropolitan area for now but expanding out from there to smaller communities in [two or three] years. Most IGE deals that we list will be business-to-consumer companies that have tangible, consumer-facing products.*

He expects most intrastate raises to be in the $25,000 to $125,000 range for the near future in Georgia.

*Most of the companies we are working with will price their deals between $250 and $1,000 per share, and will cap the number of new shareholders. I expect that most crowdfunding deals will generate between 25 and 75 new shareholders. That is a perfectly manageable size, especially if the company intelligently structures the terms of the securities to be non-voting, and redeemable.*

A redeemable security is one that gives the issuer a right to "call in" or buy back the securities at a certain price (which should be advantageous to the investors, because it provides a healthy return on their initial investments) and in certain circumstances, such as reaching a revenue or growth benchmark. They are generally restricted, which means the investor may not sell them freely in the secondary markets.

Bekiares does not expect investors to be drawn to intrastate equity crowdfunding for spectacular returns on investment. Fast-growth tech startups are not going to be the typical IGE issuers.

*For every "next Facebook" looking to raise $1 million, there are 100 mom-and-pop companies in the 50 states, looking to raise $50,000 to replace their SBA [Small Business Administration] loans. Our theory actually is that IGE will be more successfully used in smaller cities and communities. This is because those places already have built up community support networks that this concept [depends on]. That won't happen, however, until communities "get" this concept. And "getting" it is an education issue. That will spread outward from the metro areas.*

Although the Bohemian Guitars raise took little more than a month, Bekiares expects most IGE campaigns to stay open longer. "Rewards-based campaigns are generally 30 to 45 days," he says. "I expect IGE campaigns to be open for three to five months. Potential investors are asking questions, coming to events, calling the principals, and generally investigating. They can't make these decisions in 30 days. It is just going to take longer, and that is OK."

## More Intrastate Crowdfunding Exemptions

The good news is that intrastate equity crowdfunding is taking off, albeit slowly, in other states too. (See Table 4.1.)

The Michigan intrastate exemption, for example, was enacted in December 2013, and is known as the Michigan Invests Locally Exemption (MILE). The act uses the term *website platform* rather than "crowdfunding." The notable elements of this exemption, from a Michigan investor's point of view, are the following:

- Michigan-based issuers can raise up to $2 million per year via intrastate equity crowdfunding, to be adjusted for inflation.
- Investors who are accredited under federal law (with a $1 million net worth or $200,000 income threshold) may invest an unlimited amount of money under the Michigan exemption. Like the Georgia exemption, nonaccredited investors (not to be confused with "noncertified investors") who live in Michigan may invest up to $10,000 in each intrastate offering.

In May 2014, Tecumseh Brewing Company of Tecumseh, Michigan, raised $175,000 from 21 investors, both accredited and nonaccredited, on Localstake, an equity crowdfunding platform. This was not a straight-equity offering but, rather, a revenue-sharing deal whereby each investor would receive 7 percent of sales each month until he or she earned 150 percent of their investment back. The individual investments ranged from $250 to $122,000. The company held tasting events for potential investors, of course.

Intrastate equity crowdfunding is an attractive option for investors who are interested in community development and supporting local businesses. So far, the investment limits for nonaccredited investors are actually more permissive in intrastate equity crowdfunding than in Title III (interstate) equity crowdfunding.

On the other hand, issuers who want to reach investors on a regional or national scale will take advantage of Title III equity crowdfunding. The remainder of this book focuses primarily on Title III crowdfunding, although we also use comparisons with intrastate equity crowdfunding wherever they are useful.

# CHAPTER 5

# Deal Flow

**A**s soon as the SEC issues final rules under Title III of the JOBS Act, all investors, including nonaccredited investors, can browse through Title III offerings on a number of equity crowdfunding portals and broker-dealer platforms. In short, tens of millions of ordinary people will be able to buy shares in startups and early-stage companies online.

This is a dramatic departure from the restrictive (or protective, depending on your point of view) rules that U.S. investors and entrepreneurs had lived under since 1933. In this deregulated private securities environment, what kinds of companies will seek to raise capital through equity crowdfunding? What will the deal flow look like as the equity crowdfunding industry grows and matures?

In some respects, the companies that make equity offerings via crowdfunding will be the same kinds of companies that have been making equity offerings to angel investors for decades, through more traditional financing channels. For example, many of them will be companies that have raised all the money they can from founders, family, and friends (the three Fs) and still need capital to grow, but are still too small to attract the interest of commercial banks and venture capital firms. Angel investors have traditionally occupied this awkward middle funding stage. Until a few years ago, startups and early-stage companies had to struggle to find angel investors, and vice versa. Now Reg D offering platforms and Title III crowdfunding portals[1] bring equity issuers and investors together in one convenient marketplace, streamlining the financing of small, private companies.

Equity crowdfunding thus represents a new financing infrastructure (or ecosystem, as finance wonks like to call it) for the same kinds of companies that have sought angel capital for decades. But online crowdfunding, being

---

[1]Unless otherwise indicated, when we refer to equity crowdfunding portals, or simply funding portals, we mean to include broker-dealer platforms that facilitate equity crowdfunding, although there are some important differences, as we discussed in Chapter 3.

a wholly 21st century phenomenon that for the first time admits masses of non-accredited investors to the demand side, will attract companies with particular characteristics more than others. In this chapter we will explore and make forecasts about deal flow—what kinds of companies will choose to raise capital via equity crowdfunding.

## STAGES OF BUSINESS DEVELOPMENT

Different investment books and educational materials define *startup* and *early-stage* in various ways. There is not necessarily a single correct way to define them, which is fine because the boundaries between stages of business development overlap and shift over time. For the purposes of this book, we define them loosely as shown in Table 5.1.

The definitions in Table 5.1 are intended as general guidelines, with fuzzy definitions and porous boundaries. The sources of capital for each development stage vary from one industry to another. Venture capital firms sometimes get interested in innovative technology companies at the startup stage, for example, and angel investors have been known to invest at the seed stage and sometimes the expansion stage.[2] Fast-growth high-tech firms often zip through the development stages faster than consumer products firms. But in general, the primary source of equity capital for startup and early-stage companies is angel investors, whether on or outside of crowdfunding platforms.

Investment amounts grow along with development stages. According to Robert T. Slee's book *Private Capital Markets*,[3] the following are typical investment ranges in each stage:

- *In the seed and startup stages,* individual equity investors have traditionally invested $50,000 to $100,000 per deal, although the amounts have ranged lower and higher. In equity crowdfunding deals, minimum investments will be significantly lower—at the $1,000 level or possibly lower.
- *In the early stage,* angel investors historically invested $100,000 to $2 million per deal and buy both common and preferred stock as well as convertible debt. Again, equity crowdfunding investment levels will be significantly lower.

---

[2] At least one research report shows that angel investors make up to 34 percent of their investments at the seed stage. (Robert Wiltbank, PhD, and Warren Boeker, PhD, "Returns to Angel Investors in Groups," Kauffman Foundation and Angel Capital Education Foundation, 2007, p. 12.)
[3] Slee, op. cit., p. 396.

**TABLE 5.1**  Stages of Private Business Development

| Development Stage | Company Description | Traditional Capital Sources* | New Online Capital Sources* |
|---|---|---|---|
| Seed (a.k.a. proof of concept or pre-launch) | Concept and/or product development. | Founders, family, and friends (three Fs); angel investors start to show interest. | Rewards crowdfunding, equity crowdfunding up to $100,000. |
| Startup (a.k.a. launch) | Operational but still developing product or service. Little or no revenue. Typically less than 18 months old. | Three Fs, angel investors, trade credit (suppliers & customers). | Rewards crowdfunding, equity crowdfunding up to $1 million. |
| Early (a.k.a. ramp-up) | Product or service in market testing and/or pilot production, often associated with "soft" or "beta" launch. Maybe some revenue but usually operating at a loss. Less than 3 years old. | Heavier reliance on angel investors; venture capital; commercial banks begin to show interest. | Equity crowdfunding, often parallel with Rule 506(c) offerings ("hybrid offerings"). |
| Expansion (a.k.a. growth) | Significant revenue growth, maybe profit. True market potential being realized. More than 3 years old. | More reliance on retained earnings; VC groups show higher interest; commercial banks.** | Regulation D offerings: Rules 506(b) and 506(c). |
| Mature (a.k.a. later) | Profit, positive cash flow. Typically more than 10 years old. | Private equity, commercial banks, IPO. | Regulation A+ (Title IV of JOBS Act). |

* In addition to retained earnings

**Some studies show that angel investors make significant investments at the low end of the expansion stage (e.g., Wiltbank and Boeker, 2007). We expect that securities crowdfunding, especially P2P lending, will creep into the expansion stage within five years.

Primary source: Robert T. Slee, *Private Capital Markets*, 2nd edition, John Wiley & Sons, 2011, pp. 366–367. Secondary sources: Van Osnabruge and Robinson, *Angel Investing*, Harvard, 2000; Benjamin and Margulis, *Angel Investor's Handbook*, Bloomberg, 2001; Don Hofstrand, "Financing Stages for Start-up Businesses," Iowa State University Extension and Outreach, April 2013; Scott A. Shane, *Fools Gold? The Truth behind Angel Investing in America*, Oxford University Press, 2009, pp. 114–115.

- *In the expansion stage*, venture capital firms typically invest $1 million to $10 million per deal and favor preferred stock and convertible debt.
- *In the mature stage*, private equity firms typically invest more than $3 million, up to hundreds of millions, to buy common stock, usually taking more than 50 percent ownership share and often as much as 100 percent.

## Growth Potential

From an investor's point of view, it is important to categorize small businesses in terms of their long-term growth potential, as well as their stage of development. Evaluating growth potential is more subjective—and more dependent on the founders' vision and goals than on quantitative measures such as revenue and years in operation—but just as crucial to making good investment decisions. We suggest sorting companies into three main categories: lifestyle, middle-market, and high-potential.

- *Lifestyle companies* provide good incomes for their founders, but do not pursue growth aggressively. The founders of these companies are not inclined to take big risks that may jeopardize their (and their families') long-term security. They are reluctant to give up even minority control to people outside the family, preferring to keep their companies closely held (rarely seeking financing beyond community bank loans). Lifestyle companies are usually not destined to be acquisition targets (at least not until the founders retire) or IPO candidates, so they wouldn't be considered prime investment opportunities. Unfortunately for investors, the vast majority of startups—probably over 95 percent—are in this category.[4]
- *Middle-market companies* pursue growth aggressively until their annual revenues are $50 million to $2 billion,[5] and then level off or continue to seek modest growth. These companies should provide equity investors with income (in the form of dividends) and gradually increase in share value when they mature. They may also be prime opportunities for strategic investors. They may be acquisition candidates eventually, but not soon enough for equity investors looking for near-term divestment. And you can expect them to remain private (not file an IPO). In 2013 only 8 percent of middle-market companies expected to go public at any time in the future, according to a Deloitte survey.[6]
- *High-potential entrepreneurial companies* pursue fast growth aggressively. The founders want the company to be big—maybe very, very big—not only so they can earn a fortune but also because sometimes it's

---

[4]W.E. Wetzel and J. Freear, "Promoting Informal Venture Capital in the United States: Reflections on the History of the Venture Capital Network," *Informal Venture Capital,* edited by R. Harrison and C.M. Mason, Hemel Hempstead, 1994; cited in Van Osnabrugge and Robinson, op. cit., p. 20. Also Shane, op. cit., p. 31, citing the U.S. Census Bureau's Survey of Business Owners (SBO). In fact, the SBO found that only 1.3 percent of businesses less than six years old had received an external equity investment from friends and/or business angels.
[5]Definitions of *middle market* vary. This one is from "Mid-Market Perspectives: 2013 Report on America's Economic Engine," Deloitte Development LLC, p. 3.
[6]Ibid., p. 9.

necessary to get big in order to achieve economies of scale and maintain market share in a hypercompetitive environment. The founders of high-potential entrepreneurial companies typically thrive on risk taking, innovation, and the excitement of growth. Exit strategies are paramount: They aim to be acquisition targets or IPO candidates, representing jackpot-grade exit events for early investors.

In hindsight, it is easy to categorize the 1976 version of Apple Computer as a high-potential entrepreneurial company. It is quite another thing to have been Mike Markkula in 1976, visiting the scruffy founders Steve Jobs and Steve Wozniak in the garage where Apple was born and recognizing it as a high-potential startup worth investing in. It helped that Markkula had a master's degree in electrical engineering and had worked as a marketing manager for Fairchild Semiconductor and Intel, where he earned millions on stock options before he met Jobs and Wozniak. That is, Markkula had the education and experience, not to mention keen judgment of character, which enabled him to recognize Apple's potential.

That is exactly what angel investors (or their advisers) need to judge the potential of a startup: education and experience in the field where the startup operates. Studies have shown that returns on investments made by angel investors are positively correlated with the number of years of experience in the industry in which the investment was made.[7] (We will see in Chapter 6 that return on investment may not be the only motivating factor, or even the primary one, for many equity crowdfunding investors.)

You have probably heard the axiom "Invest in what you know," commonly attributed to Peter Lynch, an extraordinarily successful investor. You have a better chance of earning a good return by investing in an industry where you have knowledge and experience—this is generally true whether you invest in public or private securities.[8]

---

[7]Wiltbank and Boeker, op. cit., page 6. Note that the data and analysis that produced this correlation apply to accredited investors who belong to angel groups. "The differences between group and non-group investors are . . . unknown empirically," the authors write.

[8]Lynch ran Fidelity Investments' Magellan Fund from 1977 to 1990. During that period, Magellan was the top-ranked general equity mutual fund in America, averaging an amazing 29.2 percent return a year. Lynch is also famous for insisting that "individual investors who don't have time to learn complicated quantitative stock measures or read lengthy financial reports can research stocks as well [as] or better than most investment professionals by using the 'invest in what you know' principle to find undervalued stocks." He also famously said, "Go for a business that any idiot can run, because sooner or later, any idiot probably is going to run it." Source: *Wharton Alumni Magazine*, Wharton School, University of Pennsylvania, Spring 2007.

Traditionally, if an angel investor had no expertise in a particular field, he or she could join an angel group where other members had that expertise, so members of the group could collaborate on evaluating investment opportunities and, farther down the road, due diligence. But angel groups admit only accredited investors.

Equity crowdfunding makes collaboration possible among nonaccredited angel investors. When you register on a funding portal, you have an opportunity to ask questions and share ideas with other investors—the crowd—before you decide whether to invest. (In fact, the social networking and collaboration component is built into the SEC rules, in which the SEC repeatedly refers to the "wisdom of the crowd.") So one of the most important things you should do when you join a discussion on a crowdfunding portal is check out the education and industry experience of the investors whose opinions you take into consideration.[9]

Another reason why you, as an investor, do not need to feel confined to a familiar industry, Lynch's advice notwithstanding: New research and review tools and services are emerging in the equity crowdfunding world that will help investors scrutinize and evaluate the offerings posted on funding portals. Pioneers in this field, such as Finagraph and Zacks CF Research, developed such tools and services for the equity crowdfunding market because they anticipate a huge demand for them by investors who have never before considered buying private securities.

### Historical Angel Deal Flow

You might think that because only a small percentage of new businesses have middle-market potential, and even fewer have high-growth potential, not very many prime investment opportunities would come along each year. You would be mistaken. A *very* large number of new businesses start up each year.

As usual, the numbers vary depending on who is counting. Some researchers, such as those who receive funding from small business advocacy groups, have incentives to make assumptions and select data that yield high numbers of startups. The following statistics come from relatively unbiased sources: the U.S. Bureau of Labor Statistics[10] (BLS) and the Kauffman Foundation's Index of Entrepreneurial Activity.[11]

---

[9]Dissenting caveat: "The easiest way to lose money is by following the crowd in something that you don't understand." Lamido Sanusi, governor of Nigeria's Central Bank (reported by Elexis Okeowo in *BloombergBusinessweek*, September 12, 2013).
[10]Source: "Entrepreneurship and the U.S. Economy," undated. Available at http://www.bls.gov/bdm/entrepreneurship/entrepreneurship.htm.
[11]Robert W. Fairlie, author; released April 2014. Available at http://www.kauffman.org/~/media/kauffman_org/research_reports_and_covers/2014/04/kiea_2014_report.pdf.

- The number of new businesses in a year tends to rise and fall with the economic conditions. The BLS reports that the number of "new business establishments" peaked in 2006 at over 660,000 new establishments for the year. After a four-year decline related to the Great Recession of 2008–2009, the number of new establishments bottomed out at 505,000 in 2012. Since 2012 the numbers have been slowly recovering. These figures are limited, however, because they include only companies that have at least one employee besides a self-employed founder (i.e., one employee eligible for unemployment insurance coverage).
- The Kauffman Index (released April 2014) presents new-business numbers that are radically higher than the BLS numbers. It tracks instances of adults (age 20 to 64) who start businesses "as their main work activity"—that is, in which they work more than 15 hours per week. In 2013, about 476,000 new businesses were started *per month* (presumably yielding up to 5.7 million new businesses for the year).

The new businesses tracked by the Kauffman Index are many times more numerous than the companies tracked by the BLS, because the former includes self-employed individuals while the latter includes only employer companies. Since employers are more likely than self-employed individuals to grow, the BLS numbers are more significant for investors.

More insights from the 2011 and 2013 Kauffman Indexes of Entrepreneurial Activity:

- The industry with the highest entrepreneurial activity rate in both 2011 and 2013 was construction. The manufacturing sector had the lowest startup rate.
- The states with the strongest startup activity in 2013 were Alaska, California, Colorado, Florida, Montana, and Texas. The states with the weakest startup activity were Pennsylvania, Washington, and the Midwestern states. Note that geographic data can shift across the map fairly quickly, so in a few years there may be different states with the highest startup rates.
- The share of new businesses from "opportunity entrepreneurship" versus unemployment-driven ("necessity") entrepreneurship was substantially higher in 2013 than in 2011. The latter represents new businesses started by entrepreneurs primarily due to the difficulty of finding employment in the postrecession period. The Kauffman researchers speculate that opportunity startups have a greater likelihood of fast growth than necessity startups.

These facts and figures suggest that many companies will be in a position to benefit from equity crowdfunding. In fact, the demand may be *greater* than the figures here suggest, due to a pent-up entrepreneurial drive and need for capital. According to a 2005 Gallup Poll, 57 percent of all Americans stated they would like to own a business, but only 4 percent were actually self-employed. A big reason for that disparity was the difficulty for average would-be entrepreneurs in finding capital. This is precisely what the JOBS Act aims to fix. Accordingly, we could see an explosion of new startups as the access to capital is deregulated, thanks to the JOBS Act.

More businesses will mean more success stories, but it will also mean more failures. You have probably heard about the low survival rate for business startups. It is risky to invest in them because a large percentage of them fail in the first several years, even before they can provide any return for investors.

Sure, many businesses are shut down in their first few years, not only because some fail to earn sufficient revenue but for various other reasons—for example, founders find more lucrative opportunities elsewhere. Yet even if more than half of new businesses fail to survive beyond the expansion stage, still there are many that do survive and provide returns—in a few cases, spectacular returns—for angel investors. According to the Small Business Administration and the Bureau of Labor Statistics, about half of all new establishments survive five years or more, and about one-third survive 10 years or more. Survival rates have changed little over recent decades.[12]

Survival rates vary by industry. The healthcare and social assistance industry consistently ranks among the industries with the highest survival rates. Construction, with high startup rates since the recession, nevertheless ranks among the lowest survival rates currently.

Survival is good, but providing a return for investors goes beyond mere survival. Just because a new business survives for 10 years or more does not guarantee that its equity investors will earn the kind of return they expect. According to research by Shikhar Ghosh, a senior lecturer at Harvard Business School:

> *If failure means liquidating all assets, with investors losing most or all the money they put into the company, then the failure rate for startups is 30 to 40 percent. If failure refers to failing to see the projected return on investment, then the failure rate is 70 to 80 percent.*[13]

---

[12] "Frequently Asked Questions about Small Business," SBA Office of Advocacy, September 2012, p. 3.

[13] Carmen Hobel, "Why Companies Fail—and How Their Founders Can Bounce Back," Harvard Business School, March 7, 2011.

Thus, even if 75 percent of startups are destined to disappoint investors, that leaves something like 150,000 new businesses (25 percent of 600,000, using the BLS estimates) each year that will please investors, and a decent number of those will *thrill* investors. (Using the Kauffman Index estimates would give us 25 percent of 5 million, or more than a million, each year that would please investors.) This does not take into account the added supply of new companies that crowdfunding will inevitably add to the marketplace, providing a greater range of investment options than in the past.

That is why individual investors collectively invest tens of billions of dollars each year in startups and early-stage companies.[14] To be sure, a little less than half of that annual investment is in the form of equity financing. Roughly 56 percent takes the form of debt, a portion of which is convertible debt (which can be converted to equity when the company meets certain benchmarks). Straight debt, rather than convertible debt, is the only option for companies that are sole proprietorships and partnerships.[15]

What proportion of those individual equity investors are angel investors, and what proportion are family and friends of company founders? Two of the most authoritative sources of data on the angel investment market are the Center for Venture Research at the University of New Hampshire, and Scott A. Shane, PhD, professor of economics and entrepreneurial studies at the Weatherhead School of Management, Case Western Reserve University in Cleveland. Professor Shane estimated, based on 2004 data, that out of the approximately $80 billion per year of equity investment in small, private companies by individuals, 83 percent comes from family and friends. The remaining 17 percent—amounting to $13.8 billion per year—comes from angel investors, individuals who do not have prior relationships with company owners or managers.

As a result of Titles II and III of the JOBS Act, the money from family and friends in the earliest stages of capital formation might be dwarfed by money from the new class of angel investors, flipping the proportion on its head. Title II now allows solicitation of the general public in Regulation D, Rule 506(c) offerings—way beyond the close circle of family, friends, and

---

[14] Benjamin and Margulis, op. cit., p. 2; Shane, op. cit., p. 30.

[15] Shane, op. cit., p. 33. Professor Shane's survey of investors offered respondents only two choices on this particular question, debt or equity; he did not offer convertible debt as a distinct choice. Correspondence with Professor Shane in April 2013 led us to assume that respondents considered convertible debt as debt rather than equity. He also opined that "convertible debt would have to be a tiny portion of the total" as applied to startups.

established relationships. And Title III allows participation of all investors, *way* beyond Rule 506(c)'s tight circle of accredited investors.

The Center for Venture Research at UNH estimates that, in 2012, total angel investment in the United States was $22.9 billion, involving 67,000 issuers and 268,160 investors. In addition:

- The sectors with the highest angel investment activity in 2012 were software (23 percent), healthcare and medical (14 percent), and retail (12 percent).
- The average deal size was $341,800, and the average equity received by investors in a deal was 12.7 percent.
- The average deal valuation was $2.7 million.[16]

For comparison, Shane points out that in 2004, an additional $24 billion in equity investment in "young" companies came from venture capital firms (professional investors). Just for a sense of scale, Shane compares those *yearly* equity investment figures in small, private companies to the $25 billion average *daily* trading volume on the New York Stock Exchange (investment in large, public companies).[17]

One observation about the difference between angel and venture capital investment: Entrepreneurs have historically tended to look for equity or debt financing from business angels when their funding needs have exceeded $100,000, according to Professor Shane's research, while "companies generally go to venture capitalists when they need $2 million more."[18]

Shane also found that about 36 percent of angel investments are in companies worth more than $1 million at the time of investment. Surprisingly, about 42 percent of such investments (both debt and equity) are made in companies with valuations of less than $50,000. The area in between (valuations of $50,000 to $1 million) account for 22 percent of angel investment.[19]

**Title III Deal Flow**  All of the foregoing statistics about angel capital are B.E.C.: before equity crowdfunding. Starting in 2015, we expect, the nature of angel capital will shift for issuers and investors alike, as startups and early-stage companies can offer shares online to a much larger number of investors. Tens of millions of nonaccredited investors, in fact, who had no existing relationships with these companies (or their intermediaries) can invest in them for the first time in generations.

---

[16]Jeffrey Sohl, "2012 Angel Market Analysis," Center for Venture Research, P.T. Paul College of Business and Economics, University of New Hampshire, 2013.
[17]Shane, op. cit., pp. 38–40.
[18]Ibid., p. 62.
[19]Ibid., pp. 96–97.

What kinds of companies will seek to raise capital through equity crowd-funding portals and broker-dealer platforms? The short answer is: eventually, all kinds. In the short term, though—over the first year or two at least—a narrower range of companies will have incentives to try raising capital using the crowdfunding exemption. Once these pioneers test the waters, and perhaps Congress revises Title III to make the requirements and costs less burdensome for issuers, a broader range of companies will take advantage of equity crowdfunding to raise capital.

We can tell you what kinds of companies we think, and other people who are active in the field think, will be the early adopters in this new industry. We don't guarantee any of us are correct. Sara Hanks, a securities lawyer and the CEO of CrowdCheck (a Virginia-based due diligence and compliance service that works with broker-dealers, equity offering platforms, and crowdfunding portals as well as companies seeking funding), has said, "The only thing we know for certain about equity crowdfunding is that everything we think we know about equity crowdfunding today is wrong."

The issuers most likely to benefit from equity crowdfunding in the early days will include (but will not be limited to) the following:

- Consumer product businesses that welcome a large number of affinity investors. These are enthusiastic customers or users of their products, who will—not only to protect their investment but because they are devoted fans—spread the word and help promote the brand throughout the marketplace. In fact, some of these investors are motivated by "idea lust," whereby they simply want the product to be marketed so they can buy it; they have supported rewards-based crowdfunding projects for the same reason.
- For-profit businesses that promote or support a cause or social benefit, such as "green" (eco-friendly) products and services, sustainable energy development, low-income housing, elder care, pet rescue, and so on. Investors in these businesses will tend to be more socially than financially motivated.
- Community-based retail businesses that benefit from affinity investors who have direct connections to the business because they live in the same community and/or know the owners personally. These include gathering spots like restaurants, cafes, delicatessens, bodegas, groceries, bowling alleys, fitness centers, and hair and nail salons, as well as small real estate development and acquisition projects.
- Creative, fun, and/or glamorous projects—such as music, film, and games. Games have been the most active category in rewards-based crowdfunding, in terms of the number of campaigns and funding success. Samuel S. Guzik, a securities lawyer in Los Angeles, says

commercial film projects will be among the "best candidates" for Title III equity crowdfunding because it is relatively simple for a crowd of investors to judge whether a project is worth investing in based on the story and the film team. That's not to say the crowd can accurately predict profitability, but it can certainly decide whether the project is going to be fun and meaningful, and if so, "Let's go along for the ride!"

- High-tech startups that are too small in terms of revenue to qualify for debt financing from commercial banks, and that do not have perceived 10x growth potential (the ability to scale quickly and return 10 times the amount invested within five to seven years) to attract funding from venture capital firms. Investors may be drawn to these issuers by dreams of spectacular returns, or simply because they love gadgets and apps.

- Small service companies such as the building trades, remodeling contractors, office cleaning services, adventure expeditions (e.g., fishing trips), and so on. Barry Schuler, a late-stage venture capitalist and former CEO of America Online, says equity crowdfunding "may be ideal for a smaller [service] business . . . that can get itself to profitability on a single funding round" of $1 million or less.[20] From there, such a company would grow organically, that is, using profits to fund growth.

We want to emphasize that companies that need to raise more than $1 million are not excluded from equity crowdfunding. Some companies will raise capital through a Rule 506(c) offering, typically over $1 million, *and* a Title III crowdfunding offering simultaneously—known as a *parallel raise* or a *hybrid offering*. This strategy allows companies to seek high-minimum investments (typically tens of thousands of dollars each) from accredited, *strategic* investors—those who bring industry expertise and contacts to the table—and also low-minimum investments (as little as hundreds of dollars each) from friends, family, and total strangers at the same time.

Some equity crowdfunding skeptics admonish that growth-oriented, high-tech startups will not seek to raise capital via Title III crowdfunding because, for one reason, they need $5 million in seed funding to launch and scale quickly. The cost of launching a high-tech company, however, especially in the software, streaming media, and gaming businesses, has dropped precipitously since 2005, thanks in part to:

- Free access to powerful, open-source development software, such as Linux (operating system), PHP (content management), MySQL (database), and Apache (server control).

---

[20]Cheryl Conner, "Do You Really Want Dumb Money?," Forbes.com, November 3, 2013.

- The ubiquity of high-speed Internet access and cloud services that make virtual offices possible; startup founders and officers can work at home in different locations across the globe. This is the twenty-first-century version of Steve Jobs's parents' garage.
- Inexpensive Web infrastructure and hosting services such as WordPress, Rackspace, and Amazon Services.
- Free or low-cost distribution services like AppStore, marketing and customer service tools such as Facebook and Twitter, and sales tools such as Google AdWords and AdSense.

If launching a high-tech venture required $5 million in funding 10 years ago, it can be done today for $500,000 or in some cases as little as $50,000,[21] which are well within the equity crowdfunding raise limit. This steep drop in entry-level capital is already leading to a "tidal wave" of new entrepreneurs, says Wharton School management professor Raffi Amit.[22]

Keep in mind that companies are not limited to one round of equity crowdfunding. Many startups may seek to stage their fundraising into annual rounds of $1 million, which is permitted by the rules, or blend crowdfunding with other methods of equity or debt financing. Some conventional lenders, for example, are looking into new programs that would match a line of credit to the amount a company could raise through Title III.

The other reason high-tech startups might eschew equity crowdfunding is that having a large number of small investors could complicate their capitalization tables, which might scare away later rounds of venture capital investment. If issuers—possibly at the behest of funding portals—grant antidilution rights and no-drag-along provisions to those investors, for example, VCs might balk. (We will discuss these kinds of rights and provisions in Chapter 11.)

The problems posed by messy cap tables could be resolved in a number of creative ways, though, including deal terms that allow the issuer to buy back shares from early crowdfunding investors when the valuation reaches a certain threshold—one that is high enough to give those early investors a satisfying return.

The biggest barrier to strong deal flow, from our perspective, is not a lack of startups that need capital. It is, rather, a lack of awareness among small businesses of the advantages and benefits of crowdfunding in general. According to a TechnoMetrica survey in September 2013, only 11 percent

---

[21]Naval Ravikant, CEO of AngelList, quoted in "Bay Watched," by N. Heller, *The New Yorker*, October 14, 2013, p. 75.
[22]"The Next Generation Model for the Investor-Startup Ecosystem," *Knowledge@ Wharton*, University of Pennsylvania, April 8, 2014.

of small business owners said they were "familiar . . . with crowdfunding as a way to raise capital or access funding."[23]

That was before the launch of Title III equity crowdfunding. Familiarity with crowdfunding will certainly growing among small businesses as soon as issuers and investors are making deals on funding portals. Its advantages and benefits, as well as the disadvantages and costs, will continue to become clear as equity crowdfunding enters the mainstream of private capital markets.

We believe that equity crowdfunding is a powerful new tool for hundreds of thousands of growing businesses and tens of millions of investors. These are big numbers with the potential to effect colossal changes and innovations in our private capital markets. Maybe equity crowdfunding will get off to a slow start, and deal flow will emerge from the categories we listed here, then spread in unexpected ways. Or maybe equity crowdfunding will explode beyond anyone's expectations right off the bat, and deal flow will become a gusher, attracting investors ranging from individuals to institutions, boosting economic growth, and creating new prosperity. Spectacular things can happen when you mix new technology, prudent deregulation, and a culture that rewards entrepreneurial spirit.

Chapter 6 focuses on the other side of the deal: those tens of millions of new investors—in other words, you—and what kinds of rewards, returns, risks, and costs you can realistically expect in the new world of equity crowdfunding.

---

[23] Raghavan Mayur, president, TechnoMetrica Market Intelligence, New Jersey; confirmed in e-mail to the authors, April 4, 2014. The survey has not been repeated.

# CHAPTER 6

# Angel Investors

Entrepreneurs are among the heroes of American free enterprise. They take big risks, defy convention, drive innovation, generate new jobs, and occasionally strike it rich. Angel investors, though not quite as celebrated, accelerate the growth of entrepreneurial ventures by providing capital and sharing the risk.

Our culture did not always celebrate entrepreneurs. In the 1950s, kids were advised by their parents to avoid risk: stay in college, choose a safe career, buy a house (and a cabin up north or down south), accumulate wealth, play golf or go fishing, and leave a big chunk for your heirs. Things have changed. Since the late 1990s, startups are where the coolest things happen, where disruption begins, and where fortunes of unprecedented magnitude are hatched. Risk became hip. Some of the most celebrated and wealthiest entrepreneurs, including Bill Gates and Mark Zuckerberg, are college dropouts.

If entrepreneurs are the glamorous engines of growth in our economy, angel investors are the first tank of jet fuel for those engines (and venture capital is the later-stage rocket fuel). The colossally successful enterprises that emerged since the microprocessor changed everything (beginning with Digital Equipment Corporation, or DEC, in the 1950s) could not have scaled fast enough—that being one of the requirements for success in the intensely competitive high-tech industry—without angel investors funding those start-ups in their earliest stages.

Until recently, few people could name an angel or venture capital investor. Few people are familiar with the name Georges Doriot, whose venture capital firm American Research and Development Corporation invested $70,000 in DEC in 1957. That stake was worth $355 million when DEC went public in 1968. Today, among investors and the financial press, the most active "superangels" (some of whom have risen to become more like micro–venture capitalists) are celebrities: Ron Conway, Marc Andreessen, Esther Dyson, Paul Graham, Naval Ravikant, and others. These are people who struck it rich as entrepreneurs and then built investment portfolios of dozens or hundreds of startups, mainly in the high-tech sector.

Most angel investors are not high-octane celebrities. Most are not even active in the high-tech sector. In fact, the vast majority of them were not successful entrepreneurs, nor were most of them truly wealthy. Many angel investors, especially those who diversify their angel investment portfolios, earn respectable returns; just as important, many angels gain tremendous satisfaction from boosting entrepreneurs and startups. Some of them enjoy the action, excitement, or celebrity more than the money.

Perhaps the most famous angel investor in America today is Ron Conway, who has been investing in startups since 1998. He invested in the company founded by Larry Page and Sergey Brin when it was still called Backrub, before they changed the name to Google. His other angel investments included PayPal, Digg, Twitter, Square, BuzzFeed, and Pinterest. Keep in mind that Conway, based in San Francisco, has more resources in the areas of research and due diligence than the average angel investor, and because he writes a lot of checks his deal flow is fertile. Conway will not share publicly his cumulative return on investment, but he has said, "I invest because I love helping entrepreneurs and watching them learn and succeed."[1]

In the early years, Conway expected that about one-third of his angel investments would break even, a third would be total losses, and a third would provide excellent returns. Around 2010 his investment team "audited" the 500 or so investments he had made up to that point—*not including* the high-tech bubble years leading up to 2002. He found that closer to 40 percent of his portfolio companies had gone bust since 2002, a higher failure rate than he expected. Still, a Google here and a PayPal there tend to make up for lots of total losses.

Conway also found that the economic climate in the country does not materially affect an entrepreneur's chance for success. In other words, entrepreneurs will succeed in a slow economy if the idea and the management team are strong.[2] Still, based on others' experience, investors should use caution during slow macroeconomic growth, especially in the areas of real estate, luxury goods, and other industries that are more correlated with the overall market.

Ron Conway's abounding successes are not typical for most angel investors, so you should not create expectations for yourself based on

[1] Jay Yarow, "Ron Conway: The Scariest Man in Silicon Valley," *Business Insider,* May 12, 2011, www.businessinsider.com/ron-conway-2011-5#ixzz2zGN5WUEl.
[2] Michael Arrington interviewed superangels Ron Conway and Paul Graham for CrunchBase, posted July 30, 2012, at http://techcrunch.com/2010/07/30 /ron-conway-paul-graham/.

his results. In this chapter we will explore who typical angel investors are, what their returns and rewards have been historically, and how those might be similar or different in the new equity crowdfunding environment. More pointedly, we will explain how the most compelling benefits of equity crowdfunding for many investors will be those that are social- and community-oriented.

## ANGEL INVESTORS BEFORE CROWDFUNDING

Do the characteristics and activities of angel investors in the past mean much in terms of who should or should not invest in equity crowdfunding in the future? Yes and no.

For two primary reasons, the emergence of Title III equity crowdfunding creates a new class of angel investors who may not share characteristics with traditional angels. The first reason is that before equity crowdfunding, individual angel investors typically had to commit large sums of money to participate in an angel deal, which usually amounted to tens (sometimes hundreds) of thousands of dollars in return for straight equity or debt that could be, under specific conditions, converted to equity. By contrast, through most Title III crowdfunding portals and broker-dealer platforms, investors are able to buy in for much smaller amounts—as little as $1,000 or even much less.[3]

The second reason this new class of crowd-angels is different is based on access. Before equity crowdfunding, the average investor did not have easy access to private securities offerings. Angel deals were offered mainly to (1) angel groups, the members of which were accredited investors only; (2) professional angel investors who were well known for writing checks to entrepreneurs; and (3) strategic investors who worked in the same industry as the issuer and therefore were colleagues of or had affiliations with the issuer or its broker-dealer. Now, thanks to equity crowdfunding, many angel deals are aggregated on portals and platforms for everyone to see, no matter who you know or don't know.

The playing field for nonaccredited angel investors today is different from that of the past. We cannot predict whether return on investment will be richer or poorer in equity crowdfunding than it was traditionally. Nevertheless, it is useful to understand how angels have invested over the years and what their results—in terms of financial returns and nonfinancial benefits—have been, to get a sense of whether or not you want to join the new class of angel investors.

---

[3]There appears to be a trend toward smaller, bite-size investments on Regulation D platforms that feature Rule 506(c), also known as Title II, offerings.

## TRADITIONAL ANGEL INVESTORS

Angels invest billions of dollars in thousands of new and early-stage ventures every year. Exact figures are hard to come by in this area because angel deals involve private securities, which are not subject to the same reporting requirements as trades involving public securities. Most of the statistics about angel investors and their angel investments are estimates derived from academic surveys, research conducted by professional associations, and SEC and census data. The figures we give in this chapter come from what we consider the most authoritative sources.

An angel investor is an individual who provides capital from his or her own funds to a private business owned and operated by someone who is neither a friend nor a family member. Angel capital may be in the form of straight debt, convertible debt, or equity.

Angels represent one of several possible sources of external capital for a startup or early-stage company. The others include the founders' family and friends, venture capitalists, banks and other lenders, trade creditors, and credit cards.

As noted in Chapter 5, angels invest predominantly in companies in the startup, early, and expansion stages of development, although some do invest in the earlier (seed) and later stages as well.

Here is how venture capitalists are different from angel investors: VC firms attract funds from individual and institutional investors (all of whom are accredited investors). The fund manager uses those pooled funds to invest in portfolio companies, usually in the early and growth stages but sometimes dipping into the startup stage as well. Investors who invest money in a VC fund have no power to select portfolio companies, and they earn a return only after the fund manager takes a percentage of the capital gain (known as *carried interest*), plus a management fee. Private equity (PE) firms and hedge funds have management and fee structures similar to those of VC funds and are likewise open only to accredited investors, but they have investment portfolio strategies that are different: PE firms focus on acquiring outright (or buying controlling interest in) mature companies, while hedge funds use a broad range of investment strategies that often include both long and short positions.

Angel investors (who may be accredited or nonaccredited) make their own selections and invest directly in portfolio companies, focusing mainly on the startup and early stages, and sometimes dipping into the seed stage. So angels earn 100 percent of any income or gains derived from the investment. Angels invest in a much wider range of industries than VCs, who tend to focus more on high-growth sectors of the economy such as technology and (lately) healthcare.

According to various sources, the number of active angel investors (those who made an angel investment during the year being studied) in the United States has risen from around 200,000 in 2002 to around 300,000 in 2012. Keep in mind that, according to our definition, this figure does not include family and friends of the founders.

In terms of dollars invested, angels in the aggregate generally invest much more than venture capitalists in the startup and early stages, but much less than VCs in the expansion and later stages.[4]

A 2012 study of entrepreneurship in the United States found that 5.3 percent of American adults have invested in an entrepreneur, and that was the highest rate among the G7 countries in 2000 to 2003. Half of those American angel investors funded an immediate family member or other relative. Only 13.5 percent of all angel investors provided money to someone who was not a family member, friend, neighbor, or work colleague.[5] Note that equity crowdfunding will create a different environment entirely, where a vast majority of issuers and investors might have never heard of each other and a personal connection between the issuer and each investor is very unlikely.

More than three-fourths of investors in angel deals are nonaccredited.[6] (You will recall from Chapter 2 that under Regulation D, with the exception of Rule 506(c), up to 35 investors in each offering can be nonaccredited.) That proportion may change if more issuers use the new Rule 506(c) exemption, created by the SEC as a result of the JOBS Act, because it allows general solicitation so long as nonaccredited investors are excluded.

While nonaccredited angels outnumber accredited angels, accredited investors account for more dollars invested in angel deals, because their investments tend to be much larger. That makes sense because they have more money to start with. Accredited investors provide about 54 percent of the angel dollars invested annually.[7]

Angel investors' income and net worth vary so widely that averages ($90,000 and $750,000, respectively, when you include both nonaccredited

---

[4]Sources: Center for Venture Research, University of New Hampshire; PwC MoneyTree; as reported by the Angel Capital Association, September 2012.

[5]"Global Entrepreneurship Monitor 2012 United States Report," Babson College and Baruch College, 2012, p. 24.

[6]Scott A. Shane, *Fool's Gold? The Truth behind Angel Investing in America*, Oxford University Press, 2009, pp. 11, 36. This estimate is based primarily on the *United States Entrepreneurial Assessment*, Florida International University, Paul D. Reynolds (producer), 2004, and "survey data conducted on a representative sample of the adult age population conducted by the Global Entrepreneurship Monitor" (Babson College and London Business School), Shane told the authors in 2014.

[7]Ibid., p. 37.

and accredited angels) are fairly useless. It is worth noting, though, that only 23 percent of angel investors have a household income of more than $200,000 per year. In fact, almost 32 percent have a household income of less than $40,000 per year. Roughly half of them have a college degree, and less than one-fourth of them are retired. The typical (median) number of investments in private companies that an angel investor makes in his or her lifetime is four.[8] Two-thirds to four-fifths of angel investors are men.[9]

A growing number of U.S. angel investors are members of angel groups, which are themselves growing in number. In 2012, 15,000 investors belonged to more than 300 groups across the United States.[10] Angel groups offer the following major advantages to their members, who must be accredited investors:

- Members can collaborate on deal sourcing, selection, and due diligence.
- Thanks to their numbers and wealth, members often attract superior deal flow compared with nonmembers.
- Most groups invite entrepreneurs to present their business plans and offerings in person at group meetings, after which members privately discuss the merits of each offering—they are local versions of *Shark Tank*.
- Members who invest together as a group may provide larger amounts of capital and therefore negotiate better deal terms than solo investors.

Some of the most active angel groups have branches in more than one state: Golden Seeds, for example, has members in California, Massachusetts, and New York.

The primary disadvantages of belonging to a group are that (1) members get to know each other's investment capacity and preferences, which some would rather keep private, and (2) along with collaboration and cooperation occasionally come dissension and conflict.

### Financial and Social Motivation

Certainly one of the motives for investing in risky startups and early-stage companies is that investors can potentially earn a greater financial return

---

[8] Ibid., pp. 44–51.

[9] Maria Minniti and William D. Bygrave, "National Entrepreneurship Assessment, United States, 2003 Executive Report," Babson College and Kauffman Foundation, p. 34; and Sarah E. Needleman, "What You Need to Know to Become an Angel Investor," *Wall Street Journal*, December 2, 2013, citing as sources the University of New Hampshire's Center for Venture Research and Dow Jones VentureSource.

[10] Angel Capital Association, Kauffman Foundation, and University of New Hampshire Center for Venture Research.

than they can from investing in public stocks, bonds, and mutual funds. Friends and family are more likely than strangers to consider emotional and social motives for investing, including simple loyalty. Angel investors generally focus more on financial returns and risks. But ROI is seldom the only basis for angels' investment decisions.

> *Two-thirds of angel investors report that making money isn't their primary motivation for investing in private companies. And some angels value the non-financial benefits of investing in private companies so much that it might be better to view their activity as consumption rather than as investment, much as we look at the purchase of art or expensive homes.*[11]

Nonfinancial rewards include sharing the excitement of building new, innovative enterprises without having to work long hours.

Strategic investors often buy shares of growing companies because it allows them to make use of expertise they have developed in a particular industry or technology during their careers. Other motivations include learning about new technology before it reaches the marketplace and gaining an entrée into a company where they would like to be employed as an executive. Finally, many *locavestors* want to support the community in which they live and work, and encourage economic development.[12]

## Running the Numbers

Angel investors provided more than $20 billion in financing to more than 60,000 ventures in 2011. "A typical angel round these days might be $150,000 raised from five people," said Paul Graham, a high-profile Silicon Valley angel investor and founder of the tech accelerator Y Combinator, in 2009.[13] The typical angel round is different when the investors are members of angel groups—the median size in that case was $600,000 in 2013.[14]

The typical, or *median*, investment in a single deal by an angel investor before 2009 was $10,000, according to research by Scott A. Shane, PhD.[15] According to more recent data, the *average* angel investment made by an

---

[11] Shane, op. cit., p. 23.

[12] This term was coined by Amy Cortese, author of *Locavesting: The Revolution in Local Investing and How to Profit from It,* John Wiley & Sons, 2011.

[13] Paul Graham, "How to Be an Angel Investor," March 2009, www.paulgraham.com/angelinvesting.html.

[14] "2013 Halo Report," released by Angel Resource Institute, Silicon Valley Bank, and CB Insights, March 27, 2014.

[15] Shane, op. cit., p. 20.

individual is $37,000. Note that the average is significantly higher than the median because of a small number of very large investments (outliers, in the lingo of statistics). Remember that Title III equity crowdfunding will facilitate much smaller investment amounts from a larger number of investors.

Equity financing accounts for roughly half of the capital raised from angel investors in a typical year. Debt financing accounts for the other half, in terms of dollars. Some deals combine debt and equity, however, and about 30 percent of the deals that involve equity also involve debt.[16]

The highest-profile angel investments have always been in technology startups, and the superstar angels tend to be located in high-tech communities. Indeed, based on many recent studies of angel investment, the sectors with the most angel investment were Internet and software. But several other sectors received significant angel investment as well. For example:

- According to one study, in the third quarter of 2012, the greatest number of angel investments—in terms of both deals and dollars—were made in Internet-related companies. Those were followed by healthcare companies, mobile/telecom, consumer products and services, and others.[17]
- According to a different study, the top three sectors receiving angel funding in 2012 were software, healthcare, and retail.[18]
- In 2013, the top sectors invested in by members of angel *groups* (accredited investors only)—in terms of both deals and dollars—were Internet, healthcare, mobile/telecom, industrial ventures, software, computer hardware and services, and energy and utilities.[19]

The angel capital markets tend to be local. "Angels make between 70 and 85 percent of their investments within 50 miles of their homes," Shane wrote in 2009. The growth of online offering platforms may make the market more

---

[16] Ibid., p. 81.

[17] "Rise of the Angel Investor," InvestorPitches.com, The Pitch blog, February 26, 2013. Sources included smallbusiness.com, Angel Resources Institute (Kauffman Foundation), and Paul College at University of New Hampshire.

[18] Sarah E. Needleman, "What You Need to Know to Become an Angel Investor," *Wall Street Journal*, December 2, 2013, citing as sources the University of New Hampshire's Center for Venture Research and Dow Jones VentureSource.

[19] "2013 Halo Report," op. cit. When angel groups co-invested with other types of investors, such as VC firms, the median round size reached $1.7 million.

national and less local, but the reasons angels have historically invested close to home include these:[20]

- Angels have traditionally invested in deals that they learn about through their networks of friends, colleagues, and advisers, which tend to be geographically centralized.
- Conducting due diligence, which should include visiting the target company's premises, interviewing the management team, and "seeing them sweat," is easier when the company is closer to home.
- Some investors want to be active in their portfolio companies, sometimes requiring on-site visits. Active involvement may include serving on the board of directors; providing financial, legal, or technical advice; or assisting entrepreneurs with attracting customers, suppliers, or additional investors.
- Many angels are motivated by community loyalty and economic development.

## Where's the ROI?

Return on investment is not the only motive for investing in private securities, but it is one we can try to measure. The problem is: ROI is an elusive statistic in the angel capital markets because issuers and investors are not required to report such data. Statistics coming from academic studies are sometimes taken out of context and distorted by the media, and survey results coming from professional associations are sometimes biased because, after all, they are promoting their members' interests.

In most surveys of angel investors and their returns *before* equity crowdfunding became legal, the estimated returns on investment tend to be overstated because they fail to consider the cost of investors' time. Investors might spend considerable time sourcing deals, conducting due diligence, and negotiating deal terms before the transaction, and advising or helping the founders after the transaction. "Angel investing is not passive, like putting money into a mutual fund, a venture capital limited partnership, or a hedge fund," writes Shane.[21] Some investments require more active involvement from angels than do others, but these are rarely passive investments. Equity crowdfunding is a whole new reality, however. It is quite unlikely that equity crowdfunding investors will be obligated, or even invited, to participate in the operation or governance of the company, as we will explain further.

---

[20]Shane, op. cit., pp. 202–203.
[21]Ibid., p. 160.

We want to be careful not to create unrealistic expectations in this book, so we will give you a variety of outlooks on ROI for angel investors.

On one hand, Shane writes that "successful angel investing is quite rare." On the other hand, Robert Wiltbank writes that "the best estimate of overall angel investor returns . . . is 2.5 times their investment . . . in [an average] time of about four years," which yields a very respectable 26 percent annual return. Can they both be right?

Scott Shane has conducted perhaps the most comprehensive research on angel investing that includes both accredited and nonaccredited investors. Shane is professor of economics and entrepreneurial studies at the Weatherhead School of Management, Case Western Reserve University, and author of *Fool's Gold? The Truth behind Angel Investing in America*.[22] He is also a member of the North Coast Angel Fund, based in Cleveland.

Rather than try to estimate overall or typical angel returns, Shane draws general observations from disparate data sources. Those observations include the following:

- Roughly 0.2 percent of the companies financed by angel investors eventually go public, and in those cases the early investors can earn spectacular returns.
- Somewhere between 0.8 and 1.3 percent of angel investments end in an acquisition, where early investors can earn decent to very good returns.
- By contrast, venture capital firms experienced an IPO in about 2 percent, and an acquisition in approximately 14 percent, of their portfolio companies before 2009.

The Band of Angels, founded in 1994, is one of the most successful angel groups in the United States. Most of its 135 members (accredited investors only) are based in Silicon Valley. The Band reported in 2014 that about 4 percent of its investments over 20 years have ended up as Nasdaq IPOs and another 19 percent have resulted in acquisitions. The cumulative internal rate of return[23] for all investments over 20 years (totaling

---

[22]With respect to return on angel investment, Shane bases his research on the Federal Reserve's Survey of Consumer Finances (www.federalreserve.gov /econresdata/scf/scfindex.htm), among other sources—in other words, not solely on surveys of self-selecting angel investor respondents. Shane told the authors that research conducted since 2009 confirms the conclusions in his book. The information in this section derives from pp. 146–198 of *Fool's Gold?*, op.cit.

[23]Internal rate of return (IRR) is a measure of return on investment without adjusting for external variables such as interest or inflation. Technically, the IRR is the discount rate that will bring a series of future cash flows to the net present value of cash invested.

$228 million), including the losses suffered through the dot-com bust, is a positive 54 percent per year. (That means if you invest $1,000 today, it will be worth $1,540 in one year, $2,372 in two years, $3,652 in three years, etc.).

While 54 percent is a phenomenal rate of return, Ian Sobieski, founder and managing director of the Band of Angels, provides this caveat: "We've had more than 200 investments [actually 270]. If you take the top nine performing deals out of the basket, the IRR drops to zero. So only one in 20 really moves the needle. Since the average investor invests in only 10-or-so deals, the odds of any one angel being in a winner are only 50 percent."

Shane notes that, as with most types of investing, financial success at angel investing is "highly skewed," meaning "a few people make almost all the money." Those few people who make money at angel investing tend to be those who (1) have enough money to invest in a diverse group of startups rather than just one or two and (2) spend considerable time at deal sourcing (searching for the most promising startups) and due diligence. Shane also concluded that achieving good financial returns "tends to increase with the number of investments that investors have made." In other words, more experienced investors do better.

Shane cites the example of Luis Villalobos, a leading angel investor (with more than 50 startup investments) and founder of Tech Coast Angels, a regional group covering Southern California. Villalobos said that 6 percent of his investment portfolio accounted for 84 percent of his financial results. "Therefore, to make money commensurate with the risk of investing in private companies, investors must be diversified," Shane concluded.

Wiltbank's research takes a different approach from Shane's. Robert Wiltbank, PhD, is associate professor of strategic management at Willamette University, vice chair of the Angel Resource Institute, and partner with Montlake Capital, a late-stage growth capital fund. Wiltbank's research on angel investors was backed by the Kauffman Foundation's Angel Returns Study, the NESTA Angel Investing Study, the University of Washington, and Willamette University.

In 2012, Wiltbank described the results of his survey of individual angel investors—all of whom are accredited and members of angel groups—in which he asked them to disclose the financial results of their angel investments over a 15-year period.[24] We must take into consideration that the respondents were self-selecting; in other words, we might hypothesize that investors who had lousy returns were less likely to respond to the survey.

---

[24]Robert Wiltbank, PhD, "Angel Investors Do Make Money—Data Shows 2.5x Returns Overall," TechCrunch, October 2012, http://techcrunch.com/2012/10/13/angel-investors-make-2-5x-returns-overall/.

In October 2012, based on his survey data, Wiltbank looked at more than 1,200 angel investments in the United States and the United Kingdom that resulted in what we call a termination event, where investors sold, redeemed, or forfeited their shares and realized a gain or loss. These events ranged from the company going out of business (possibly a total loss for investors) to an acquisition (possibly a loss but more likely a gain) to an IPO (probably a big gain). Based on what those investors told him, Wiltbank reported the following:

- In any single investment, an angel investor was "more likely than not to lose their money, i.e., to earn less than a 1x return. However, once investors had a portfolio of at least six investments, their median return exceeded 1x."
- When you aggregate all the data, these angel investors in the United States and the United Kingdom produced a gross multiplier of 2.5x their investment, in a mean time of about four years. In other words, an angel investment of $1,000 today would typically be worth $2,500 in four years, which represents a 26 percent annual return. Keep in mind that Wiltbank surveyed only accredited investors who belong to angel groups (who were willing to discuss their investments), who represent less than 25 percent of all angel investors in the United States. Also, these returns do not account for the time investors spent researching and managing their investments.
- As a rule of thumb, "angel investors probably should look to make at least a dozen investments" to diversify their portfolios in terms of one or more of the following: industry or sector, geography, vintage, and/or stage of development.
- "This is critical," Wiltbank wrote. "Each investment has to be done as though it's your only one." Do not lower your standards at any point just because you are building a diversified portfolio and assuming that diversity in itself will guarantee good returns.
- "Ninety percent of all the cash returns are produced by 10 percent of the exits." This proportion applies to venture capital as well as angel capital. In fact, this proportion is essentially constant everywhere, not just in the high-tech centers of Silicon Valley or Boston, and across all industries.

Keep in mind that those survey results tend to represent investments by wealthy investors who target fast-growth and high-potential companies, rather than companies that strive for steady long-term growth, dependable (rather than volatile) profitability, and longer time before an exit for investors. The latter are probably underrepresented in Wiltbank's data, as they are more likely to be rejected by angel groups (because of their longer exit horizon), so they are consequently more likely to filter down to equity crowdfunding as a path to financing. Rejection by angel groups does not necessarily make them bad investment opportunities; in fact, some of them may be less risky than the fast-growth startups that accredited investors chase. Although their returns may be less spectacular, they can yield income (from profits) over a longer term, as well as respectable capital gain.

## ANGEL GROUPS AND ANGEL CROWDS

Considering the evidence, you would logically conclude that angel investors who belong to angel groups have an advantage over those who don't. And since nonaccredited investors are excluded from those groups, nonaccredited angel investors are at a disadvantage.

But equity crowdfunding creates a new kind of angel group—the crowd—to which all investors can belong. The SEC declared in October 2013, when it released its *proposed* rules for Title III (on page 376): "A premise of crowdfunding is that investors would rely, at least in part, on the collective wisdom of the crowd to make better informed investment decisions"—which is why "we propose to require intermediaries to provide communication channels for issuers and investors to exchange information about the issuer and its offering."

When you sign up for and become a member of an equity crowdfunding portal (or equity crowdfunding platform operated by a broker-dealer), you have the ability to collaborate with other members through three methods:

- In Q&A forums you can ask questions of issuers. Your questions and their responses are posted for all members to see, or at least the members who have indicated an interest in that issuer's offering.
- Portals also enable crowd members to engage in discussions among themselves, share research, and invite their professional advisers to join the discussions.
- Crowd members can and often do contact each other off-platform to engage in private discussions. Almost certainly, equity crowdfunding investor meet-up groups will form in major cities across the country, just as angel groups have.

## WISDOM AND MADNESS OF CROWDS

How will these online collaborations among nonaccredited investors (who are presumed by the U.S. government to be less sophisticated in the private securities markets) compare with angel group collaboration? Equity crowdfunding on a national level is too new in the United States to provide data for empirical studies or even much anecdotal evidence. But we have anecdotal evidence from Australia, where equity crowdfunding has operated for years successfully with participation of "unsophisticated" investors.

The Australian Small Scale Offering Board (ASSOB) is an equity crowdfunding platform that allows all investors to participate in private offerings, regardless of income or net worth. From its launch in 2004 to April 2014, around 300 issuers raised more than AU$138 million (about US$128 million) on the platform. ASSOB reports that about 50 to 60 percent of the firms that received funding in its first five years (2008–2012) are still "operational" in 2014.[25] There have been no reported incidences of fraud (as defined by Australian securities regulators).[26] It should be noted that ASSOB accountants conduct reviews of the issuers' financial information, and the platform performs substantive due diligence on potential offerings before accepting any.

We do have some nascent anecdotal evidence about crowd wisdom in U.S. intrastate equity crowdfunding. Adam Lee is the CEO of Bohemian Guitars of Atlanta, the first company to raise capital from both accredited and nonaccredited investors on an equity crowdfunding platform in U.S. history. The platform was SparkMarket, which uses the new Invest Georgia Exemption (see Chapter 4 for details). During Bohemian Guitars' successful campaign to raise $50,000 in 2013, says Lee, the nonaccredited investors asked questions that were in some cases more relevant and challenging than the questions asked by the accredited investors on the platform.

Even if all of the crowd members are nonaccredited investors, inexperienced in the private securities markets, can an equity-crowdfunding crowd really offer advantages comparable to those offered by angel groups? We propose that the answer is yes, under certain conditions—three conditions, to be exact.

---

[25]Paul Niederer, CEO of ASSOB, in an e-mail to the authors on June 15, 2014.
[26]Richard Swart, "The Truth about Crowd Selection & Crowdfunding Success," CrowdfundInsider.com, April 21, 2014. According to Paul Niederer, CEO of ASSOB, issuers can raise up to $5 million per offering. Up to 20 "unsophisticated" investors can participate in each offering; the Australian definition of *unsophisticated* is similar to the American definition of *nonaccredited*. The average raise has had fewer than 20 investors. As of April 2014, only five countries, in addition to Australia, allow "small investors" to buy equity shares on a crowdfunding platform: France, Ireland, the Netherlands, Switzerland, and the United Kingdom.

The premise of James Surowiecki's book *The Wisdom of Crowds* is that:

*Under the right circumstances, groups are remarkably intelligent, and are often smarter than the smartest people in them. Groups do not need to be dominated by exceptionally intelligent people in order to be smart. Even if most of the people within a group are not especially well informed or rational, it can still reach a collectively wise decision.*[27]

Looking at investors particularly, Surowiecki shows that even if "investors, as individuals, are irrational, it's still possible that when you aggregate all their choices, the collective outcome will be rational and smart."

The circumstances have to be right, though. Under the wrong circumstances, the crowd can be an irrational, destructive mob. Scottish author Charles Mackay wrote a book about mass manias and collective follies, the classic *Extraordinary Popular Delusions and the Madness of Crowds*, published in 1841. Mackay described stock market bubbles and riots where "aggregating individual decisions produces a collective decision that is utterly irrational." And the American financier and adviser to U.S. presidents Bernard Baruch (1870–1965) famously said, "Anyone taken as an individual is tolerably sensible and reasonable—as a member of a crowd, he at once becomes a blockhead."

So what are the circumstances under which a crowd—specifically a crowd of average investors on a Title III funding portal—will be wise rather than mad? Surowiecki identifies three such conditions: diversity, independence, and decentralization.

- *Diversity* means that members of the crowd have a wide variety of perspectives, knowledge, experience, and sources of information. Funding portals typically let members see the profiles of the other members who take part in discussions, so you can evaluate the diversity of the backgrounds and expertise of the people with whom you collaborate. Smaller groups tend to be less diverse.[28] If a portal accepts members who do not provide their true names and contact information, or if issuers do not

---

[27] James Surowiecki, *The Wisdom of Crowds*, Anchor Books, 2004, pp. xiii–xiv. The quote in the following paragraph is from p. 230.
[28] A 2013 study found that "the validity of evaluations by crowds [can be made greater] through increasing the number of individuals within the crowd." Christoph Hienerth and Frederik Riar, "The Wisdom of the Crowd vs. Expert Evaluation," WHU–Otto Beisheim School of Management, Innovation and Entrepreneurship Group, Germany, 2013.

require verification of members' identities, be wary of making investments there.

- ▪ *Independence* means crowd members are free to express their own opinions, without suppression or intimidation. The funding portal should not limit the kinds of communication among members, beyond basic civility and lawful expression (e.g., members should not be permitted to commit libel or slander).
- ▪ *Decentralization* means there are no dominant leaders or moderators unduly influencing the crowd. If you find that the operator of a funding portal tends to moderate discussion forums, for example, or tries to set an agenda for discussions, that would diminish the effectiveness of crowd wisdom.

Theoretically, at least, crowdfunding portals can be ideal environments for crowd wisdom when they encourage those three conditions. In addition, portals should require investors to use their real names, and their identities should be verified, when they participate in on-platform discussion forums. Keep in mind that, in some instances, if a crowd member suspects a scam, he or she may tend to abandon the offering rather than voice concerns—so expressing such concerns should be encouraged.

A classic example of crowd wisdom appeared in the public stock market following the *Challenger* space shuttle tragedy on January 28, 1986. At 11:39 a.m. eastern time, 74 seconds after liftoff at Cape Canaveral, the *Challenger* blew up and its crew was killed. News of the disaster spread instantly. Within minutes, investors started selling off the stocks of the four major contractors that had worked on the *Challenger* launch: Rockwell International (which built the shuttle and its main engines), Lockheed (which managed ground support), Martin Marietta (which manufactured the ship's external fuel tank), and Morton Thiokol (which built the solid-fuel booster rocket). By the end of the day, Morton Thiokol's stock had fallen by 11.9 percent, while the other three were down only around 3 percent. Although NASA had not speculated publicly as to the cause of the failure or which contractor might have been responsible, investors collectively deduced a higher probability that Morton Thiokol would be liable. (The next day, the *New York Times* stated that there were "no ideas yet" regarding the cause of the disaster.) Six months later, a presidential commission revealed that defective O-ring seals on the booster rockets, made by Morton Thiokol, were responsible for the failure.

There was no evidence that Morton Thiokol insiders (or its competitors, for that matter) dumped the company's stock or gave tips to investors that day. The only clue, available to a very limited number of outsiders, was that three months before the disaster, Morton Thiokol had "made a broad call for assistance" to the Society of Automotive Engineering in solving a problem involving its O-ring. Whether that call for assistance was factored into buying decisions by investors on January 28 is unknown, but, if so, that evidence was very quickly disseminated and accurately processed by the market.[29]

Thus, an aggregation of diverse investors, each operating independently in a decentralized market, had somehow singled out one NASA contractor for liability within hours of the disaster, months before rocket scientists and physicists officially determined the cause.

We can't guarantee that the equity crowdfunding crowd will be wise in the exactly same way, because it is such a new system. On the other hand, funding portal technology will create new efficiencies in the dynamics of crowd wisdom. For example, portals will allow side-by-side comparison of investment offerings. Broker-dealer equity crowdfunding platforms may allow investors to sort and rank investment criteria, which they can share and discuss. And some sites will let investors evaluate and rate each other (in much the same way that Amazon.com lets users evaluate product reviews), to help you decide whose opinions are reliable.

## NEW ANGEL INVESTORS

Now you know something about equity crowdfunding (Chapter 3), the kinds of startups and early-stage companies that you will be able to invest in via equity crowdfunding (Chapter 5), the nonfinancial motives that have spurred angel investors to buy shares in such companies in the past, as well as the potential financial rewards and returns, along with the risks. You know that diversifying your angel portfolio and collaborating with the crowd are keys to financial success for equity crowdfunding investors. Do you think you are cut out to be one?

To help you answer that question, we have identified 10 kinds of angel investors who have potential for a satisfying experience in equity crowdfunding. They are listed as follows, ranging from mostly social to mostly financial motivations for investing:

- *Social impact investors.* Socially motivated investors who are passionate about supporting a cause- or ideology-oriented company. Examples include "green" (eco-friendly) products, renewable energy

[29]Michael T. Maloney and Harold Mulherin, "The Stock Price Reaction to the Challenger Crash," SSRN, December 7, 1998, http://papers.ssrn.com /sol3/papers.cfm?abstract_id=141971.

development, low-income housing, elder care, for-profit drug rehab clinics, and organic lawn care. Investors in this category may be less concerned about valuation, exit strategy, or even return on investment, and more concerned about the social benefits and the sense of belonging to a committed group of people who think alike. Investors who previously contributed funds on donation- or rewards-based crowdfunding platforms will follow the same issuers to new equity-based platforms.

- *Locavestors.* Members of a community—at the neighborhood, local, or regional level—who have a shared connection to a business that they depend on and want to "own a piece of." These are also known as *affinity investors,* and they may know the business owners personally. The businesses tend to be gathering spots like restaurants, cafes, delicatessens, bodegas, groceries, microbreweries, bowling alleys, fitness centers, and hair salons, or a business whose owner who has been the victim of a tragedy or perceived injustice.[30] Investors may be motivated by broad community development goals. Like socially motivated investments, this category will have some carryover from previous rewards-based crowdfunding campaigns.

- *Demography-driven investors.* On a national level, they want to show support for businesses owned by war veterans, college alumni, women, diaspora members, coreligionists, or (on a more local level) inner-city minorities, for example. In fact, some funding portals will develop around niches like these.

- *Creatives.* Investors who want to join creative, hip, or glamorous projects such as music, film, and publishing. These investors are slightly more concerned about fun and prestige than profit. In an equity crowdfunding context they may have an opportunity to offer creative input into the project, especially in the promotional phase.

- *Fans.* Enthusiastic users of a consumer product or brand—loyal fans—who want to help ensure the future availability of the product or brand as much as they want to earn a share of the profit or capital gain. At an earlier stage of product development, this type of investor experiences "idea lust" and wants to help get a new product to market so they can consume it before anyone else. Gadgets, games, hobbies, 3D printers, Apple electronics, fitness, cooking, recreational supplies and equipment, sports teams, clothing, and fashion accessories fit into this category, among others. These investors are e-commerce-savvy,

---

[30] In her book *Locavesting,* Amy Cortese writes: "The adage that what's good for General Motors is good for the country may not hold true in these days of outsourcing, downsizing, and wage stagnation. But what's good for the local family farm, merchant, or startup truly is good for the community." (Op. cit., at 864, Kindle edition.)

have backed projects on rewards-based platforms like Kickstarter, and have no hesitation about sharing a personal profile, participating in discussion groups, and conducting large transactions on-platform.

- *The Leading Edge.* Technology-oriented angels who want to invest in high-tech startups to help drive innovation (because it is truly exciting to be "ahead of the curve"), help brilliant entrepreneurs succeed, and possibly own a share of the next big thing (because this is where returns on investment can be most spectacular). In addition to investors of modest income and net worth, we will probably see some venture capitalists poking around in funding portals looking for early access to high-potential startups.[31]

- *Moderate-income investors seeking portfolio diversification,* tens of millions of whom now can invest small amounts (hundreds rather than thousands of dollars) in private securities. The JOBS Act made this possible for the first time in decades. Moderate-income investors with low risk tolerance should also consider diversifying into peer-to-peer lending platforms, where the risks are fixed but returns are potentially better than those for bonds and the money market.

- *"Patient money."* These are value investors who look for long-term growth rather than a short-term exit. They will invest higher amounts (thousands of dollars per deal and a series of deals over the years), prefer established businesses that have solid growth strategies, and spend more time conducting comprehensive due diligence and identifying realistic exit strategies. They will invest not so much in fast-growth high-tech startups (which typically need further rounds of venture capital financing to raise tens of millions of dollars, often resulting in dilution of share value for early investors) but, rather, in companies that can become self-sustaining (using retained earnings rather than external capital sources) after one or two rounds of equity crowdfunding. These companies may include commercial and agricultural real estate; service providers such as building contractors, healthcare, cleaning services, and auto repair; or franchisees.

- *Wildcatters and speculators* in boom-or-bust industries such as oil and gas exploration (e.g., a single oil pump), small-scale mining of precious metals, or prepatent inventions (e.g., batteries, solar panels). These are operations where a hit (or a patent) results in huge gains for investors, while a miss results in a total loss; there is typically no middle ground. Such speculators must have a high tolerance for risk.

---

[31]Some Regulation D offering platforms (e.g., CircleUp, according to Ryan Caldbeck, CEO) report that venture capital and even private equity investors have made investments in early-stage companies on their platforms.

■ *Followers* of well-known or highly rated lead investors, a.k.a. "smart money." If you saw that Mark Cuban invested $250,000 in a startup that produces enterprise software, you might be tempted to follow his lead without even conducting much due diligence, under the assumption that the billionaire must have done the due diligence. Many investors will follow others whom they consider smart, or will follow their friends' lead as a matter of camaraderie. We can't say that this is the most prudent way to invest, but we wouldn't discourage you from doing it as long as you understand the risks involved in leaving the due diligence to others whom you trust.

In addition to these 10 categories of equity crowdfunding investors, it is likely that some large corporations and institutional investors will invest in early-stage companies via equity crowdfunding. Some corporations are already affiliating with Regulation D offering platforms to sink money into startups that might someday become suppliers, strategic partners, or even acquisition targets. An example is Cisco Systems, the networking equipment manufacturer in San Jose, California. Through its Entrepreneurs in Residence program, Cisco invests in some of the issuers listed on EarlyShares, the Miami-based Reg D and soon likely to be Title III platform. Cisco looks for startups in the cloud services, website analytics, "big data," and related areas.

Institutional investors (such as pension funds, university endowments, and banks) will seek to diversify, perhaps in an exploratory sense, by buying shares in early-stage companies, especially in the technology, consumer products, and real estate sectors. They have prodigious resources for conducting due diligence. If you are aware that an institutional investor is participating in a Q&A forum or discussion on a crowdfunding portal, pay close attention to their questions and comments.

## TWO KEYS TO ANGEL INVESTING SUCCESS

Whether or not you fit into any of the investor categories described here, you still need two traits to be a successful investor in equity crowdfunding: judge of character and patience.

When you invest in a company that has a limited track record in terms of revenue, or even product distribution, you need to judge whether the founder (or founding team) has what it takes to succeed. Experienced angel investors commonly "bet on the jockey, not the horse." For example, founders who have been involved in startups in the past—whether those startups have succeeded or failed—are more likely to succeed in the future than founders with no startup experience.

Even if they do have what it takes, it's still a long way to market penetration and profit, but the talent and commitment of the founders underlies all the other variables of success. You need to be able to judge whether the founders and executives are honest, talented, reliable, durable, and committed to making customers and investors (and regulators, in some cases) happy. Fortunately, the equity crowdfunding regulations require owners and key employees to fully disclose information about their backgrounds.

Even if you have never made an angel investment before, "you are already a better angel investor than you realize," writes Y Combinator founder Paul Graham. "Someone who doesn't know the first thing about the mechanics of venture funding but knows what a successful startup founder looks like is actually far ahead of someone who knows term sheets [documents that spell out the terms of a deal] inside out."[32]

Good founders, according to Graham, are "relentlessly resourceful." They "make things happen . . . but not always in a pre-defined way." They have a "healthy respect for reality" and adapt to circumstances, sometimes pivoting into new directions. They "do not get discouraged and give up."

Graham's view is echoed by legendary angel investor Ron Conway: The business idea might change—in fact, it will change—but "the people are the foundation of the company." We will provide more guidance on researching and evaluating founders in Chapter 12.

In addition to being a good judge of character, to be a successful angel investor you need patience. In equity crowdfunding, under Title III, when an investor buys shares in a company, he or she must hold those shares for at least a year before trying to sell them, with some exceptions. Even after the first year, those shares may be difficult to sell—who will buy them? There may not be a ready market or exchange for them; in other words, they are illiquid.

In the past, angel investors typically had to wait seven to eight years before an exit or liquidity event occurred or selling their shares became realistic,[33] if, in fact, the companies still existed after eight years. It is possible that this timeline will be condensed in the equity crowdfunding markets, but that is yet to be seen. For now, assume that the money you invest in equity crowdfunding deals will be off-limits to you and your family for several years.

---

[32] Graham, op. cit.

[33] Various sources, including Benjamin and Margolis, *Angel Investor's Handbook*, Bloomberg, 2001. However, Slee states that investors in startups can typically expect five years before an exit, while investors in expansion-stage companies can expect four years before an exit. (Robert T. Slee, *Private Capital Markets*, John Wiley & Sons, 2011.)

If you are impatient and a poor judge of character, you will be better off investing in public securities like stocks, bonds, and mutual funds, which are relatively liquid, and pass this book along to someone else. If your goal is to be a smart, patient angel investor with a diversified portfolio of startup and early-stage companies (and a several-year liquidity horizon), get ready for an exciting opportunity.

# CHAPTER 7

# Equity Crowdfunding Portals

## How to Navigate the Websites That List Title III Offerings

Intermediaries known as funding portals and broker-dealer platforms lie at the heart of the equity crowdfunding experience. This is where issuers and investors find each other. These intermediaries provide various tools, forums, and services to facilitate compliant offerings, disclosures, communication, and transactions between issuers and investors.

In fact, under Title III of the JOBS Act of 2012, an issuer may not make an equity offering via its own website or directly to investors; it must use an intermediary's portal or platform.

Funding portals, as defined in Title III, are websites that are registered with the Securities and Exchange Commission (SEC) and the Financial Industry Regulatory Authority (FINRA) for the purpose of hosting equity crowdfunding activities: offering, disclosure, investor registration, communication, transaction, and so on.[1]

There are important distinctions between funding portals and broker-dealer platforms that feature Title III offerings. Funding portals are a new type of intermediary created by Title III, while broker-dealers have been established market makers for many decades. A broker-dealer can be an individual or a company.

Broker-dealer platforms are authorized to do, while funding portals (which are not owned or operated by broker-dealers) are prohibited from doing, the following: offer investment advice or recommendations to investors; solicit purchases, sales, or offers to buy securities offered or displayed on its website or portal; compensate employees, agents, or other persons for such solicitation or based on the sale of securities displayed or

---

[1]For registration purposes, the SEC considers funding portals as "limited-purpose brokers," i.e., brokers that do not hold or maintain "customer funds or securities." Source: SEC proposed rules for Title III crowdfunding, November 2013, p. 209.

referenced on its website or portal; and hold, manage, possess, or otherwise handle investor funds or securities.[2]

## SUITABILITY AND DUE DILIGENCE

Broker-dealers (B-Ds) must comply with the Know Your Customer Rule (FINRA 2090) and the Suitability Rule (FINRA 2111), which we mentioned in Chapter 2. Together these FINRA rules require broker-dealers to collect sufficient information about each investor to determine that investor's risk profile and whether particular investments are suitable for that individual. To accomplish that, the broker-dealer operating an equity crowdfunding platform should review applicant companies' business plans and screen out offerings that it believes are generally unsuitable for its registered investors.

Broker-dealers are subject to strict standards of due diligence, with respect to how they select issuers and equity offerings to be listed on their platforms. That does not *necessarily* mean you will not find high-quality issuers and good investment opportunities on funding portals; they may or may not conduct due diligence according to the same high standards. When you visit a broker-dealer platform, though, you know exactly what its due diligence standards are because they have been published by the SEC and FINRA (as we explained in Chapter 2). Broker-dealers must adhere to those standards or face disciplinary action.

Both funding portals and B-D platforms may establish *objective* criteria for accepting and rejecting issuers that apply to their portals (i.e., they may curate their offerings based on, for example, industry, geographic location, quantifiable performance metrics, product testing results, patents issued, and market data). B-D platforms may use *subjective* criteria (such as the founder's management style, credibility of claims regarding competitive advantages, soundness of business strategies, independence of one or more board members, and so forth). The SEC has not clarified yet whether, or to what extent, funding portals may use any subjective criteria in accepting and rejecting issues.

How can you tell funding portals and B-D platforms apart? They may be very similar in appearance, because they use the same kind of website architecture, design, and navigation structure. You may not be able to distinguish between them readily, unless you read the "About Us" page and/or the fine

---

[2]SEC Division of Trading and Markets, JOBS Act FAQs, May 7, 2012. This definition has been added to the Securities Exchange Act.

print in the footer on the home page. If you are unable to determine whether a site is operating as a broker-dealer, you can (1) contact the platform's staff and ask about their broker-dealer status or (2) visit FINRA's BrokerCheck page (http://www.finra.org/Investors/ToolsCalculators/BrokerCheck/) and conduct a search to see if the platform is registered as a broker-dealer or merely as a portal.

If you consider registering as an investor on a non-broker-dealer funding portal, ask the principals exactly what kind of screening and selection process they use before they approve an issuer's application and list an offering. Some portals use third-party services such as CrowdCheck, a Virginia-based due diligence service provider, to perform due diligence and/or conduct background checks on the owners and officers of issuers. If the platform claims to conduct its own due diligence in-house, make sure the principals have relevant experience in the securities or investment banking industry so that their due diligence is effective. Keep in mind that you (along with the crowd) may still need to conduct your own due diligence before you invest, even if the platform is a broker-dealer. Do not presume that due diligence performed by the intermediary supports your personal objectives and risk tolerance. We provide guidance on due diligence in Chapter 12.

All intermediaries—funding portals and broker-dealer platforms alike—must conduct background checks on officers, directors, and 20 percent equity holders of each issuer, to reduce the risk of fraud. Intermediaries must disqualify an issuer if one of its officers, directors, or "participants" (such as promoters) in the offering is a "bad actor," as defined by the SEC (a convicted felon, person subject to a finance-related injunction or restraining order, person subject to SEC disciplinary action, etc.). Likewise, all funding portals and broker-dealer platforms are subject to antifraud and antimanipulation provisions of federal securities laws and regulations.

## FUNDING PORTALS SPOOKED BY TITLE III LIABILITY ISSUES

As of February of 2015, some of the major players in the crowdfunding industry, such as Indiegogo and EarlyShares—which have publicly expressed their desire to support Title III offerings on their rewards-based and Reg D platforms—are still not totally committed to Title III, mainly because the SEC has yet to clarify two critical issues: (a) statutory liability for intermediaries, and (b) acceptance/rejection of offerings based on subjective criteria.

*Statutory liability for intermediaries.* Title III (and its counterpart, Section 4(a)(6) of the Securities Act of 1933), implies—but does not definitively state—that funding portals might share liability with issuers for not only fraud but also material inaccuracies and omissions (possibly even unintentional ones) in the offering materials that issuers post on the portals. The SEC is expected to clarify, in its final rules, whether (or to what extent) portals will, in fact, bear responsibility for issuers' deceptions or mistakes.

Joanna Schwartz, CEO of EarlyShares, told the SEC (during the 2014 comment period for the SEC's proposed rules under Title III) that intermediaries certainly should make a strong commitment to investor protection through education, due diligence, compliance, and fraud prevention. But requiring intermediaries equally to share liability for issuers' deceptions or mistakes would place a "potentially insurmountable burden on all funding portals." Even with high standards of due diligence, said Schwartz, funding portals "cannot reasonably verify every statement (or material omission) as it pertains to issuers on their platforms. The cost to comply, insure, and/or defend against this liability is significant and misaligned with the role of a funding portal...."*

*Approval of offerings based on subjective criteria.* As we pointed out earlier in this chapter, broker-dealers may review issuers' applications and accept issuers on their platforms based on both objective and subjective criteria. Non-broker-dealer funding portals may use objective criteria, but it is not clear to what extent, if any, they may use subjective criteria.

Because evaluating subjective criteria might be construed as giving investors advice about the *suitability* of offerings for investors, Title III seems to prohibit non-broker-dealer portals from using subjective criteria.** Recall from Chapter 2 that only broker-dealers can give suitability advice. The SEC is expected to clarify, in its final rules, to what extent portals may use subjective criteria.

Schwartz commented to the SEC that portals ought to be able to "disqualify certain issuers for a combination of objective and subjective reasons." Otherwise, a portal might have to accept all applicants (issuers) that qualify under the portal's narrowly stated objective criteria even if the portal believes the issuer has a ridiculous business plan and therefore would not represent a good investment for anyone.

Primarily (but not necessarily exclusively) because of these uncertainties about portal liability and using subjective criteria for approving issuers, EarlyShares, Indiegogo, and other major players in the crowdfunding industry have not committed to Title III offerings until those rules are clarified by the SEC. If the SEC maintains that intermediaries share liability equally with issuers for not only fraud but material inaccuracies and omissions (even unintentional ones) as well, then—worst case scenario—equity crowdfunding might be stalled until Congress makes revisions to Title III.

*Comment letter from Joanna Schwartz to the SEC dated February 3, 2014. See the full text at www.sec.gov/rules/proposal/2013/33-9470.pdf.

**Securities and Exchange Commission, Crowdfunding, Proposed Rules 227.402(b)(1), September 23, 2013.

## Revenue for Platforms

Equity crowdfunding portals and B-D platforms may be independent enterprises (like EarlyShares and Indiegogo) or funding arms of larger enterprises. The latter includes portals owned by municipalities, chambers of commerce, "main street coalitions," and civic organizations that want to inject capital into businesses in their areas, and universities that want to fund entrepreneurs who spin out of the academic environment.

Whether they are for-profit or not, equity crowdfunding portals and platforms may earn revenue in the following ways:

- A funding portal can charge an issuer a flat fee, usually on a monthly basis, for posting an offering on the platform. Or the portal can charge the issuer a "success fee," a percentage of the capital raised on the platform. Portals should disclose to investors how they charge issuers (whether a monthly fee or a percentage of the funds raised), but they do not have to disclose the amounts of those fees. Typically, the success fee is in the 5 to 10 percent range—a higher percent for larger raises—although it can vary according to the type of startup as well (e.g., real estate ventures and startups with valuable hard assets may pay lower fees).
- Broker-dealer platforms can charge the same kinds of fees and percentages as portals do, although the percentages might be slightly higher because they typically provide consulting services to issuers. In addition, broker-dealers may compensate their employees and agents based on the amount raised by issuers.
- Both kinds of platforms can charge issuers a flat fee for background checks and due diligence reports.

On most crowdfunding sites, investors do not pay registration fees. The only charges they *might* have to pay, aside from their actual investments, are transaction fees to third-party payment services such as PayPal, which can range from 1 to 3 percent.

Title III of the JOBS Act, and the SEC rules implementing the act, establish the following additional requirements for equity crowdfunding intermediaries:

- An intermediary may not pool investors' funds into a centralized investing entity. In other words, each individual investor will invest directly in the company that offers shares.[3]
- Non-broker-dealer funding portals may not have a financial interest in an issuer that uses their platform and may not compensate any third parties (including promoters, finders, and lead generators) for identifying potential investors.
- Equity crowdfunding portals may not (but broker-dealer platforms may) receive, manage, or hold investor funds. All portals must use an independent escrow service for that purpose and release the funds to the issuer only when the offering is successfully funded. The money is returned to investors if a campaign is not fully funded.
- Intermediaries must make reasonable efforts to ensure that issuers comply with offering limits (e.g., $1 million per year), ensure that the personal information collected from investors is kept private and secure, and make an effort to ensure (it is not yet clear how they will do this) that investors do not exceed their annual limits based on income and/or net worth.

## Purebred and Hybrid Platforms

Some equity crowdfunding sites will focus solely on Title III offerings. Some will combine rewards-based and Title III crowdfunding on one site, and some will combine Regulation D and Title III crowdfunding—they are called *hybrids*.[4] An example of the latter (D/III) may be EarlyShares,

---

[3] A proposed revision to this rule, introduced in the U.S. House of Representatives in May 2014, would allow intermediaries to create funds, in which investors could pool their capital so that the intermediary would invest in an offering as a single entity. From an investor's point of view, such an arrangement may give the entity more negotiating strength and result in better deal terms, but then the investor would have indirect access to the company in which he or she invests.

[4] As we described in Chapter 2, Regulation D platforms may feature Rule 506(b) offerings, Rule 506(c) offerings, or both. The latter are also known as Title II offerings, where general solicitation is permitted.

which launched in 2012 as a Reg D offering platform, focusing on growth companies and real estate projects. Some sites combine straight debt, convertible debt, and equity. An issuer may list Reg D and Title III offerings simultaneously, known as *parallel offerings*. An issuer may also give tangible rewards to its equity investors as an element of its equity offering,[5] as some have done on EarlyShares. When you register on a hybrid Reg D and Title III platform, you will gain immediate access to all Title III offering information. Both accredited and nonaccredited investors can invest in Title III offerings on a hybrid platform. But you must register before you can gain access to Reg D offering disclosures, and you must verify your accredited investor status before you can invest in those deals.

On a pure Title III equity crowdfunding portal, you do not need to declare your investor status to gain access to offering information. Thus, you will *not* be obligated to provide information about your income and net worth before you can invest. Intermediaries bear some responsibility to make reasonably sure investors do not exceed their annual investment limits based on income and net worth.

All this nomenclature—platforms, portals, hybrids—can get confusing. So to keep things simple, from now on, unless we need to point out distinctions between them, we will refer to all platforms and portals that feature Title III offerings as "equity crowdfunding sites."

### The Equity Crowdfunding Ecosystem

A constellation of service providers support equity crowdfunding sites, including the following, which are typically identified on the sites as "strategic partners":

- *Stock transfer agents.* Registered with the SEC, these firms manage the registration and transfer of securities from issuers to investors after transactions are conducted on the sites. Examples are VStock Transfer and eShares. You will not need to find or hire these sorts of firms, or any others on this list, because they provide these services to the intermediaries and/or the issuers through the portals by prior arrangement.
- *Escrow agents.* Title III requires that equity crowdfunding sites use third-party escrow services to (1) hold investors' money until a deal closes or (2) return the money to investors if the deal is not fully funded.

---

[5]There may be income tax implications of receiving tangible rewards in an equity investment.

Some, such as BancBoxCrowd, specialize in crowdfunding escrow accounts. Issuers, not investors or intermediaries, pay the escrow agents' fees (and intermediaries do not earn royalties or commissions on those fees).

- *Due diligence services.* Not all equity crowdfunding sites have expertise on staff to conduct comprehensive due diligence on issuers. Many platforms, and even some broker-dealers, engage outside securities lawyers, CPAs, researchers, and investment professionals to review prospective issuers' offering documents, financial disclosures, business plans, deal terms, executive profiles, and other information before accepting their applications to be listed. The platform typically charges issuers a fee for this service, and issuers sometimes make resulting due diligence reports available to prospective investors. CrowdCheck is a prominent example of due diligence firms that specialize in crowdfunding issuers and offerings.

- *Risk management services for investors,* also known as investment insurance. On some sites, after you make a commitment to invest in a company, you will have the option of buying a policy that provides coverage in the event that you lose money as a result of bankruptcy or dissolution. All the information you need—about the insurer, policy coverage, premiums, and benefits—is integrated into the equity crowdfunding site (there will be a link to the insurer's website so you can check it out). You can either select the coverage you want or decline. See more about this in Chapter 11.

- *Educational content providers.* Title III mandates that intermediaries provide content to educate investors on the risks of investing in private securities and then survey their registered investors to ascertain that they understand those risks before they can invest on the site. This is the first time in history that such a mandate has been issued, and the SEC has yet to clarify how this educational system will work.

Most Title III equity crowdfunding sites have a somewhat standard appearance. Just like rewards-based platforms and Reg D platforms, the home page typically shows several of the most popular and/or newest offerings. From there you have to "drill down" to find a full listing of offerings. If a site has more than a couple dozen listings total, it should be easy to search through them according to industry or sector, time left in the offering before the deadline, and maybe region as well. Hybrid platforms should, in addition, let you search offerings according to the type of crowdfunding project: rewards, debt, Regulation D equity (for accredited investors only), and Title III equity (for all investors). Especially if you are not an accredited investor, you should be able to search Title III offerings without having to scan a whole lot of Reg D offerings along the way. Some sites let you search according to minimum investment amount as well and combine the search criteria so that you can, for example, look for Title III investments in the Midwest, focusing on the healthcare industry, with a low minimum investment.

It is important that, before you become a registered investor on an equity crowdfunding site and enter your personal information, you should be sure the site is registered with FINRA as follows:

- A broker-dealer, as mentioned earlier, should show up as registered on FINRA's BrokerCheck page (http://www.finra.org/Investors /ToolsCalculators/BrokerCheck/).
- A funding portal should be registered with the SEC and FINRA.
- The site should *not* show up on the SEC's list of "unregistered soliciting entities" that have been the subject of investor complaints (http://www.sec.gov/investor/oiepauselist.htm).

Before you register as an investor, look in the footer (bottom of the home page), the "About Us" page, and the contact page, and make a note of the full corporate name under which the site does business, along with the names of its principals. If that information is not readily available, that's probably a red flag. When you do find that information, check out the site by conducting an Internet search, looking for independent reviews or favorable mentions in the media. Another way to tell if a site is reputable is if you see at least two or three offerings that have gained "traction"—meaning they have reached their funding goals or attracted substantial commitments from investors. If a site is too new to have attracted much in the way of commitments, check out the principals' backgrounds and make sure at least one of them has experience in the securities or investment banking industry—then perform an Internet search to make sure their reputations are not questionable.

## Generalists, Specialists, and Aggregators

In the early days of Title III equity crowdfunding, we can expect to see generalized sites that list offerings in a variety of industries across the country, as well as niche-oriented sites that focus narrowly on a particular industry, region, or demographic sector.

As we explain in Chapter 8, if you are investing in private securities for the first time and want to maximize your return on investment, you can manage (try to reduce) your risk by:

- Investing in more than one company (ideally 10 to 15 over a number of years) to achieve diversification.

- Investing in the industries where you have working knowledge, so you can better judge the viability of an issuer's business plan and competitive advantages and assess the risks involved.

From a risk management perspective, you might be more comfortable and have better results by narrowing your searches to a few specialized equity crowdfunding sites within your niche, as well as one or two generalized sites that list issuers in your niche. It may seem adventurous to search for investment opportunities on a high-tech-oriented portal, but—again from a risk management perspective—if you are not tech-savvy, you should approach those opportunities as gambles rather than smart investments.

We started this discussion with "In the early days of equity crowdfunding . . . " In the later days of equity crowdfunding, we expect that some specialized sites will find that life in the niches can be brutal. Along with a narrow focus comes a smaller market, and it's difficult to earn sufficient revenue with insufficient customers. So after the first two or three years, you will probably see many of the niche players being acquired and subsumed by generalized crowdfunding sites, and some of them being aggregated into a "site of sites" along the lines of Kickstarter's Curated Pages.[6]

In addition to generalist and specialist equity crowdfunding sites where you can invest, you will find directory-type websites that provide comprehensive lists of investment portals and platforms, searchable by (1) industry or sector, (2) type of crowdfunding (rewards, donation, Reg D, Title III, etc.), (3) location, (4) minimum investment amount, (5) offering type (preferred stock, LLC units, convertible debt), and other criteria. Some of these directory sites feature reviews and ratings of crowdfunding platforms. They might help you find portals that are appropriate for your investment objectives, but, again, check out the reputations of these directory sites and their principals (and the reviewers) before you follow their guidance.

You will also find websites that publish research and reviews of issuers whose offerings are listed on equity crowdfunding sites. These review websites, such as Zacks Investment Research, can evaluate issuers based on information that is generally available online, in the business press, or through personal interviews. As is true with stock analysts and reviews of all kinds of products and services, reviews of Title III issuers are highly subjective and sometimes biased. We will talk more about independent research sources in Chapter 10.

---

[6]https://www.kickstarter.com/discover/curated-pages.

## ORIENTATION TO EQUITY CROWDFUNDING SITES

The best way to become familiar with equity crowdfunding sites is to explore a few of them. You can browse certain areas of a site without registering as a member. On most sites, from an investor's point of view, here is the content that you can see without registering:

- A list of the current offerings, with the following details for each Title III offering: company name and location, and industry category; equity or convertible debt; funding goal in dollars, funding deadline, minimum investment, amount of capital already committed to the offering, and percentage of the goal attained so far; a short description of the business, a videotaped pitch (usually under 10 minutes) and team profiles (including founders, executives, partners, key advisers); the company's proprietary business plan, financial projections, deal terms, and risk disclosures.[7]
- Information about the crowdfunding site itself, its principals, its due diligence standards and/or issuer selection process, terms and conditions of use, privacy policy, how the investment process works, and how the site earns revenue.
- Educational content as mandated by the JOBS Act, which should include the fundamentals of equity crowdfunding, Title III basics, explanation of risks and returns of investing in private securities, and other investing fundamentals.

Participation in the discussion forums and Q&A forums (where investors ask questions directly to issuers and their replies are open to all participants) is available only to registered members of the site. Upon registration, you will be prompted to set up a profile, similar to the way many social networking sites work. Initially you may enter as little or as much personal information as you wish in your profile. You can start with a skeleton profile (name and contact info) and add more personal information once you feel comfortable on the site.

Be aware that other registered investors (and some issuers) will view your profile and possibly conduct a more thorough online search of your background—maybe even call you for a brief chat to judge whether they can rely on your opinions. So eventually you will want to fill in your profile

---

[7]This information is also available on the company's Form C, published on EDGAR, the SEC's searchable database of company filings: https://www.sec.gov/edgar/searchedgar/companysearch.html.

with (only accurate) information that will help other investors, with whom you will collaborate on due diligence, to judge that you are reliable. Be careful in the discussion forums not to unfairly disparage an issuer or other investors—they will be reluctant to share information and opinions with anyone whose profile is incomplete or suspiciously cryptic, or who rants and raves or unfairly criticizes a company or another investor.

## Terms and Conditions of Use

When you register on an equity crowdfunding portal or platform, you must acknowledge that you have read, and accept, the site's terms and conditions of use. This is one instance where you *really should* read the terms before you click "accept." Accepting those terms and conditions, and completing the registration, constitutes a legally binding agreement between you and the site. Following are condensed versions of some of the most important terms and conditions common to equity crowdfunding sites:

- The registration information that you submit must be accurate and truthful. Most, if not all, Title III portals require "real name only" registration. In any case, your user ID cannot be offensive, vulgar, or obscene.
- You are responsible for protecting the confidentiality of your user ID and password.
- You must be an adult to invest in an offering on the site.
- Your activities on the site must comply with laws relating to taxes, securities, and contracts.
- Statements of material fact that you make on the site, in discussions and forums, must not be misleading or untrue.
- You must not reveal personal information about another investor.
- You must not "further disclose" or otherwise disseminate private and confidential disclosures, to which you have been granted access, about offerings on the site.
- You acknowledge that your investment may or may not produce a favorable result.
- You are responsible for conducting due diligence on, and assessing the risks of, the investment opportunities presented on the site. If you incur a loss, you can't hold the issuer or the intermediary liable (in the absence of fraud or negligence by those parties).
- The site may suspend or remove an offering at any time for any reason, and shall not be liable for losses or damages that result therefrom. (If you have committed money in escrow to such an offering, you would receive a refund.)

## The Investor Dashboard

Once you register on an equity crowdfunding site you will have access to your account, sometimes presented as a "dashboard," where you can build or revise your profile, change your account settings, and maintain an archive of your interests and activities on the site. We will show you a couple of hypothetical examples based on the design of the EarlyShares site. We chose EarlyShares because we believe it exhibits high standards of professionalism and compliance.[8] EarlyShares launched in April 2012, when it was one of the first equity offering platforms in the United States (though it could not feature Title III offerings at that point). The platform started with 506(b) offerings and expanded to 506(c) offerings in December 2013. Its first successful 506(c) offering was Boatsetter, an Airbnb-like service for boat owners and renters, which raised $1.104 million from 24 investors (whose funds were pooled into an investment vehicle called EarlyFund-Boatsetter LLC) over about six months. Notably, Boatsetter offered rewards, in the form of discounts on boat rentals, to its investors. (EarlyShares currently allows issuers to integrate rewards-based crowdfunding campaigns with their equity offerings, but not to list freestanding rewards-only campaigns.) Joanna Schwartz, EarlyShares' CEO, was previously the founder of Silver Hill Financial, a commercial mortgage lender with 550 employees and $1 billion in annual originations.

From the EarlyShares dashboard, you will see the following information for Title III offerings (assuming the final SEC rules are favorable, as discussed in the sidebar):

- *Current offerings that you have expressed interest in.* When you come across an offering that you might want to invest in, on that offering page you can check a box to "watch" the offering's progress. A section of your dashboard titled "Offerings I'm Watching" (also called a "watchlist") shows company names, descriptions, and updated information about each of your selected offering's committed capital and funding goal (see Figure 7.1). This is a convenient feature especially on sites that list dozens of offerings in various categories. You can follow the funding progress of equity offerings that you selected while you decide whether or not to invest in them.
- *Offerings that you have committed to investing in.* This section of the dashboard shows offerings that you have pledged to invest in, with instructions for transferring money into escrow. After you send your

---

[8] In Figures 7.1 and 7.2, the issuers' names and offering details are fictional. Neither author has any personal, professional, or financial interest in or commitments to EarlyShares.

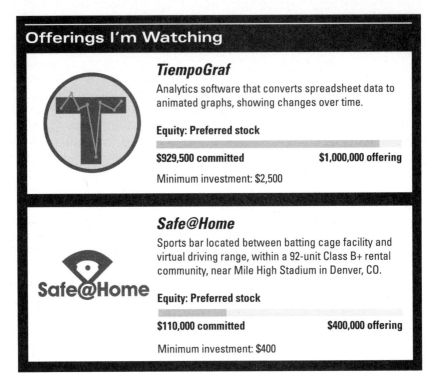

Offerings I'm Watching

**TiempoGraf**
Analytics software that converts spreadsheet data to animated graphs, showing changes over time.

**Equity: Preferred stock**

$929,500 committed                              $1,000,000 offering

Minimum investment: $2,500

**Safe@Home**
Sports bar located between batting cage facility and virtual driving range, within a 92-unit Class B+ rental community, near Mile High Stadium in Denver, CO.

**Equity: Preferred stock**

$110,000 committed                              $400,000 offering

Minimum investment: $400

**FIGURE 7.1** Dashboard Lets You "Follow" Selected Offerings
Sources: Used with permission from EarlyShares.com

payment, you must wait for the offering to reach its funding goal before the deal closes. The progress bar continues to show how close the offering is to closing (see Figure 7.2). If the offering fails to reach its funding goal, escrow money is refunded to committed investors.

■ *Closed offerings that you have invested in.* After the offering reaches its funding goal, the deal closes, escrow money is released to the issuer, and you are finally an equity investor. The dashboard keeps an archive of the deals you have invested in on this site, with access to all deal documents, postfunding notifications from the issuer, and ongoing discussion forums.

■ *Accounting of the money you have invested on this site over the past 12 months.* Using an embedded calculator, this feature helps you keep track of your invested capital to be sure you do not exceed your yearly limit—on this particular site at least—based on your income and net worth. (Each investor is ultimately responsible for tracking his or her total capital invested in Title III deals and complying with yearly investment limits, on one or more sites.)

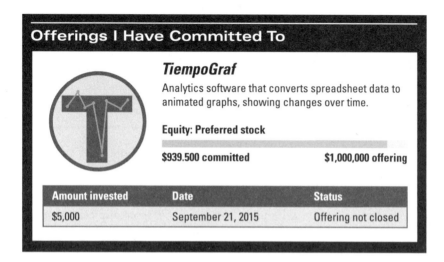

**FIGURE 7.2**	Dashboard Tracks Your Commitments to Invest
Sources: Used with permission from EarlyShares.com

## Application for Issuers

As an investor, you should become familiar with an equity crowdfunding site's application process for issuers. On most sites, registered members can see the application that issuers must complete if they want to list their offerings. The application will give insight into the intermediary's screening process. See the sidebar in this chapter for an example of a comprehensive application.

Before an issuer's application is accepted, an equity crowdfunding site must conduct background checks on the issuer's team: officers, directors, 20 percent equity holders, and "participants" in the offering. If any one of these team members is a "bad actor," the offering is disqualified. The issuer may reapply after removing any bad actors from the team.

In the case of EarlyShares, background checks are farmed out to Crowd-Check, the due diligence service. On behalf of EarlyShares, CrowdCheck also reviews the applicant's records to confirm that its board of directors authorized the offering of shares, its articles of incorporation (or operating agreement in the case of an LLC) are on file with the state, its capitalization table is accurate, it is not involved in disruptive litigation, its intellectual property is registered as claimed, and other key compliance issues. The issuer pays CrowdCheck's fee directly for this service.

In later chapters we will describe more features of an equity crowd-funding site, including: (1) Q&A and discussion forums, where you can communicate with the offering teams and collaborate with other investors on due diligence, and (2) transaction processes.

## ISSUER APPLICATION REVEALS SITE'S SELECTION CRITERIA FOR OFFERINGS

Before you invest on an equity crowdfunding site, take a look at the application that an issuer must fill out to get its offering listed on that site. The application will reveal much about the criteria used in the site's screening and selection process.

Some equity crowdfunding sites have different applications for issuers in different industries. A real estate developer will fill out one kind of application, while a technology company will fill out a slightly different application on the same site, for example.

Following is a summary of the information that an issuer in the "growth company" category must submit in its application on the EarlyShares Reg D platform.*

- Industry (select from a list).
- Company name, address, website URL, social media presence.
- Company overview.
- Length of time in business.
- U.S. state in which the offering is based.
- Target funding (also called the *raise*) in dollars.
- Amount of capital already invested by owners.
- Amount of capital invested in previous financing rounds by friends, family, angel investors, and/or venture capital firms.
- Funding round currently applying for (seed, angel, series A, series B, series C or later).
- Commitments for a portion of the raise currently applying for.
- Current stage of company or project (pre-prototype or concept, prototype, pre-revenue, post-revenue but not profitable, post-revenue and profitable).
- Number of people on the team.
- Background checks on team members completed? Could any be disqualified under SEC or FINRA regulations?

- Offering name.
- Contact person (name, phone number, e-mail, address).
- Proposed funding completion date.
- Business concept/mission.
- Proposed use of funds to be raised.
- Competitors and competitive advantages.

In addition to filling out this information, applicants must upload documents containing the following information:

- Business plan.
- Historical and projected financials.
- Management team profiles.
- Deal terms and disclosures if currently midround.
- Subscription documents.

Just because a site's application requests a lot of information doesn't mean the site's staff uses the applications most judiciously to select the best offerings. Check the staff profiles to make sure they have the education and experience needed to screen out potential fraud and bad actors. If profiles are not available, you can't be sure their screening and selection process is judicious.

Note that the information in the application is only a portion of the information that ultimately becomes available to investors on the equity crowdfunding site once the offering is listed.

*As of June 2014; subject to change. Summarized with permission of EarlyShares.com, Inc.

# CHAPTER 8

# How to Invest, Part I: Portfolio Strategy

## A Three- to Five-Year Plan for Building an Equity Crowdfunding Portfolio

**A**ngel investors have various motives for making risky investments in startups and early-stage companies. Those motives can be financial (seeking portfolio diversification and superior returns), personal (supporting particular entrepreneurs), social (boosting community development, renewable energy, etc.), expressing brand loyalty, driving innovation, and others.

This chapter is for investors whose motives are largely financial and who want to learn how to diversify intelligently and maximize their return on investment.

Focusing on return on investment (ROI) does not mean totally ignoring personal and social motives. But successful angel investors caution that you should identify your primary motive before you begin. If your primary motive is personal or social, then seek to maximize your intangible rewards, but do not expect your equity crowdfunding investments to be financially rewarding (and be pleasantly surprised if they are). Conversely, if you really want to achieve superior ROI, then your personal and social motives should take a backseat.

Becoming a financially successful angel investor requires a disciplined focus on the fundamentals that we cover in the next few chapters. Because equity crowdfunding investments are risky and illiquid, if your motive is primarily financial, we advise that you make such investments *only* if you learn and apply these fundamentals.

### PRIVATE SECURITIES RISK AND REWARD

In this chapter, first we address how equity crowdfunding investments should fit into your overall investment portfolio. Then we offer guidance on budgeting: How much money should you allocate to this new asset class each year?

We also help you set expectations for the next several years, during which your equity interests will rise and fall in value, maybe soar, maybe crash.

All investments in securities involve risk. A U.S. Treasury bond is considered the least risky investment because it is backed by the United States government, which has rarely (or never, depending on how you define *default*) defaulted on a debt. That's not to say it never will default, but the risk of that happening is less than just about any other securities risk in the world today. By comparison, an investment in public securities (whether corporate bonds or stocks, i.e., debt or equity) is generally riskier than government securities. But an investment in private securities is generally the riskiest of all. That is, the chances of a private company defaulting on its debt or leaving shareholders holding worthless stock is greater, generally, than the chances of a public company doing so.

The more information you have about a company, the better able you are to measure and monitor the riskiness of its securities.

Another risk factor is that small businesses are more vulnerable than large ones to natural disasters, or the sudden death or disability of a founder or CEO. Larger companies are more insulated from such micro- and macro-economic shocks because they have more locations, a deeper management structure, and a wider range of products and services that can buffer a company from disruptions in supply or demand.

Why would anyone—anyone motivated primarily by financial returns, that is—invest in risky securities if they can (more easily and with greater liquidity) invest in less risky ones? Because taking such a risk gives investors an opportunity to earn commensurately higher returns.

When you park your money in a savings account at an FDIC-member bank, you earn interest at a very low rate. Why would you do that? Because your money is safe (it's insured up to $250,000) and extremely liquid (you can get access to it almost immediately). You trade higher returns for less safety and liquidity. As your investment vehicle moves up the risk ladder—government bonds, public stocks, private securities—you want to earn higher returns for taking on greater risk.

When a bank loans money to borrowers who have low credit scores, the bank sets a higher interest rate than when it loans money to borrowers with high credit scores. When a borrower has a greater likelihood of defaulting, the lender should be rewarded for taking a chance on that borrower. Likewise, when you invest capital in a startup, you should expect an opportunity to earn a much higher return than an investment in a public stock, as a reward for taking a chance on that entrepreneur.

We can sum up by saying all investments involve risk. Securities issued by small, private companies are generally riskier than securities of large, public companies. In return for investing $x$ dollars in a small business, you should expect a chance to earn a return that is greater than investing $x$ dollars in the public stock market. Where the risk is *very* much greater, you should hesitate to invest unless the possible return is *very* much greater as well. Issuers of private securities must be willing to reward their investors handsomely—first by offering sufficient equity percentages and second by working hard to make the business succeed—in return for taking a chance on them.

So the first principle of risk for investors is: Higher risk should be rewarded with higher return, or, more realistically, the *opportunity* to earn a higher return.

## RISK AND DIVERSIFICATION

The second principle of risk is: The riskiness of investing in private securities should not be judged in isolation. You should weigh the riskiness of an investment, or of a particular class of investments (in this case, startups and early-stage companies), in terms of how it affects the overall risk in your entire investment portfolio.

By adding diversification to your portfolio, private securities (which can appear risky in isolation) can potentially *reduce* overall portfolio risk when done judiciously.

Diversification is not putting all your eggs in one basket. Here is an example that will help clarify what diversification means in an investing context. Let's say you have a 401(k) retirement fund, and you invest all your retirement savings in the stock of your employer. This is certainly an expression of loyalty, and you can be assured that working hard from 9:00 to 5:00 (or any other shift) helps your company earn profits, which in turn maximizes the value of your retirement fund. It seems like a very synergistic investment—you work hard for your company and your company rewards you with a salary and portfolio growth. But there is danger here: Your retirement portfolio is not diversified. If your company suffers a setback and its stock price plummets, your *entire* portfolio suffers. In the worst-case scenario, your company goes bust, your portfolio crashes, and you lose your job—total disaster. This actually happened to some Enron employees when the company declared bankruptcy in December 2001, as well as employees at many other companies over the years who failed to diversify their 401(k) plans.

In 1999 and 2000, investing in Enron seemed like a smart bet. But putting all their eggs in that basket resulted in financial catastrophe for Enron investors who failed to diversify.[1]

---

[1] As a result of Enron's bankruptcy, Enron employees lost $1.2 billion in retirement funds and Enron retirees lost $2 billion in pension funds. In that same year, Enron executives received bonuses totaling $55 million and cashed in $116 million in Enron stock.

That is why the first and foremost rule of investing is: Diversify your portfolio.

Diversification means investing in different asset classes (stocks, bonds, mutual funds, money markets, real estate, etc.), in different sectors of the economy (energy, utilities, healthcare, manufacturing, retail, natural resources, media, services, technology, etc.), maybe in global markets as well as U.S. markets. Even in the bond market you can diversify by allocating funds to corporate, municipal, and variously rated bonds that offer commensurate yields. Diversification assures you that if one sector of the economy suffers, your entire portfolio won't be a disaster. If you were invested heavily in technology stocks in 1999, for example, the dot-com bust could have wiped you out; loading up in real estate investments in the lead-up to the 2008 recession would also have set you back decades in your financial performance.

## ALTERNATIVE ASSETS

In addition to the asset classes mentioned in the preceding paragraph, accredited investors have had the privilege and the means to invest in alternative asset classes, further diversifying their risks. Alternatives include private equity, venture capital, angel capital, hedge funds, and tangible asset funds (which invest in farmland, machinery and equipment, natural resources, etc.).

Alternative assets offer investors a special kind of diversification, known as noncorrelation. Alternatives typically do not rise and fall with the broader markets. When the country goes through a general economic downturn and most mainstream asset classes level off or fall in value, noncorrelated alternatives will tend *not* to follow the mainstream, but can maintain their own momentum or otherwise move independently of macroeconomic pressures.

Certain kinds of hedge funds, for example, are positioned to earn a positive return even when most stocks and bonds are losing value. By taking offsetting short and long equity positions (see sidebar), these hedge funds can make money in falling as well as rising markets. In 2013, when the public stock market indexes soared (the S&P 500 gained about 16 percent), hedge funds posted lackluster gains (about 7 percent). But in the mini-recession of 2000 through 2002, when the S&P fell an annualized 17 percent, hedge funds returned a positive 7 percent. And in 2008, the heart of the deep financial crisis, the S&P 500 was down a whopping 38 percent, while hedge funds fell only 19 percent.[2] Thus, hedge funds exhibit a lack of correlation with the general market, effectively diversifying portfolio risk.

## LONG AND SHORT POSITIONS

If you believe the price of XYZ Corporation stock will rise, you can exploit your belief by purchasing shares of XYZ stock. You buy XYZ today and, if the price rises in the future, you can sell the same shares for a capital gain. Of course, it is also possible that the share price will fall, but that's the risk you take.

If you believe that the price of ABC Corporation is going to fall, how can you exploit that belief? If you already own shares of ABC, then you can sell. If you sell and the price indeed falls, then you have avoided a loss. But what if you don't already own ABC stock? If you strongly believe ABC stock will fall but you don't own any ABC shares, then you can sell ABC short.

When you sell a stock short, you first borrow the shares from your broker and then sell them. Let's say you sell 100 shares at $12 per share (you receive $1,200 on the sale). Three months later the price falls to $5 per share, and you decide it's a good time to buy 100 shares (which cost you $500) and return those 100 shares to your broker. Your short sale has been successful: You received $1,200 and spent $500, so you earned the difference, which is $700 (not including broker's fees).

When you sell short, or take a short position, you are betting that the stock price will fall. When you buy long, or take a long position, you are betting that the stock price will rise.

What happens if you sell short and the stock price rises and keeps rising? Then at some point, to avoid further loss, you must buy the shares at a higher price, return them to your broker, and lick your wounds.

### Disproportionate Risk

Selling short is inherently riskier than buying long, which is why few individual investors, other than professional investors, engage in short selling. Why is short selling riskier?

When you buy XYZ shares long, the worst-case scenario is that XYZ's share price falls to zero, and you lose your entire investment. But

---

[2]Data from Preqin and HFRX.

the upside is unlimited: The price can double or triple or (theoretically) keep rising infinitely. (See Table 8.1.)

**TABLE 8.1**   Comparing Long and Short Positions

|  | Long Position | Short Position |
|---|---|---|
| Direction of bet | Share price will rise | Share price will fall |
| Upside | Unlimited (price keeps rising) | Limited (price falls to $0) |
| Downside | Limited (price falls to $0) | Unlimited (price keeps rising) |
| Cost | Broker fee | Broker fee + loan interest |

Remember that short-selling means betting that the price will fall. When you sell ABC short, the best-case scenario is that the price falls to zero—it can't fall any further. The downside, however, is unlimited: The price can keep rising infinitely, in which case you must eventually spend a fortune to return your shares to the broker. Not only that, but you usually have to pay interest or a fee to the broker for the time you borrow the shares. Moreover, as soon as the share price rises significantly, your broker will probably require that you start covering the margin (the difference between your sale price and the current price); this is known as a *margin call*.

All things considered, short selling is a strategy that sophisticated investors employ cautiously. Some hedge funds and institutional investors, for example, manage risk by taking offsetting long and short equity positions, especially in volatile sectors of the economy. Volatile sectors today include information technology, renewable energy, and small-cap stocks (companies with less than $1 billion in market capitalization).*

The lesson here is about the use of various alternative assets in portfolio diversification, not necessarily about the need for average investors to sell short. In fact, in equity crowdfunding there is no way to take a short position on a Title III offering.

*Sectors with lowest volatility include regulated utilities and consumer staples (products that people use every day, like food and clothing).

Likewise, venture capital has exhibited a lack of correlation with public stocks. Morningstar researchers found in 2002 that "the correlation coefficient between VC (venture capital) and public stocks is estimated to be 0.04 percent," which is essentially zero.[3] This noncorrelation does not have the same basis as hedge funds—VC funds do not take offsetting long and short positions. But share values of venture-backed startups and early-stage companies do not tend to drift upward and downward in response to macroeconomic forces that affect public stock values.

We could not find research on correlation measurement between angel capital and public securities. But because of the similarity of angel and venture capital stages and deal structures, the noncorrelation characteristics should be similar as well—assuming sufficient diversification within the angel investment portfolio. In other words, angel investors likely have a similar experience as venture capital funds and hedge funds, in that they do better than the overall market during periods of decline and also do reasonably to very well when broader markets are in the black.

Before 2014, as a practical matter, only accredited investors could invest in most alternative asset classes. Thanks to the JOBS Act, now nonaccredited investors can diversify into one alternative asset class, angel capital, via equity crowdfunding. So diversification into a noncorrelated asset class is now possible for everyone.

## ASSET ALLOCATION

The first step in developing a diversified portfolio is determining how much of your nest egg ought to be allocated to the various investment classes.

Some family offices (the investment arms of very wealthy extended families) and institutional investors (such as university endowments)—both of which employ teams of professional investment managers—invest up to 20 percent of their money in alternative assets. That would not be a good idea for individual investors. While alternatives generally offer the potential for significant upside (in some cases, spectacular returns), they also present high downside risk (in some cases, catastrophic losses). If a family office loses 20 percent of its assets, the member families are still wealthy, if somewhat disgruntled. The pain would probably be much greater if 20 percent of *your* investment portfolio went down the drain, especially if your retirement savings or your children's college tuition were battered in the process.

---

[3]Peng Chen, Gary T. Baierl, and Paul D. Kaplan, "Venture Capital and Its Role in Strategic Asset Allocation," *The Journal of Portfolio Management*, Winter 2002, pp. 83–89.

Investment advisers almost universally advise moderate-net-worth individuals to allocate no more than 5 to 10 percent (a few go as high as 15 percent) of their portfolio (not including the primary residence) to alternatives. If you are not a millionaire, "alternatives" essentially means equity crowdfunding.

For example, a growth-oriented, fairly risk-tolerant investor with stable income might allocate 65 percent of his or her portfolio assets to public stocks and stock mutual funds, 25 percent to fixed-income securities such as bonds and money markets, and 10 percent to alternatives. On the other hand, a retired investor who is more concerned with wealth preservation (less risk-tolerant) might allocate 55 percent to fixed income, 40 percent to stocks and mutual funds, and 5 percent to alternatives for the sake of diversification. Everyone's risk tolerance and allocation strategy is different; yours will depend on your family income and expenses, net worth, age, short-term liquidity needs, long-term estate planning considerations, and other factors. Asset allocation is an area where you need advice from a good financial planner, estate lawyer, and/or accountant who is familiar with your situation and objectives.

In addition to strategically allocating your investable money into diverse asset classes, you should try to diversify strategically within each asset class. If your alternative investments consist entirely of equity crowdfunding deals, then you should think about doing a number of such deals over the course of several years. Some accredited angel investors set their sights on making at least five angel investments each year, with a goal of 20 to 25 deals in their portfolios at any given time. Because some of those investments will crash and perhaps one or more will result in profitable exits, those angels need to keep investing in deals each year to replenish their inventory of angel deals, at least until their overall portfolio allocation strategies change. Experience has shown that this level of activity can yield excellent returns, but it does require a long-term commitment, spreading out your angel investments over a period of several years, and in most cases a lot longer.

Nonaccredited investors should not necessarily set 20 deals as their goal. A dozen equity crowdfunding deals, accumulated over a period of three to five years, would probably constitute a full and proper angel investment portfolio for the vast majority of investors.

There are two schools of thought on whether you should diversify your angel portfolio in a "panoramic" way, which means investing in various industries, geographic regions, and development stages (startup, early, and growth). Some angels try to diversify every which way. Others believe that you should focus your angel portfolio on industries that you understand and geographies that let you conduct due diligence and monitor your investments without incurring outrageous travel expenses. In the world of equity crowdfunding, much due diligence and monitoring is done online, so travel might not be a concern. But we agree that an understanding of the issuer's industry gives you an edge in selecting and investigating equity crowdfunding offerings, and you need every edge you can get. You are already achieving broad portfolio diversification by investing in angel deals, so you don't need to take diversification to a level where it creates more risk than it moderates. This approach is well articulated by David S. Rose in his book *Angel Investing*.

Rose warns, however, that if you invest in two or more small companies in a particular industry, you should avoid investing in direct competitors. You don't want one company to be using your invested money to fight against your interest in another company. Also, you have to be "excruciatingly careful about not sharing confidential information across two [competitors], or in any way advising or guiding one of them based on privileged knowledge of the other."[4]

Every library has shelves full of books dealing with the notions of diversification and asset allocation for average Americans. Books published before 2015, however, will not consider the availability of this new class of alternative investments—equity crowdfunding—for every American.

## DRY POWDER

As we explained in Chapter 3, the total amount of money that you can invest each year in equity crowdfunding deals (whether on one funding portal or a number of portals) is limited, depending on your income and net worth (see sidebar).

---

### ANNUAL INVESTMENT LIMITS IN EQUITY CROWDFUNDING

To review the information that we first presented in Chapter 3, here is how you determine the maximum amount of money that you can invest in equity crowdfunding deals in a 12-month period:

- Individuals with annual income and net worth of $40,000 or less can invest up to $2,000 in equity crowdfunding per year.

---

[4]David S. Rose, *Angel Investing: The Gust Guide to Making Money and Having Fun Investing in Startups*, John Wiley & Sons, 2014, pp. 137–138. Rose's book is written mainly for accredited investors, but we believe this approach is valid for all investors.

- Individuals with annual income or net worth greater than $40,000 and less than $100,000 may invest 5 percent of their income or net worth, whichever is greater. (The range is $2,000 to $5,000 per year.)
- Individuals with income or net worth of $100,000 or more can invest up to 10 percent of their income or net worth, whichever is greater, but not more than $100,000, per year.

When an issuer lists its offering on a funding portal, the issuer sets a minimum investment amount. (The portal might set an absolute minimum across the entire platform.) You may invest more than the minimum amount, depending on how excited you are about the company's growth prospects. Some smaller issuers with modest valuations will likely accept investments as low as $100, while some more established companies will set a minimum of $1,000 or more.

Based on your asset allocation strategy, assuming you will spread your angel investments out over a few years, you should calculate how much money you can devote to equity crowdfunding investments in the current year, and roughly how much you'll have to invest each year over the next few years. This is not PhD-level finance, but it's easy to overlook this essential budgeting process. It is essential, that is, if you've decided to be a disciplined investor.

Figure you will make fairly small bets in the first year or two (or in your first few deals), while you are learning how to be a smart angel investor. After you become more skilled at reviewing offerings and judging suitability of investments, you might decide to increase the size of your bets.

Keep in mind that one or more of the companies that you invest in this year may need another round of equity financing in the next few years in order to expand. It is quite common for fast-growing companies to go through a series of equity funding rounds, typically named in sequence: the seed round, the Series A round, the Series B round, and so on. If you believe in your company and want to keep supporting it—especially if you want to avoid any dilution of your equity percentage—you should reserve some cash for follow-on rounds. This reserved cash is known among angels VCs as "dry powder." David Rose points out that issuers often provide incentives for its investors to participate in follow-on rounds, and sophisticated angels typically reserve 50 percent of their original investment for that purpose.[5] (We will further discuss dilution and follow-on incentives in Chapter 11.)

---

[5] Ibid., pp. 45, 95.

## SEVEN STEPS TO BUILDING YOUR EQUITY CROWDFUNDING PORTFOLIO

Start with a three- to five-year plan. You will probably adjust and revise it from time to time, so don't feel you are stuck with the first draft of your plan.

1. Determine your allocation to alternative investments. In most cases, it is appropriate for a household to have 5 to 10 percent of its total investment portfolio in alternatives, including equity crowdfunding.*

    *Let's say the total value of your investment portfolio today is $P, and you plan to allocate A% of your portfolio to equity crowdfunding. Then your allocation to equity crowdfunding is $PA ÷ 100.*

2. Develop a long-term plan. Most people will spread out their crowdfunding investments over three to five years. It is important to be patient and selective, waiting for offerings that are most likely to result in strong ROI and/or social impact.

    *Let's say you plan to build your equity crowdfunding portfolio over Y years.*

3. Develop your first-year budget. For planning purposes, figure you will invest roughly equal amounts of capital each year in equity crowdfunding deals until you build your portfolio. The actual yearly amount can change depending on the quality of deal flow and other variables. (Be sure this yearly investment amount falls within the limits permitted by Title III. See the previous sidebar "Annual Investment Limits in Equity Crowdfunding.")

    You will invest roughly $PA ÷ 100Y in the first year, where:

    *P = Total portfolio value today in dollars*

    *A = Percent of your portfolio allocated to equity crowdfunding*

    *Y = Years to build your equity crowdfunding portfolio*

4. Identify your true investment motivations. You (and your family) may want to focus solely on ROI, or you may be more interested in the social impact of your investments. It is important that you are clear about your motivation and do not try to optimize any particular investment for both ROI and social impact. You can hold a mix of ROI and social impact investments, but each investment should be optimized for one or the other.

5. Your goal is to build a portfolio of 10 to 15 crowdfunding investments—or perhaps fewer if you are purely a social-impact investor. If you spread these over three to five years, you will invest in an average of roughly two to five deals per year. Remember that you might need to reserve some cash (dry powder) for follow-on deals after the first year—that is, investments in subsequent rounds for a company where you invested in an earlier round.

6. Diversify your equity crowdfunding portfolio. Even though your investments in equity crowdfunding represent diversification of your *overall* portfolio, it is still a good idea to diversify the risk *within* your equity crowdfunding portfolio. If that sounds redundant, remember (from Chapter 6) that successful angel investors achieve good ROI by implementing this dual level of diversification. Diversifying could mean investing in a variety of industries, regions, and/or stages of development. Some angels believe you should stick to an industry where you have knowledge and expertise, and diversify only in terms of regions and stages.

7. Implement, review, crunch numbers, and adjust your plan every six months ideally, or yearly at least. Over the course of five to seven years, chances are some of your crowdfunding investments will tank and be total losses, some may result in (hopefully very profitable) exits, and some will still be illiquid. Replace the total losses and exits with fresh crowdfunding investments, assuming you are comfortable in this asset class. If your crowdfunding portfolio is providing very good returns (beating your overall portfolio returns or the broad market indexes, for example), consider increasing your allocation to this asset class, to as much as 15 percent. If you are unhappy with your returns, consider lowering your allocation or winding down.

---

*Financial planners usually advise that you reserve six months of expenses, in case of emergency, in a savings or other fairly liquid account. If you do not have such a reserve, then you should subtract that amount from the value of your investment portfolio before calculating a 5 to 10 percent allocation to alternatives.

## BEFORE YOU PULL THE TRIGGER

Once you determine how much money you can allocate to equity crowdfunding investments over the next 12 months, you are ready to visit one or more funding portals and search for suitable investment opportunities. Two caveats before you begin:

First, do not feel compelled to spend all of your first year's allocation in the first year. It's not a use-it-or-lose-it proposition. Be patient and wait for investment opportunities that you believe in and feel comfortable with—you will be stuck with them for at least a year and more likely several years, as they are relatively illiquid securities. Keep in mind that as the new equity crowdfunding industry gains acceptance among entrepreneurs and broker-dealers, the deal flow will increase and the quality of deals will improve over the next five years or so.

Second, before you pull the trigger and make a commitment to invest, be sure you have realistic expectations about what will happen with your investments over the next several years. There are four main areas of concern: returns, liquidity, employment, and exits.

## Return on Investment

As we showed in Chapter 6, angel investors who are members of angel groups enjoy average returns in the neighborhood of 25 percent per year, and some as high as 50 percent, with the highest returns being generated in the technology sector. They achieve impressive ROI numbers by gaining access to high-quality deal flow, assiduously conducting due diligence, and diversifying their angel portfolios with at least a dozen investments over a period of several years.

In the first year or two of equity crowdfunding, you probably can't expect such high-quality deal flow. In fact, it is uncertain whether equity crowdfunding will ever attract the same quality of deals as angel investor groups do. As the industry gains acceptance among issuers and broker-dealers, however, high-quality issuers may gravitate more toward equity crowdfunding because of the efficiency with which they can reach large numbers of investors. The government will, we predict, within a few years improve the law—raising both the offering limits and the investment limits, and lowering the cost of compliance for issuers—which will attract a better grade of equity offerings and more growth-stage companies.

And you will become more successful as you learn the ins and outs of angel investing via equity crowdfunding. Meanwhile, you have a chance to earn decent returns, but don't expect that your returns in the first few years will equal those of experienced angel investors.

Remember that there is a brutal downside to business startups and angel investing. According to research conducted by Shikhar Ghosh at Harvard

Business School (which we introduced in Chapter 5), 30 to 40 percent of startups wind up in liquidation, resulting in a total loss for investors.[6] Among the sectors with the highest failure rates are information technology and retail; among the lowest failure rates are real estate, healthcare, and agriculture.[7]

Can the smartest angel investors consistently predict which startups will be winners? Definitely not. Consider the experience of Bessemer Venture Partners, one of the nation's oldest venture capital funds. Bessemer may have invested in Staples, LinkedIn, and Skype when they were startups, but they took a pass on Apple, eBay, FedEx, Google, Intel, Intuit, PayPal, Compaq, and StrataCom (which was acquired by Cisco). Don't expect that you will develop a sixth sense for which startups will succeed and which will flame out! Draw on your own entrepreneurial and financial experience when possible, and welcome input from the crowd (and other sources of news and insight) to develop a broader perspective on the equity crowdfunding investment opportunities.

If you are investing in startups mainly for social or ideological reasons, keep in mind that it is "practically impossible," says David Rose, "to optimize for both financial return and social impact" on the same investment.[8] If you are focusing on the social impact of your investment, forget about optimizing for ROI, and vice versa. You might participate in some deals purely for social motives and other deals purely for ROI.

## Liquidity

When you invest in a public stock, your investment is relatively liquid. If you have an emergency need for cash, you can sell your stock a week after you buy it, and you can easily find a buyer for your shares in the appropriate public stock exchange. In many markets, except during the worst of economic conditions, you can buy real estate and flip it within a few months, making it not quite as liquid as public stocks. All kinds of capital assets (tangible or intangible property that has value) can be liquidated when necessary, though not always immediately. In equity crowdfunding, however, in most cases you must hold your investment for one year, making it relatively illiquid. Even after the one-year holding period, unlike public stocks, you may have a hard time finding a buyer for your shares, as the secondary markets for private

---

[6]Carmen Nobel, "Why Companies Fail—and How Their Founders Can Bounce Back," *Working Knowledge*, Harvard Business School, March 7, 2011, http://hbswk.hbs.edu/pdf/item/6591.pdf.

[7]Statistic Brain, January 1, 2014 (citing *Entrepreneur Weekly*, Small Business Development Center of Bradley University, and University of Tennessee Research), www.statisticbrain.com/startup-failure-by-industry/.

[8]Rose, op. cit., p. 190.

securities are not well established. Finding a buyer is the first challenge. The second challenge is getting a good price for your shares. It is much more difficult for a buyer and seller to agree on the valuation of a small startup than the valuation of a public company whose share price is a matter of daily reporting. (We will talk more about secondary markets in Chapter 14.)

When you invest in a growing business via equity crowdfunding, your long-term goal should be to hold your shares until there is a liquidity event or exit (see "Exits" section for details). With rare exceptions, these exits don't typically happen in the first few years. The Angel Capital Association found that, among its members (accredited investors only), the average time before a "positive exit" was almost nine years.[9] Experienced angel investors and academic researchers estimate the typical time to liquidity variously at 3 to 10 years, depending on the industry and the company's stage of development at the time of the investment.

## Employment

In the traditional angel investment world, early investors—who typically bought tens or hundreds of thousands of dollars' worth of equity in a startup—might expect to help the founders, and protect their investments in the process, by providing professional expertise or industry connections. They are called *strategic investors* or "smart money." Those who invested the largest sums might expect to win a seat on the board of directors or gain employment as a consultant or even as an executive in the startup. There are, not so rarely, angel investors who essentially want to buy a job.

In the new equity crowdfunding world, you are one of hundreds of small investors in a startup (to the tune of hundreds or maybe low thousands of dollars' worth of equity). You can't expect to participate in the company's management in the same way that traditional angels often do. You can politely offer your management expertise and ideas, but there is no assurance that issuers will look to their equity crowdfunding investors for that kind of help. An exception is in the area of promotion: The company might (and, in some cases, should) ask you to be an unpaid "brand evangelist" for its product or service, and give you the materials and instructions for how to do that. Participating in that way protects your investment.

If you apply for a job with the startup through the normal channels, you might get special consideration because you are an investor, but don't count on it—the founders are (or should be) laser-focused on becoming profitable above all else, not inclined to do you any favors if it doesn't optimally benefit their bottom line.

---

[9]Ibid., p. 104.

## Exits

Based on Shikhar Ghosh's research at Harvard, more than half of all startups will enjoy some measure of success. That does not mean they will provide good returns for investors. Some of them will chug along profitably, they will not require subsequent rounds of equity financing from venture capitalists, and for any number of reasons (e.g., they don't penetrate the market widely enough) they will not become acquisition targets. A vast majority will never grow big enough to go public. So the mere fact that your portfolio company achieves profitability—while it may offer you income in the form of dividends—does not mean you will be able to sell or redeem your shares for a capital gain (at a higher price per share than you paid). If you need cash and must sell your shares, you may have to settle for a slight (or not so slight) loss. Or, if you really enjoy being an owner and/or believe strongly in the company's long-term future, you may be able to buy up shares from other early investors who want to cash out.

If you are fortunate, your investment will result in an exit that yields a positive return, typically one of the following three types:

- *Buyback of shares by the company* in the event of a subsequent venture capital funding round. This outcome depends partly on the terms of your investment in the company—some deals require or allow issuers to buy back shares, at a specified price (or based on a specified formula) that benefits early investors, before they accept future VC funding. The reason for a buyback is that VCs often want their portfolio company's capitalization table "cleaned up" before they invest.

  If your deal terms do not contain a buyback provision, the issuer may offer to buy your shares back at a price that you must then negotiate. Issuers in those circumstances will typically be hungry for VC money and therefore be willing to make early investors a good offer.

  To be in a position to receive VC funding, a startup or early-stage company must exhibit a potential for rapid growth. Some VCs may perceive a successful equity crowdfunding campaign as a sign of market acceptance or proof of concept, but most VCs will not rely on the crowd's due diligence—VCs will conduct their own comprehensive due diligence.

- *An acquisition by a competitor or larger company.* As we said in Chapter 6, according to Scott A. Shane's research, around 1 percent of angel investments result in an acquisition. Among angel groups (whose members must be accredited investors), the percentage is higher: The Band of Angels, which we introduced in Chapter 6, reports that 19 percent of its angel investments have resulted in acquisitions.

  There are many reasons that an established business might want to buy a startup outright even before it is profitable: as a shortcut to fast growth (e.g., to expand its sales territory or product line), to achieve vertical integration (e.g., a manufacturer acquiring a supplier or distributor), to achieve horizontal integration (e.g., buying out a competitor to gain its market share, also known as consolidation, common today in the banking and pharmaceutical sectors), for access to proprietary research, to acquire patents or other intellectual property, to bring in a brilliant founder or stellar management team (also known as an acqui-hire), to gobble up future competitors preemptively, and other motivations. In a few cases, acquisitions can be driven by vanity, where middle-market executives like to brag about their merger and acquisition (M&A) conquests.

On a national level, acquisition transactions vary widely, but in a typical private company acquisition the purchase price is in the $30 million to $50 million range.[10] This suggests that early investors should aim to invest at a valuation in the low single-digit millions, in order to earn strong returns—assuming that only a few in 10 investments will result in a successful exit.

On a regional level, however, there is another world of smaller-dollar M&A transactions, which is where exits are more likely to occur for equity crowdfunding investments. But do not rule out the possibility of a higher-profile, larger-dollar acquisition in your most promising deals.

Acquisition-minded companies keep a keen eye on startups in their respective industries. Some companies in the consumer products, technology, and entertainment fields have already established strategic partnerships with equity crowdfunding portals, where they mentor founders of promising startups and get an early peek at possible future suppliers and acquisition targets. For example, Cisco Systems, through its Entrepreneurs in Residence program, is partnering with the EarlyShares platform to support startups with "the next big ideas" in Internet development.

The hottest sector in the United States for M&A activity (deal count) in the first three months of 2014 was commercial services, followed by technology services, finance, consumer services, manufacturing, and healthcare (in a comparison of 21 sectors).[11]

- *An IPO.* Not all entrepreneurs dream of filing an initial public offering; some would rather stay midsize, or even get big but stay private, for various reasons. The two main reasons for wanting to go public are (1)

---

[10]Ibid., p. 106.
[11]"U.S. M&A News and Trends," *Flashwire U.S. Monthly*, FactSet Research Systems, April 2014.

to reward the founders and early investors by generating huge returns and making them rich and (2) to make it easier to raise capital on regular basis in the vastly more efficient and liquid public markets.

Even among the most sophisticated angel investors the IPO is rare, though. The Band of Angels reports that about 4 percent of its investments over 20 years have resulted in IPOs. Shane's research (see Chapter 6) indicates that roughly 0.2 percent of all the companies financed by angel investors eventually go public.

Industries with high IPO rates (percent of startups founded each year that go public, according to 2009 data) include pharmaceuticals, communications equipment, computer and office equipment, medical instruments and supplies, electronic components and accessories, and measuring and controlling devices.[12]

Over the four-year period 2010 through 2013, the industries with the most IPOs were technology (163), financial (101), energy (90), healthcare (87), and consumer (63).[13] In both 2013 and the first quarter of 2014, however, the industry with the most IPOs was healthcare.[14]

It is important that you have realistic expectations when you start investing in startups via equity crowdfunding. You should be pleasantly surprised if one of your portfolio companies achieves a positive exit within three or five years, and you should not kick yourself too hard when one or two or three of your companies go belly-up before you experience a positive exit.

As we showed in Chapter 6, angel investors who take a disciplined approach to diversification, selectivity, and due diligence can earn very good returns. You should assume that if you do not take seriously those tasks (and the other fundamentals we cover in the next few chapters), then you will not earn the kinds of returns that disciplined angels earn. Maybe that's not your primary concern; maybe you want to help drive innovation, promote community development, boost clean energy solutions, or just "own a piece" of your favorite company. In any case, now you have realistic expectations and a seven-step plan.

---

[12]Scott A. Shane, *Fools Gold? The Truth behind Angel Investing in America*, Oxford University Press, 2009, p. 192.

[13]"IPO Industry History," Renaissance Capital LLC, posted in 2014 at http://www.renaissancecapital.com/ipohome/press/ipoindustryhistory.aspx.

[14]Kyle Anderson, "IPO Market Charts," *Money Morning*, March 6, 2014, http://moneymorning.com/2014/03/06/ipo-market-charts-industries-booming-new-companies-2014/. In 2013, the industries with the most IPOs were healthcare (43), financial (40), technology (40), energy (20), and consumer products and services (18).

# CHAPTER 9

# How to Invest, Part II: Identify Suitable Offerings

In Chapter 8, we discussed portfolio strategy and laid out a seven-step plan for building an equity crowdfunding portfolio. Before you register on an equity crowdfunding site and start looking for offerings to invest in, we urge you to think seriously about the first four steps of the plan to develop your first-year budget and identify your motivation for investing in startups and early-stage companies.

Your primary motivation may be social or financial—that is, you may be motivated primarily by the social impact of your investments or primarily by the potential return on investment. We want to reiterate here that you should not reasonably expect to achieve both social and financial objectives in the same investment or to the same degree of success—if it happens to work out that way, consider yourself very lucky. Instead, most opportunities will be *principally* one or the other.

Portfolio construction, which we talked about in Chapter 8, is about finding a mix of investments. You can hold a mix of social-impact and financial-return investments, but each investment should be optimized for one objective or the other.

## NARROW DOWN YOUR SELECTION OF OFFERINGS

Before you pinpoint the kinds of offerings you will consider investing in, browse through the offerings on a few equity crowdfunding sites to get a feel for what kinds of companies appeal to you—and why.

The following two lists (derived from the "New Angel Investors" section of Chapter 6) show a breakout of social motivations and a breakout of financial motivations. This will help you narrow down your selection of offerings that are suitable for your portfolio.

## Social and Personal Motivations

- *Ideology.* You are passionate about supporting a cause- or ideology-oriented company, and you enjoy a sense of belonging to a committed group of owners who think alike. Examples include "green" products, renewable energy development, low-income housing, elder care, for-profit drug rehab clinics, organic lawn care, religious music, and film. Issuers may form *benefit corporations* (B corps), which is possible in California, Illinois, Massachusetts, New York, and several other states. Due diligence will emphasize the authenticity and credibility of management's commitment to the cause. With Internet search and social media tools, it is fairly easy to dig into the backgrounds of the people involved; thus, in many cases you'll be able to tell whether the management team has a mature history of work in a particular area or are just wannabes.

- *Brand loyalty.* You are an enthusiastic user of a product or line of products under one brand—a loyal fan—and you want to help ensure the future availability of the product or brand. At an earlier stage of product development, you want to help get a new product to market so you can be among the first people to use it. Examples in this category include gadgets, games, hobbies, 3D printers, Apple electronics, fitness, cooking, recreational supplies and equipment, sports teams, clothing, and fashion accessories. Due diligence will emphasize the company's ability to produce and market at a sustainable cost and competitive price.

- *Deserving entrepreneur or demographic group.* You want to show support for entrepreneurs whom you personally admire or businesses owned by war veterans, college alumni, women, diaspora members, coreligionists, or (on a more local level) inner-city minorities, for example. Due diligence will focus on founder and executive team profiles—their education, experience, credentials, integrity, and record of success.

- *Community development.* You share a connection with members of a neighborhood, local community, or regional advocacy group and wish to "own a piece of" a business on which that community depends. Such businesses tend to be gathering spots like restaurants, art studios, cafes, delicatessens, bodegas, groceries, microbreweries, bowling alleys, fitness centers, hair salons, theaters, and stadiums. Alternatively, you wish to join a community in supporting a business whose owner has been the victim of a tragedy or perceived injustice. You may be motivated also by broad community development goals, such as job creation and neighborhood renewal. Due diligence will emphasize a strong business plan. This is a crossover category, as some financially motivated investors prefer to be near the companies that get their money so they can conveniently be active in the business and keep an eye on it.

- *Creative endeavor.* You want to join a creative, hip, or glamorous project such as music, film, theater, or publishing. You may have an opportunity to offer creative input into the project if you are a major investor, or in the promotional phase of the project at least. In evaluating deal terms, you will be concerned with access to meetings, rehearsals, movie sets, and premieres.
- *Innovation.* You want to invest in startups, especially in (but not limited to) the high-tech industry and any business sector that is adapting to new technology, to help foster innovation. This crosses over into financial motivation also, because it is where returns on investment in a few lucky deals can be spectacular. The key here is a deep understanding and intended use of the end product.

## Financial Motivations

- *Fast growth potential.* These offerings are more likely to result in a shorter-term exit (via acquisition or IPO) and larger (possibly spectacular) returns, but are also more likely to be crushed by competitors in the early stages, burn through seed capital, and need more rounds of financing (which may result in dilution of share value or the need to invest more capital in later rounds). Examples are technology and healthcare. If you do not understand the technology and/or the business model, then this is more akin to gambling where the odds are against you.
- *Long-term (slower but steadier) growth potential.* You represent "patient money" and look for established but still early-stage businesses that have solid growth strategies. Due diligence will be comprehensive, with special focus on whether the business can become self-sustaining (use retained earnings rather than external sources of capital) and identifying realistic exit strategies. These companies include commercial and agricultural real estate; service providers such as building contractors, healthcare, cleaning services, and auto repair; and franchisees.
- *Speculation in boom-or-bust industries.* This includes operations such as oil and gas exploration (e.g., a single oil pump), small-scale mining of precious metals, or prepatent inventions (e.g., batteries, solar panels). A hit (or a desired patent) will result in potentially huge gains for investors, while a miss will often result in a total loss; there is rarely a middle ground. Such speculators, known as wildcatters in the oil and gas industry, must have a high tolerance for risk. Some knowledge or experience in the field is necessary for due diligence and for identifying the opportunities that have higher probability for success.
- *Strategic investment.* If you are a consultant or professional adviser, investing in a small business might help you reel it in as a prospective client. You might invest in a company because you want to get a job

there. If you currently own or manage a business, you might sink money into startups that could become your company's suppliers, strategic partners, sources of R&D, or even acquisition targets. In Title III offerings, where there may be hundreds or thousands of investors in a deal, you may have to invest a noticeably large amount to gain the recognition you need from the issuer. This category may hit ethical or legal issues. In general, "vertical" investments—those related to you in the chain of goods or services—are fine, but "horizontal" investments, which are essentially competitors (whether direct or indirect) are likely to be barred by the issuer—and may be illegal. If an issuer suspects you are motivated by a job hunt, it may reject your application as well.

■ *Follow the smart money.* Experienced angel investors and venture capitalists, small incubators and accelerators, corporate entrepreneurship programs, and even institutional investors will be cherry-picking some of the best deals on equity crowdfunding sites. Their participation in an offering is sometimes highly visible. While there is no guarantee that these sophisticated groups will do complete due diligence and apply the same variables that you would apply, this is a very intriguing investment type for those who want to invest but don't have the time or experience to perform due diligence on their own. Following "smart money" is one fairly prudent way to invest, although it is never a sure thing—even the most successful angel investors make bad investments *most* of the time. We don't want to discourage you from following the smart money, as long as you understand the risks involved in leaving the analysis and due diligence to others.

We suggest that you begin searching for suitable offerings in an industry where you have experience and knowledge, at least in the first few years. As you gain confidence in your ability to select good deals, you might want to broaden your scope, for greater diversification, to other industries where you feel you can study and become knowledgeable.

Also, don't be afraid to pull in the experience and investment skills of friends and colleagues—especially successful business executives and entrepreneurs, business lawyers, and accountants—and from those you can network with online. Consider visiting chat rooms and discussion groups for crowdfunding investors, both on- and off-platform (including LinkedIn groups), before making investment decisions. Get a feel for members of those groups who are well informed and insightful and who ask good questions, and don't hesitate to initiate one-on-one conversations with them. While you cannot wholly rely on the perspectives of people you don't totally know and trust, you can factor their ideas into the bucket of information you use prior to making final selections.

## SELECTING EQUITY CROWDFUNDING SITES

We also suggest that you begin searching for suitable offerings on two kinds of equity crowdfunding sites: (1) those that focus on the industries where you have expertise (or the locality or region that you want to support) and (2) those that have a broader focus, including your industry, but have a reputation for attracting high-quality offerings.

Two more considerations are important when choosing crowdfunding sites on which to register. First is whether the site is a broker-dealer, or has a contractual relationship with one, and therefore is held to a strict standard of due diligence and has the ability to post only companies that it thinks are of higher quality.

Second is whether the site offers an insurance-type policy that covers the risk of bankruptcy and dissolution (see sidebar "Investment Insurance Covers Bankruptcy and Dissolution"). Not all sites offer such coverage. If you are more comfortable investing with that kind of protection, it is important that you check the availability of such a policy on a crowdfunding site before you invest there. If you feel comfortable "exposed," then availability is not an issue.

In all likelihood as this new industry develops there will be high-profile front-runners in the field; you can research which are the top-rated, most visited sites that raise the most capital. Referrals from friends or using rating websites can be useful. In the end, a major part will be to choose the portals that offer the investments in which you are most interested. Despite that, do not underestimate the importance of using reputable sites, since some of them will effectively "prescreen" offerings to the extent legally permitted and you can rely on that prescreening to at least weed out the bottom layer of companies.

### INVESTMENT INSURANCE COVERS BANKRUPTCY AND DISSOLUTION

A couple things make investing in startups and early-stage companies riskier than other securities. First, as compared with more mature companies, they tend to have lower capital reserves on which to draw when cash flow is squeezed. Second, they are less diversified, because they typically have just one flagship product, and their success depends directly on the outcome of that single product.

From an angel investor's point of view, there are two kinds of failure: (1) failure to generate enough profit to provide a satisfactory return (in the form of dividends and/or capital gain) to investors and (2) the ultimate failure, a bankruptcy or dissolution. Now at least one company has developed a form of investment insurance that covers bankruptcy and dissolution through the first 6 to 18 months after you invest—via an equity crowdfunding site—in a private company.

> *Bankruptcy* is a legal proceeding governed by Title 11 of the United States Code, available to both individuals and companies. Companies that file bankruptcy are commonly, but not necessarily, insolvent. Companies are eligible to file two types of bankruptcy: Chapter 7 always results in a liquidation of a company's assets. Chapter 11 may also result in liquidation, but it can instead result in a repayment plan under which creditors are paid less than the full amount of their claims. Both chapters have the immediate effect of halting the collection activities of a company's creditors, and both chapters almost always result in a total loss for equity holders, according to Chicago lawyer Jonathan Friedland, who practices in the areas of bankruptcy and restructuring. It is also possible for creditors to file an involuntary bankruptcy petition against a company.

> *Dissolution* is when a company terminates its existence as an independent legal entity. The most common reason for dissolution is not having enough projected revenue to continue operating in a solvent manner; in that case, the company will simply pay its outstanding bills, settle all liabilities, and stop doing business. Another reason could be an acquisition, where the legal entity is dissolved but the employees and assets are transferred to the acquiring company. Investment insurance covers the cessation of business, not a transfer due to acquisition.

Peach, Inc., (formerly Asurvest, Inc.,) was the first (and, as of October 2014, still the only) company to create a viable insurance product for crowdfunding investors.* (Technically, the company calls its product a "risk management policy" rather than "insurance.") The company foresaw that equity crowdfunding would open the door to investment in private securities for tens of millions of nonaccredited investors who had little or no experience in this arena and who would tend to be nervous about the high risks. This kind of insurance can soften the risk a bit and lubricate the new equity crowdfunding machine, which otherwise might start off sluggishly due to investor caution.

The policy does not explicitly cover cases of fraud, that is, in the event that a company is charged with criminal fraud by a prosecutor or is sued for civil fraud by a customer or shareholder. That is not feasible for an insurance policy, because adjudication of the case might take many months or years, and, meanwhile, the defendant is presumed innocent (in the case of a criminal charge). However, the existence of a fraud investigation might push the company closer toward bankruptcy or dissolution if it is already tipping in that direction.

## How It Works

Asurvest's product, which it brand-named Peach, is offered in much the same way as flight insurance is offered when you book an airline reservation online. Here is how Asurvest (and, presumably, its competitors in the future) structures its product:

1. **Investor opts in.** On an equity crowdfunding site, an investor decides to invest a certain amount of money in a startup. As soon as the investor commits to this investment, he or she can opt in or out of the Peach insurance policy.
2. **Investor chooses the term and premium.** The investor opts in and—without leaving the crowdfunding site—selects from a menu of terms (coverage periods) and corresponding premium amounts (estimated and subject to change), as shown in Table 9.1.
3. **Investment round closes and policy is effective.** When the investor commits to the investment and the insurance policy, he or she transfers the money (the investment amount plus premium) to the crowdfunding site's escrow agent. Later, when the startup's funding round closes, the funds are released by the escrow agent, the premiums are immediately received by Asurvest, and the policy goes into effect. If the startup fails to reach its funding goal, all the funds are returned to investors.
4. **Startup goes bankrupt and investor files claim.** If the startup files for bankruptcy or dissolution within the selected term, the investor files a claim with Asurvest. The insurer can verify the filing within one business day and issue a benefit check to the investor.
5. **Insurer pays benefit to investor.** The insurer sends the investor a check in the amount of the investment minus a 10 percent deductible. There is no claims process, as the benefit is released automatically.

**TABLE 9.1**    Asurvest (d.b.a. Peach) Terms and Premiums

| Term (months after investment) | Premium (pct. of investment amount) |
| --- | --- |
| 6 months | As low as 6.5% |
| 9 months | 7.2% |
| 12 months | 8.4% |
| 15 months | 9.0% |
| 18 months | As high as 12% |

As an example, say the investor invests $1,000 in a startup and opts into the Peach insurance plan with a six-month term. The policy costs 6.5 percent, or $65, so the investor's total cost is $1,065. The startup goes bankrupt in five months. The investor files a claim with the insurer, which verifies the bankruptcy filing and sends the investor a check for $900 (the investment amount minus 10 percent deductible). Net result: The investor has lost $165 ($1,065 minus $900, or roughly 17 percent of the total cost). Without the insurance policy, the investor would have lost the entire $1,000 investment.

The policy is not transferrable. So if you select a 15-month term and you sell the stock after just a year, the last three months of the policy will be canceled.

Not all equity crowdfunding sites will offer this kind of insurance policy. Asurvest is selective about which sites it supports. If you are new to angel investing and feel more comfortable with such coverage, you may want to start investing solely on portals that offer this kind of policy.

*The authors have no professional or financial relationship with Asurvest or its officers or employees.

## GET GOOD ADVICE FROM INFORMED ADVISERS

We would never discourage you from seeking advice from your professional financial adviser on how to plan your long-term investment strategy. Keep in mind, however, that advisers who are not thoroughly familiar with the risks, rewards, and economics of Title III equity crowdfunding will tend to reflexively warn you *not* to invest in Title III deals, because they are novel. Some of them will fear that you might hold them partly accountable for your losses if they don't dissuade you from making risky investments, some of which *will* be losses. Money managers and stockbrokers may also have an incentive to advise against Title III deals because they do not earn commissions on crowdfunding transactions.

As we write this chapter in the winter of 2015, we are still dismayed by how many professionals—CPAs, family lawyers, and certified financial planners among them—do not know what crowdfunding is, or do not understand the difference between rewards- and equity-based crowdfunding, much less the details of Title III of the JOBS Act.

If you are unsure about how much money you should allocate for alternative investments like equity crowdfunding each year, definitely ask for professional help with allocation. That's the first decision you need to make in order to maintain control over your investment strategy and build a diversified portfolio over the next several years, without taking undue risks or incurring losses that will cause your family financial hardship.

After equity crowdfunding portals and platforms have launched, we believe financial advisers will be better informed about Title III equity crowdfunding, although some will still be squeamish about encouraging their clients to participate. A smart adviser will be able to explain clearly the risks and the possible rewards, and discourage you *only* if you don't thoroughly comprehend those concepts. Still, some advisers will accept the value of equity crowdfunding investments only after being urged to do so, a few of them kicking and screaming, by their investor clients.

## TYING IT ALL TOGETHER

Some first-time equity crowdfunding investors might get overwhelmed by the task of finding good investment opportunities that fit their portfolio strategies. If you feel that way, simplify the process by breaking it down into three simpler steps. First, identify your motives for investing, whether social, financial, or a mix of the two. Second, spend time browsing portals and reading reviews of them online, and select one or two that appear highly professional and feature the kinds of offerings you are looking for. Third, refer to Chapter 8, and make sure you stick with your portfolio strategy and stay within your budget for crowdfunding investments.

# CHAPTER 10

# Equity Crowdfunding Securities

**W**hen you browse an equity crowdfunding site, you will see basic information about each offering: the name and location of the company, a description of the product or service, team profiles, the type of securities, and other confidential deal terms and disclosures. In Title III deals, the types of securities will be predominantly corporate stock (usually preferred shares), LLC membership units, and convertible debt (actually a hybrid of equity and debt).

We will explain the basics of preferred stock and LLC units first, as they are straight equity and are more common than convertible debt in angel investments. Convertible debt was used in less than 8 percent of investment rounds in which angel investors participated, according to a 2002 study at the University of Chicago's Booth School of Business.[1]

## STRAIGHT EQUITY: STOCK AND LLC UNITS

If you are new to private securities, your investment portfolio probably consists mainly of public company stocks (equity-based securities), corporate and municipal bonds (debt-based securities), and various mutual funds (bundles of public stocks and/or bonds). The public stocks in your portfolio are likely shares of common stock, rather than preferred stock, because common shares offer the potential to earn greater returns when the companies behind them are consistently profitable.

When a public company—usually a corporation—needs to raise capital, it must decide whether to borrow money or sell equity, or both. (Public companies may take other forms, such as real estate investment trusts, but

---

[1]Andrew Y. Wong, PhD candidate at the Booth School of Business, "Angel Finance: The Other Venture Capital," January 2002. Wong is now a principal in the Analysis Group in Chicago.

most are corporations.) Deciding which is the best option at a particular time depends on the company's financial condition, its capital structure (the amount of equity and debt financing it already has on its books), the intended use of the new capital, what's going on in the capital markets (such as interest rates), and other factors.

When a private company—which might be a corporation, limited liability company (LLC), or other legal entity—needs to raise capital, it decides whether to borrow money or sell equity based on pretty much the same factors that public companies consider. In terms of selling equity, if the private company is a corporation, it can issue various classes of stock, including common and preferred shares. If it is an LLC, it can sell membership units, sometimes called membership shares. Both corporations and LLCs can issue convertible debt.

At least for now, the only kind of corporation that can raise capital via equity crowdfunding is the traditional C corporation. Subchapter S corporations, the newer flow-through entities that many small companies organize under, are effectively barred from participating in Title III equity crowdfunding because (1) the number of S corporation stockholders is limited to 100, while the number of C corporation stockholders is unlimited, and (2) S corporations can issue only one class of stock, whereas C corporations can issue any number of classes—the two major categories of which are *common* and *preferred*.[2] We hope the IRS changes the rules governing S corporations to make them eligible for equity crowdfunding, or else creates new a new entity specially tuned to Title III governance.

## Common and Preferred Stock

When founders incorporate their company, they issue common stock to themselves. Common stock is considered "pure equity," as it entitles shareholders the right to vote on management issues at annual shareholders' meetings.

Aside from voting, common stock is the type of investment that is most directly tied to actual profitability and growth of a corporation. Common stockholders may or may not receive dividends when the company is profitable, depending on management's decisions about distributing profits. But most investors—at least those whose portfolios are allocated more for growth than for fixed income—focus on stock price more than dividends,

---

[2]Another major limitation, not relevant to equity crowdfunding at this time, is that all the shareholders in an S corporation must be individual U.S. citizens or certain qualified trusts, rather than companies, funds, or special-purpose investment vehicles.

as capital gains depend solely on the price per share. Common stock prices fluctuate freely with the performance of the company: In a period of sustained profitability and growth, the price per share normally climbs. (Share prices of stock in public companies are reported daily, while the share price of a private company is not generally known until shares are transferred, which might be seldom.)

Preferred stock is considered a more conservative investment, as the price per share does not fluctuate as freely as that of common stock in the public stock exchanges—though prices of both preferred and common shares could fluctuate wildly in private secondary markets if they are traded at all. So it offers less opportunity for capital gain. But if you are investing in a startup or early-stage company, where the risk of failure is high, preferred stock offers other advantages, such as liquidation preferences (which we will explain in Chapter 11). Most deal terms allow angel investors to convert their preferred shares to common shares when the company achieves certain milestones.

In the public stock market, preferred stockholders usually receive dividends (depending on the terms of the stock issue) when the company is profitable,[3] and those dividends tend to be higher than for common stockholders, which makes preferred stock more attractive for retirees whose portfolios are allocated more for income and wealth preservation than for capital growth. The yearly dividends for preferred shares are usually fixed, such as 8.5 percent of the price paid per share, while the dividends for common shares, if any, are tied to the company's performance each year, and then only after the fixed dividends are paid to the preferred stockholders. If the company goes bankrupt or dissolves (two forms of liquidation), preferred stockholders almost always have a claim to company assets ahead of common stockholders (but behind bondholders and some creditors). If enough assets are available, preferred stockholders will recover the amount of their investment and sometimes an annualized total return (but no more).

On the other hand, in the public stock market, preferred stockholders generally do not have direct voting rights, so it's not considered "pure" equity.

Preferred stock prices for public companies are reported daily just as for common stock, but preferred prices—because the investment is more conservative—are less responsive to general market volatility.

Founders and managers of startups and early-stage corporations generally offer preferred stock rather than common stock when they raise equity

---

[3]When budgets are tight, a company can suspend preferred dividends (it cannot suspend bond payments). But preferred shares typically earn dividends cumulatively, so the company must distribute suspended dividends to preferred shareholders eventually. This is not as common for startups as for publicly traded companies.

capital. For one thing, it lets them maintain a certain degree of control over the company because preferred shareholders do not necessarily have voting rights (although they may have a representative member of the board of directors who is elected from the class of preferred shareholders). For another, investors often *insist* on buying preferred shares because of the preferences in the event of failure, as well as the chance to convert to common shares under certain conditions.

Think of it this way: Preferred stock for startup companies can be a "win-win" for both the founders and the investors. The founders can retain control if preferred shares have few or no voting rights. On the flip side, preferred shareholders have better protections against downside risk, thanks to liquidation preferences, but also tend to enjoy the upside if the company succeeds later on, as the shares can be converted to common stock.

For that reason, if you invest in preferred stock in an equity crowdfunding deal, pay close attention to conversion rights. The downside of *not* being able to convert to common stock is that the amount of money you can earn in the event of an acquisition (another form of liquidation) will be limited. In the event that the acquisition price is low, then preferred shareholders get their investment back and common shareholders might get nothing much. But in the event that the acquisition price is very high, then preferred shareholders still get their investment back and common shareholders have a very gigantic pie to slice up. So make sure you have an option to convert preferred to common shares in the event of an acquisition.

A private company may issue different classes of preferred stock in successive rounds of equity financing, where each class has a unique set of rights, preferences, and other terms. The classes are typically known as Series Seed Preferred, Series A Preferred, Series B Preferred, and so on.

If you are considering investing in a later round (after the seed round), take the time to compare the rights of your class or series with those in previous rounds. This will help you identify how strong your class of investors will be in the organization.

### Drawbacks of Corporations

The corporate structure has evolved into a powerful way not only to finance an enterprise but to govern it as well. The same structure that gives a corporation those advantages, however, also gives it disadvantages in the context of equity crowdfunding.

The origins of today's corporations go back as far as the Roman Empire. Modern versions arose in Europe in the 1600s, and the corporate structure migrated to the American colonies, where it evolved along with the American republic. U.S. corporations are similar to our federal system of government, where power is divided among three branches: executive, legislative, and judicial. Corporations similarly divide power among directors, officers, and shareholders. The roles of these three corporate branches have been further defined over the years as a result of new statutes and court decisions. From a shareholder's point of view, this highly evolved structure has the effect of making corporate governance fairly uniform, understandable, and pre-dictable. But it is also quite rigid from the point of view of founders of startups, where they want to keep governance highly centralized in order to empower leaders to make quick decisions and pivots. Not only that, but the diffused corporate structure of governance, with its board meetings, share-holders notifications and votes, reporting requirements, and double taxation (first on profits and second on dividends), can be prohibitively expensive for lean startups. That is why many startups and early-stage companies operate as sole proprietorships, partnerships, limited liability companies, and other simpler, more flexible structures that allow centralized governance and are less costly to operate. Of those simpler entities, only the LLC provides lia-bility protection for investors and can sell shares via equity crowdfunding.

## Limited Liability Companies

The LLC is a relatively new legal entity, first created in Wyoming in 1977. It combines the personal liability protection of corporations with the flow-through tax advantages of partnerships and S corporations. (In fact, the flow-through tax treatment is only one of the various taxation options that LLCs may select, but it is the most common.)

Owners of LLCs, whether they are founders or investors (and whether the investors are active in running the business or passive), are known legally as members of the LLC, and their equity is called *membership interest* or *units*. An LLC can have an unlimited number of members and can issue various classes of membership interest.

Most states allow two major types of LLCs: member-managed and manager-managed. Member-managed LLCs function much like a general partnership, where all members participate in the management of the company. In manager-managed LLCs, much like limited partnerships, one member (or a small committee of members) makes the most important decisions, while all other members are passive and have limited or no participation in management. In this respect, manager-managed LLCs are an alternative to old-style limited partnerships (in which general partners run the company and limited partners do not), with added liability protection—in addition to more flexibility in other areas of governance.

Regarding liability protection, all LLC members, including both active and passive investors, are *not* personally liable for acts and debts of the LLC.

This "veil" of personal liability protection is not absolute: The LLC veil can be pierced under the same circumstances that a corporate veil can: when an active member commits fraud, fails to deposit taxes withheld from employee wages, treats the LLC as an extension of his or her personal interests, and so on. Of course, a member can personally guarantee a debt of an LLC and be on the hook, which is common for new companies, but the veil is otherwise a strong one and generally safeguards personal assets from business risk. It is quite unlikely that a passive member of an LLC, or a passive stockholder of a corporation, would be subject to personal liability for the company actions.

An LLC's operating agreement establishes the internal governance of the entity. Operating agreements are similar to corporate bylaws, but they are much more flexible and unorthodox than bylaws. Also, LLCs do not rest upon centuries of legal precedent and standardization as do corporations; thus, it is really the operating agreement alone (without that comprehensive legal framework) that creates the "constitution" for how an LLC is governed.

An LLC operating agreement should include how the company is managed and how it allocates profits and losses among its members. Unfortunately, too many startup LLCs do not include that information, or do so inadequately, and those LLCs present a challenge for investors, especially with respect to evaluating deal terms and conducting due diligence, which we will explain further.

Management may decide that different classes of membership interest receive different proportions of profits and losses. So if you invest in an LLC membership unit that represents 2 percent ownership, it is possible that you would receive less than 2 percent of the profit or loss. But in the long term, you might consider that trivial relative to the increase in value of the unit, in the event of an exit whereby you earn a large gain on your investment.

The operating agreement also establishes whether the LLC is member-managed or manager-managed, which is an important distinction in the context of equity crowdfunding. As we mentioned earlier, generally in a member-managed LLC, all members—including passive investors—can vote on major decisions that, according to the operating agreement, require such a vote. In a manager-managed LLC, only the designated managers—which may be members or nonmember employees—can vote. An LLC that intends to raise capital via equity crowdfunding must be manager-managed if it does not want to allow hundreds or thousands of passive members, mostly strangers, to vote. Keeping track of many dispersed members so that they can be contacted each time a vote is required would be an administrative burden.

The tax advantage of LLCs is that the company itself typically does not pay income tax because company profits and losses flow through to the individual members (including passive investors), usually in proportion to their ownership interest (known as their *distributive share*). That income must be claimed on their individual tax returns. By contrast, C corporation income is said to be taxed twice, once on the corporate tax return and again when income is distributed as dividends on the stockholders' tax returns.[4] Thus, LLCs and their owners avoid that so-called double taxation. And a distributive share of LLC losses (which are to be expected in the early years of a startup) can be deducted from investors' taxable income on their individual tax returns—because losses flow through just as income does. Each year the LLC issues a tax form, typically a Schedule K-1 (similar to corporate 1099-INT forms), to each member showing that member's distributive profit or loss. Remember, when dealing with tax issues, a loss can be a good thing, since it can be deducted from other income and reduce your overall tax obligations for that year.

There are two minor hitches to this tax advantage. First, passive members—that is, those who are not active in running the business—can deduct flow-through losses only from *passive* income such as interest, dividends, certain rents and royalties, and pensions. Members who are employees of the LLC, by contrast, can deduct flow-through losses from their salaries and wages (earned income).

The second hitch relating to the pass-through tax advantage is that an LLC's operating agreement may provide that yearly profits and/or losses will be distributed to members *not* in proportion to their ownership interest. (This provision would affect not only your pass-through income and loss for tax purposes but also your ultimate calculation of return on investment.) Talk to your personal accountant before you invest in an LLC, to fully understand whether a loss can be used on your tax return, what income can be offset by a loss, and how an LLC's profit might affect your tax situation. For this purpose you should ask your accountant, assuming confidentiality guidelines permit, to review the issuer's operating agreement.

## LLC Drawbacks

In the context of equity crowdfunding, there are three kinds of drawbacks to LLCs: tax-related hassles, lack of incentive options for employees, and barriers to future venture capital and IPO financing.

The first problem with LLC income taxation, from the investors' point of view, is that members must pay income tax on flow-through profits even

---

[4]If an LLC has more than 100 members, it may lose the ability to pass income through to members. LLCs can elect to be treated as C corporations for tax purposes, but that is rare.

if none of the profits are actually distributed. In other words, the company may earn a profit in 2014 but use it to pay expenses in 2015, or it may keep it in the bank, to be used for future business development. In that situation, members do not receive any portion of the income but still must pay their distributed share of income tax on the profit. (By contrast, C corporation stockholders pay income tax on dividends only when they actually receive the cash.) This problem can be overcome by designating, in the deal that investors make when they buy LLC membership, that each year the company shall distribute enough of the profit for members to at least pay income tax (if the company makes a profit).

The good news is that if the LLC is earning a profit, the membership units are probably gaining value. If the LLC investment turns out to be a home run, then all this tax rigmarole might seem trivial.

Another drawback of LLCs is the difficulty of giving employees equity incentives such as options on membership interests (similar to corporate stock options). In entrepreneurial businesses, employers often pay employees with options as well as cash, in order to motivate them toward strong growth—and this in turn aligns those motivations with investors' interests. So the ability of the company to grant options to employees is important for investors as well as for the company itself. Corporations can grant options to employees fairly easily and with favorable tax consequences. But for LLCs, granting options is complex and the tax consequences are not necessarily as favorable.

Another drawback is that LLCs present certain liquidity and exit barriers for investors because (1) venture capitalists typically do not want to invest in LLCs since many of their limited partners, such as pension funds and nonprofit organizations, do not want flow-through income, and (2) only corporations can go public. An LLC can still be acquired by another company, but that possibility may be limited by the difficulty of swapping LLC units for stock shares in a merger-oriented acquisition.

It is possible for an LLC to convert to a C corporation when the need to raise venture capital or issue incentive options to employees becomes more urgent than preserving the flow-through tax advantages and flexible management structure. In fact, converting the form of entity is quite common. If planned well, such a conversion is possible to accomplish without too much expense, disruption of the business operation, or adverse tax consequences in some states (including California and Delaware).

But businesses that expect to grow quickly, especially in the technology and healthcare industries, know that they will eventually need to raise venture capital—and they eventually hope to go public—so they typically incorporate initially, rather than convert from an LLC. Even if they know that they must first do an angel capital round (perhaps via equity crowdfunding), they will still incorporate with an eye to one or more subsequent VC rounds.

Future financing is not the only consideration. Many companies incorporate because case law in the area of corporations is much more extensive than case law in the area of LLCs, so that questions and disputes about rights and obligations of corporate officers, directors, and shareholders are easier to settle than questions about rights and obligations of LLC members and directors.

In Chapter 9 we identified social and financial motives for investing via equity crowdfunding. If your motives center on ideology, brand loyalty, an entrepreneur, a demographic group, community development, creativity, or innovation, then you are primarily a socially motivated investor. If that's true, then a company's LLC status should not be a barrier to investment if you strongly believe in the ability of the team to achieve its mission and execute its business plan.

If your motives center on financial return, high-growth potential, voting rights, aligning with smart money, or a strategic opportunity, then before you invest in an LLC make sure the founders and managers have a smart plan for conversion to corporate status at least a year before a future VC funding round or an IPO.

## Stock or LLC Units: Which Is Better for Investors?

Which of the two kinds of straight-equity securities—stock or LLC units—is a more attractive investment? Actually, that is the wrong question. The right question is whether the company is operating under the structure—either corporate or LLC—that will best help it achieve its goals, first; and, second, whether the company has clarified in its offering documents how investors will share in the profits and gains. "Both corporations and LLCs can present simple or complex offerings—corporations by the nature of their various classes of equity, and LLCs by the nature of their operating agreements," says New York securities lawyer Vanessa J. Schoenthaler. "So I don't think the form of entity itself should be the primary concern to investors when evaluating an investment opportunity. I think a good rule of thumb, for all investors, is that if you can't understand the issuer's corporate structure and the rights and obligations associated with the security that the issuer is offering, then it's probably not a good investment opportunity for you."

Chapter 11 explains the most common terms and conditions of straight-equity offerings that you will find on crowdfunding sites.

## CONVERTIBLE DEBT, THE HYBRID SECURITY

Whether issued by a corporation or an LLC, convertible debt starts out as a loan to the company from the investor, in the form of a note that can be traded later for shares of stock or LLC units. Some convertible notes give investors the *option* to convert to equity, while others *require* investors to convert, typically on the occurrence of some specific future event that involves a valuation and/or transfer, such as a round of equity financing. When properly structured, convertible notes give investors the best of both worlds—liquidation preferences if the company becomes insolvent, capital gain if the company grows and gets acquired. It also presents an important advantage for issuers, especially startups that are pre-revenue, which we will explain.

Of course, the ultimate objective for investors, when they buy into the deal, is to end up with equity instead of debt. So although it begins as debt—and, unfortunately, in many cases ends as debt, too, due to a startup failure—this security belongs in a book about equity crowdfunding.

The basic mechanics of convertible debt are easy to understand, but then the variables can get complex. Let's say you invest $1,000 in Startup City, Inc., in an equity crowdfunding deal whereby the issuer promises to pay you $x$ percent interest every month and then repay your principal in three years. If, at any point before the maturity date (within three years), a group of angel investors or a VC fund invests in Startup City, you have an opportunity to convert your $1,000 note, plus accrued interest if any, into Startup City stock. So far, the concept is simple. The fact that an angel or VC wants to buy stock means they believe the company has strong growth potential.

But how many shares will you receive for your $1,000? Looking at it another way, what is the price per share at the time of conversion? That is the primary question to be answered in the convertible note, which—like a term sheet for straight equity—lists all the terms of the investment. This is where it gets complicated.

The reason it's complicated is that when you invested, the valuation of the company was not discussed. The valuation was probably very difficult to calculate at that time, because the company did not have enough revenue or other metrics to use as a basis for the calculation. And that is the beauty of convertible debt for entrepreneurs: The company can attract investors without having to propose or negotiate a valuation.

The deal you made when you invested did not specify a conversion price per share, because it was impossible at that time to forecast when another round of financing would occur, how well the company would perform in the meantime, and, thus, what price per share the later investors would agree to pay—and price is ultimately based on valuation.

The price per share that you (and other early, convertible-debt investors) pay to convert is derived from the price that later, straight-equity investors pay when they buy straight equity.

Let's say this later round of investment comes two years after you invested, Startup City has become profitable, and the new investors agree to pay $1 per share of preferred stock, valuing the company at $4 million. Would you be satisfied paying $1 per share for 1,000 shares? Heck no. Early investors took a much greater risk, investing when the company was not yet profitable, than later investors. You should be rewarded for taking a big risk and providing seed capital to the company when it wasn't so attractive to angel investors, not be penalized by having to pay as much for stock as the angels who waited until the investment wasn't as risky. This fairness issue is typically resolved in one of two ways: discounts and caps.

- *Discounted convertible note.* One way to reward early investors is by discounting the price that they must pay to convert when later investors buy stock. The convertible note states, in its list of terms, that you can convert debt to equity, in the event of a subsequent round of equity financing, at a discount that is typically 10 to 30 percent of what the new investors agree to pay per share. In the Startup City example, if you have a convertible note with a 20 percent discount, you would have an opportunity to convert to stock at 80 cents per share.
- *Convertible note with a cap.* Another way to reward early investors is to cap the hypothetical valuation, on the basis of which the stock price is calculated for early investors who convert just before the subsequent round of equity financing. In our example, if your convertible note caps the valuation at $2 million, then you would pay half the price per share as the later investors who value Startup City at $4 million. Since the company was *probably* worth no more than $1 million when you invested, this seems like a fair deal.

The two terms can be combined in a discounted convertible note with a cap. But these discounts and caps have to be carefully planned, because if they are too advantageous to the investor, they could backfire for the company. If the discount is too high or the cap is too low, future angel investors—and especially VC funds—would balk at investing alongside crowdfunding investors who get inordinate bargains with the exact same rights, where the difference in valuations is remarkable. Alternatively, later equity investors will want a bargain, too.

For issuers, this scenario would be a mixed blessing: The company has become profitable, its valuation has soared to several million, and VCs want to invest; but a large group of earlier equity crowdfunding investors are ready to convert at a much lower valuation (and, therefore, a much lower stock price), which scares the VCs. For this reason, some convertible debt offerings specify that the issuer can pay off the note, with interest, at any time. Doing so would eliminate the investors from the seed round, clearing the way for a Series A round. For seed investors who bought convertible debt, assuming the interest rate is high enough (which it certainly ought to be), an early payoff is better than parking that money in a savings account, but the original objective of owning equity in the company will be defeated. So if you invest in a convertible note, first make sure the interest rate is sufficient to make you happy in this payoff scenario, or specify in the deal terms that the issuer may not pay off the loan before the maturity date without consent of a majority of the investors. After all, if your objective is to earn good interest on your savings, you—that is, nonaccredited as well as accredited investors—can more safely invest in debt-based crowdfunding deals, also known as peer-to-peer lending (see Chapter 1).

Another scenario is where Series A investors establish a valuation that is less than the cap that is specified in seed investors' convertible notes. Here the seed investors are happy (although the issuer is not quite *as* happy) because their conversion price is nice and low.

The scenarios in the previous two paragraphs, where the company becomes profitable, grows quickly, and attracts Series A investors, is not the most likely one, however. Two equally likely scenarios are where (1) the company does not become profitable enough to attract the interest of angels or VCs, and the conversion event does not occur before the loan's maturity date, in which case the convertible-debt investors merely get paid off with interest; and (2) the company is not profitable at all and can't pay off its creditors, in which case the convertible-debt investors may have senior status over other creditors but may or may not receive payments, depending on the company's financial condition. The worst case, of course, is that the equity crowdfunding investors lose most or all of their investment.

One of the keys to a successful investment in convertible debt is assessing the possibility that the issuer will, if the business is successful, attract future rounds of straight-equity financing. Without that possibility, it's just a loan.

In this chapter we covered the fundamentals of equity crowdfunding securities. If you scratch below the surface, you will find many variations and complications. To make smart equity crowdfunding investments, you probably won't need to learn much more than you just did.

# Deal Terms

**W**hen you find a Title III equity offering that seems attractive in terms of its industry, location, product or service, team profiles, and idea with growth potential—the factors that are visible to everyone on the site—your next step is to request access to the confidential offering documents, deal terms, and other disclosures.

If you are new to the world of private securities, it is easy to be confused by the vocabulary used to describe offering documents and terms. We will start by distinguishing between prospectuses, private placement memorandums, term sheets, and equity purchase agreements. In general, these documents summarize the information that investors need to make an informed investment decision.

*Prospectus.* When a company issues stock and offers it to the public on a stock exchange, the financial and legal terms of the offering are presented in a document called a prospectus. The prospectus is distributed to prospective investors and also filed with the SEC with Form S-1 or F-1. Most prospectuses are dozens of, and sometimes well over 100, pages long and contain the following information, all of which is material to an investor's ability to make a fully informed decision whether to invest:

- Offering terms, including the date of the public offering, number of shares authorized to be issued, price per share (if it's an IPO), class of stock (common, preferred, etc.), intended use of the proceeds of the offering, shareholder rights and restrictions, distribution of dividends, liquidation preferences, and policies regarding dilution of shares in the event of future equity financing.
- Overview of the company and its operation; business plan or strategy; economic studies and market analysis; profiles of officers and directors, including their compensation and employment agreements; list of major company assets, permits, licenses, intellectual property, major contracts, and so on.

- Details about the company's financial condition, including financial statements, forecasts, and analysis; capitalization table (stock classes and major shareholders) and capital structure (debt and equity financing).
- Disclosure of foreseeable risk factors, including competition, economic threats, related-party transactions, conflicts of interest, and pending litigation.
- Explanation of underwriting process and other legal matters.

Prospectuses are also required for offerings of other public securities besides stock, including bonds and mutual funds.

*Private placement memorandum.* When a private company issues stock (if it is a corporation) or membership interest (if it is a limited liability company) and offers it to investors under an exemption from SEC registration (such as a private placement or Regulation D offering), the terms of the offering as well as information about business operations, financial condition, and risks are sometimes presented in a document called a private placement memorandum (PPM). The offering may be in a seed or angel round, Series A round, or subsequent rounds of private financing. For very large offerings (in terms of dollars raised), and for offerings where sophisticated angel investors, VC firms, and/or institutional investors participate, the investors often insist on seeing a PPM, although entrepreneurs might look at PPMs as a time-consuming and expensive burden. PPMs set forth much the same information as a prospectus—with the addition of a subscription agreement—but are less formal and generally a lot shorter.

A subscription agreement is the contract that both parties sign and to which the investor attaches a check when the deal is consummated.

Actually, the only time a PPM is required by law is when at least one nonaccredited investor participates in the private offering. (PPMs are not filed with the SEC.) For that reason, some issuers choose to limit an offering to accredited investors only, to avoid the time and expense of producing a PPM. Even when all investors are accredited, however, especially when they are institutional investors, they may insist that the issuer produce a PPM as part of the deal negotiations.

*Term sheet.* For smaller private offerings, especially when the issuer is a startup or early-stage company listed on a Web-based offering platform, PPMs tend to be viewed as expensive overkill, and issuers will simply produce a term sheet for prospective investors. The term sheet is a list of offering terms (equivalent to the first item in the preceding list of prospectus contents), with a subscription agreement appended either at the end of the term sheet or as a separate document. Investors may still ask for and receive detailed information about the business operations, intended use of the proceeds, financial forecast, cap table, and so on, but in a less formal, somewhat abbreviated, and more piecemeal format—that is, through various informal documents, correspondence, and conversations.

When a private company makes an offering via a Title III equity crowdfunding site, it provides to potential investors the same kinds of information that investors want to see in a smaller Reg D offering, all within the confines of the offering portal or platform: a term sheet, a separate purchase agreement (the equivalent of a subscription agreement), and various other offering documents and disclosures, typically in PDF format.

As we discussed in Chapter 7, the information that issuers provide to investors on equity crowdfunding sites is segregated according to two levels of accessibility. Cursory deal terms, general descriptions of the business and team profiles are typically available to all who visit the equity crowdfunding site. But the complete deal terms, business plan, financial reports and forecasts, risk disclosures, and other confidential documents are positioned behind a digital gate, through which only registered prospective investors may enter.

In this chapter we will explain the deal terms that most commonly appear in Title III offerings. Chapter 12 will help you navigate through the business plans, financial reports, and disclosures.

## NEGOTIATIONS AND STANDARDS

When an issuer offers private securities to certain known prospective investors, directly or through a broker or agent—that is, not to anonymous investors through a crowdfunding site—in most instances the issuer draws up the PPM or term sheet and presents it to the investors. Occasionally the reverse is true: Investors, typically those who are in a strong bargaining position because they represent a large pool of capital or an angel group or VC fund, draw up the offering terms and present them to the issuer. From that point, the parties on both sides of the table may negotiate the terms until they either reach a final agreement or walk away from the deal. Rarely is the first draft of the offering terms a final draft.

On Web-based offering platforms and portals, however, where much of the process is automated, issuers *always* present the deal terms to the crowd of mostly anonymous investors, and terms are largely nonnegotiable. You either accept the terms and invest or reject the terms and continue shopping for attractive offerings. In rare instances, if potential investors overwhelmingly disapprove of one or more terms, they might compel the issuer to revise the terms of the equity offering. If that occurs in the middle of a raise—that is, after some investors have already committed to the deal—then the committed investors should have an opportunity to either withdraw their commitments or upgrade their investments according to the new terms.

As in all other industries, the offering terms vary from one kind of deal to another. Deal terms for a preferred stock offering are different from the terms for a convertible debt offering, for example. There is no single standardized set of terms for all kinds of equity offerings, just as there is no single standard lease for all kinds of commercial real estate.

Within each of those narrower categories of equity securities, however, the terms for one deal may, to some degree, resemble the terms for many other deals, especially within a particular industry. Thus, some professionals in the securities, entrepreneurial, and investment communities have composed standardized or "model" term sheets for certain categories of offerings. Entrepreneurs on a tight budget can save a lot of money by using or adapting the appropriate model term sheet, rather than paying a lawyer to draft one from scratch.

On the other hand, deal terms may be idiosyncratic—and the term sheet must be composed from scratch—if an issuer is particularly innovative, or if the investors have peculiar preferences, or if the relationship between the parties is unusual.

Investors should be careful when they see idiosyncratic term sheets with unfamiliar terms. Those offerings may still be good investments, but the cost of making those investments might be higher (thus, the return on investment lower) if you have to hire a lawyer to explain the unusual terms.

If you plan to invest in more than one or two equity crowdfunding deals, you should become familiar with the common offering terms. Here are some of the most reliable model term sheets for offerings of preferred stock in the $250,000 to $1 million range:

- The Kauffman Foundation's Entrepreneurship Resource Center recommends a "Series Seed Term Sheet" for offerings of preferred stock. Available at www.seriesseed.com/posts/documents.html.[1]
- The Angel Capital Association, which represents accredited investors and angel groups, and the National Venture Capital Association provide model term sheets for preferred stock offerings. The ACA model is annotated with explanations and options.
- The Crowdfunding Professional Association provides a model term sheet for Title III equity crowdfunding offerings, available at www.cfpa.org.
- Techstars, a high-tech accelerator, provides a model term sheet for a preferred stock offering, composed by the law firm Cooley LLP. Available at www.techstars.com/docs/.

---

[1]Recommended by Thom Ruhe, Director of Entrepreneurship, Kauffman's ERC: www.entrepreneurship.org/resource-center/series-seed-financing-document.aspx.

- The Gust Series Seed Term Sheet is a model for preferred stock offerings, provided by Gust.com, the platform for startup financing used by angel groups, VC funds, and entrepreneurs. It is available as Appendix D in David S. Rose's book *Angel Investing* (Wiley, 2014).

Model term sheets for convertible debt are used primarily in the high-tech sector. Here are some reliable sources of model term sheets:

- A convertible debt model is provided by the Startup Company Lawyer, a website hosted by corporate and securities lawyer Yoichiro Taku, a partner in Wilson Sonsini Goodrich & Rosati in Palo Alto, California. www.startupcompanylawyer.com/?s=term+sheet.
- Techstars provides a model term sheet for convertible debt offering, composed by the law firm Cooley LLP. Available at www.techstars.com /docs/.
- Y Combinator, another high-tech accelerator, provides an alternative to convertible debt known as "simple agreement for future equity." available at www.ycombinator.com/documents/.
- The Gust Convertible Note Term Sheet is available as Appendix C in Rose's book *Angel Investing*.

The way for an entrepreneur to use a standard or model term sheet is not simply to fill in the blanks on page 1 with names and dollar amounts. They are meant to be modified and adapted throughout as needed, because every deal is different, just as every commercial rental property is different and calls for a customized lease.

Some equity crowdfunding sites are developing their own sets of standardized deal terms and urge their issuers to use or adapt them. EarlyShares plans to go a step further and *insist* that issuers use its standard term sheets (one for straight equity and another for convertible debt, with variations for different industries), with minimal adjustments, so that investors do not have to spend hours studying new terms and learning what they mean every time they invest on the site—they have to study the terms only the first time they invest on that site, and then evaluate each deal on the basis of the variables: price, shares authorized, valuation, and so on.

## DO ALL THOSE TERMS REALLY MATTER?

You might be asking, "Do I really need to read every one of these terms and understand them before I make an equity crowdfunding investment?"

The cautious approach, and the approach that your lawyer will advise you to take, is: "Yes, of course, you should understand each and every provision of the term sheet (and other offering documents) before you make a risky investment in a startup."

On the other hand, let's be realistic. For a single $100 investment, do you want to spend half a day (minimum) studying the legal jargon beyond the price and valuation on page 1 of the term sheet? After all, dozens of other investors—some of whom claim they have studied the deal terms assiduously—have already committed money to the same investment. What difference do all those rights and restrictions and preferences and contingencies make if the company you invest in grows and gets acquired by Amazon or Facebook—you're going to hit the jackpot regardless of this or that deal term, right?

Indeed, even some experienced angel investors admit that they don't pay all that much attention to the terms beyond price and valuation, as long as the terms are fairly standard and there are no ambiguities. What really matters is the business concept, the ability of the entrepreneurs to execute the business plan (and pivot to a new plan when necessary[2]), and a sizable market for the company's product or service. Paul Graham, one of America's premier angel investors and founder of tech accelerator Y Combinator, wrote this in 2009:

> Don't spend much time worrying about the details of deal terms, especially when you first start angel investing. That's not how you win at this game. When you hear people talking about a successful angel investor, they're not saying, "He got a 4x liquidation preference." They're saying, "He invested in Google."
>
> When angels make a lot of money from a deal, it's not because they invested at a valuation of $1.5 million instead of $3 million. It's because the company was really successful.
>
> I can't emphasize that too much. Don't get hung up on mechanics or deal terms. What you should spend your time thinking about is whether the company is good.[3]

No doubt some people will invest in equity crowdfunding deals for reasons other than ROI, such as showing support for entrepreneurs they admire,

---

[2] For a dissenting viewpoint on pivoting, see "The Perils of the Pivot," by Sara Hanks, May 6, 2013, at http://www.crowdcheck.com/blog/perils-pivot. Hanks, a securities lawyer and the CEO of CrowdCheck, warns, "If you take money from people who think you are going to undertake Project A and you end up undertaking Project B, those investors may think that you've committed securities fraud." To avoid liability, issuers should disclose that there is a chance it will have to pivot if circumstances change, and "explain what Plan B might be."

[3] Paul Graham, "How to Be an Angel Investor," March 2009, http://www .paulgraham.com/angelinvesting.html.

owning a piece of the local hangout, or just plain adventure. For those people, studying deal terms might seem like a needless burden.

Nevertheless, keep in mind that investing in private securities is risky, starting up a new business is risky, and the purpose of deal terms is to minimize the risk for both sides. Whether you invest for ROI or any other reason, every term in the deal has a significant purpose relating to the resolution of a potential problem, dispute, or question that might (and often does) arise after you invest your money. You are free to ignore any or all deal terms. But please read the following brief explanations of the most common terms, and see if maybe you don't appreciate how they can protect you from loss and improve your ROI.

Strong recommendation: If you are investing repeatedly on an equity crowdfunding site that uses one or two standardized term sheets (one for straight equity and one for convertible debt, for example), it is worth your while to learn the meaning of the most important terms that apply to a number of your investments—including valuation, stock option pool, liquidation preferences, voting controls, and antidilution provisions.

One other thing to keep in mind before you decide to challenge any terms of the offering on a crowdfunding site: Financing is only the beginning of a relationship—hopefully, one that will last several years—between you and the company in which you invest. If you decide to challenge one or more terms, do so as diplomatically as possible—your goal is to end up on the same team.

## DEAL TERMS FOR STRAIGHT-EQUITY OFFERINGS

Following are definitions and explanations of the most common terms that you will encounter in offerings of stock and LLC units on equity crowdfunding sites. They are presented in four categories: (1) economic terms, (2) control terms, (3) terms relating to liquidity events, including future rounds of financing and exits, and (4) other terms.

One of the first terms you will see at the top of page 1 of a term sheet is the type of security being offered. The most common securities offered in equity crowdfunding are stock, LLC membership units, and convertible debt (which is actually a hybrid of equity and debt). We explained the basics of those securities in Chapter 10. Straight equity is much more common than convertible debt in angel investments.

## ECONOMIC TERMS

The first page or two of the term sheet sets forth the most important economic terms: price per share of stock or LLC membership unit, company valuation (or percentage of ownership offered per incremental amount invested), target amount of capital being raised, minimum investment amount, investment increments accepted, and deadline for the raise.

Most investors will study those initial offering terms and see if they make sense before reviewing the full term sheet and conducting any due diligence. You might decide you ultimately don't need to study the entire term sheet, but it is absolutely essential that you study and understand the economic terms on page 1. If you don't understand the legalese, ask the issuer to provide an explanation of the terms in plain English—or Spanish or whichever language the offering is written in. If the issuer won't comply with your request, ask a lawyer or financial adviser, one who is experienced in private securities trans-actions, to explain the terms to you. This professional advice might cost you a few hundred dollars, but it is absolutely necessary—and it should carry over to future equity crowdfunding investments, because many issuers (especially if they are listed on the same crowdfunding site) will use similar deal terms.

If you still do not understand the economic terms on the first page, *do not invest* unless you take a very reliable "follow the lead investor" approach, which we discussed in earlier chapters.

Also, do not assume that because the crowdfunding site is reputable the deal terms must be fair. Some sites do indeed insist that their issuers offer fair terms, and some even require their issuers to use (adapt) a standardized term sheet that their legal team has drafted. But some sites are more con-cerned with the freedom of issuers to construct term sheets than the safety of investors.

**Price per share and minimum investment.** The first terms most investors look for, aside from the type of security being offered, are the price and minimum investment. If the minimum is higher than you are qualified to invest under Title III (based on your income and net worth), you're out of luck. Keep in mind that you may want to make more than one investment in your first year of equity crowdfund investing, in order to diversify the risk.

Many offerings state a certain price per share of stock or per unit of LLC membership. The price alone is not very meaningful unless you also know the percentage of ownership that a share or unit represents. Issuers who are extra-thoughtful will give you both of these figures, but many do not. In any case, they must give you enough information—such as the company's (proposed) valuation and the total number of existing shares or units—to calculate the percent of ownership that you get when you buy a share, using one or more of these formulas:

$$100 \div \text{Total shares issued} = \text{Percent ownership of each share}$$

$$\text{Investment amount} \div \text{Company valuation}$$

$$= \text{Percent ownership for that amount}$$

To make these formulas meaningful, we need two definitions:

- *Total shares issued* means all shares held by the issuer, granted to employees and directors, sold to investors, and authorized for sale (and held in reserve as employee options) in the current round of financing.
- *Company valuation* is the value on a specific date as proposed by the issuer or, in some cases, as estimated by a third-party valuation analyst hired by the issuer. For private companies, valuation is a subjective measure; the earlier the stage of company development, the more divergent various people's estimates of value might be. In a private securities offering, valuation is usually stated in premoney terms (that is, the value before the current round of financing), although it is sometimes stated in both pre- and postmoney terms. (Premoney valuation plus the amount currently being raised equals postmoney valuation.) You should use postmoney valuation in the second formula.

The issuer should disclose what approach, method, or multiple it used to estimate its valuation, and the date on which the valuation was effective—as it can change from month to month. (See the "Startup and Early-Stage Valuation" sidebar.)

Angel capital valuations typically fall into the $500,000 to $3 million range, although outliers certainly come along.

How do you know if the price is fair? Of course, investors (buyers) want the price to be low, while issuers (sellers) want the price to be high, as in any free-market transaction. Some inexperienced, starry-eyed entrepreneurs assign their startups exaggerated valuations, often with sincere optimism but sometimes with avarice. You should try to judge whether the valuation seems reasonable, as the price is derived from the valuation, but not try to narrow it down too precisely. As we mentioned in Chapter 10, the key to success in angel investing is not necessarily buying in at bargain prices but buying shares of potentially great companies.

The next logical question is, How much equity should the company sell in its first round of financing? Angel investors who invest in a startup's initial financing round typically acquire 20 to 35 percent of the company in which they invest collectively.[4] If the company offers more than 35 percent in its seed round, it might be hurting its ability to have shares left over for future equity financing rounds and still maintain control.

---

[4]Scott A. Shane, *Fool's Gold? The Truth behind Angel Investing in America*, Oxford University Press, 2009, p. 98.

## STARTUP AND EARLY-STAGE VALUATION

Valuation is one of the most important terms of an angel deal, but it is also one of the slipperiest. That's because it is very difficult to figure out the value of a company without much history, especially if it has not yet earned much revenue or positive cash flow.

Public companies are easier to value because they have a discrete market capitalization: Share price multiplied by number of shares outstanding equals the capitalized value (to oversimplify a bit). There are other measures of value, such as book value (the value of a company's assets minus its liabilities as shown on its balance sheet), that can be used for certain management and investment purposes.

A private company whose shares are rarely traded does not have an easily discerned share price, so it is almost impossible to calculate its market cap on a given day. Professional appraisers and valuators use three approaches, and various methods within each approach, to estimate the value of middle-market companies, usually defined as those with revenues of $50 million to $1 billion—although some define the middle market as low as $5 million. Selecting the appropriate approach (or combination of approaches) and methods is as much art as science. The three approaches are the following:

- **Asset approach.** This is an estimate based primarily on the market value of the company's productive assets (taking into account appreciation or depreciation), minus its liabilities. For some startups the assets might be predominantly intellectual property such as registered patents and trademarks, manufacturing or food processing equipment, retailers' inventory, or land for energy exploration, for example.

- **Market approach.** The valuator compares the subject company to similar companies whose values are known due to recent acquisitions. This approach works best for local businesses where "comps" are located in the same area. The estimate is derived by adjusting for various risk factors, such as management experience and the competitive environment.

- **Income approach.** Value is estimated by forecasting cash flows over 10 or more years and discounting the total income stream to present value. The discount rate is "built up" using a risk-free rate (based on government bonds, for example) plus various company-specific and broader economic "risk premiums."

In startup and early-stage companies, it is quite common that there are not enough assets, comparable business acquisitions, or income to use as the basis for reliable valuation estimates. So valuation is very subjective for startups, skewing more toward art than science. Angel investors use shortcut valuation approaches, along with a strong dose of intuition, to judge whether the issuer's proposed valuation is in the right ballpark.

One such shortcut method, used for an early-stage company with some profit history, is using industry multiples to derive rough valuation estimates. Aswath Damodaran, a business valuation expert and professor of finance at New York University's Stern School of Business, publishes annually updated value multiples for dozens of industries from advertising to utilities, in terms of EBITDA (earnings before interest, taxes, dividends, and amortization) and, more simply, EBIT. Near the low end, for example, the oil and gas industry value multiple is about 9.4 times EBIT, while, climbing the value ladder, the biotechnology value multiple is about 50 times EBIT, the multiple for the e-commerce retail industry is 79, and the real estate development multiple is around 112.[5]

A valuation method for pre-revenue companies, used primarily in the technology industry, involves adapting the market approach using financial data from venture capital and angel funding rounds instead of acquisitions. This requires inside knowledge of angel and VC deals and the valuations involved, or access to databases and surveys conducted by the Angel Resource Institute, CB Insights, Gust, and others. Comparable valuations are the starting point—from there you would raise or lower (usually lower) the estimate by assessing various risk factors, such as the strength of the issuer's management team, stage of development, size of the market, competitive pressures, and economic trends.[6]

Keep in mind that these methods of valuing startups and early-stage companies provide rough estimates at best. If you have experience in a particular industry, you may be familiar enough with startups in that industry to assess the reasonableness of an issuer's proposed valuation without having to use databases, risk factors, and college-level mathematics.

[5]Current value multiples, expressed in terms of EBITDA and EBIT, are available at the website of New York University's Stern School of Business: http://people.stern.nyu.edu/adamodar/New_Home_Page/datafile/vebitda.html.
[6]This method and others are described in detail by David S. Rose in his 2014 book *Angel Investing*, John Wiley & Sons, pp. 98–104.

One valuation method you should be very cautious about using is the black-box-type "tool" that some websites (and even some funding platforms) offer, where you simply enter a dozen or so financial performance–related numbers and check a few boxes and the website automatically spits out a dollar figure. If the issuer claims that it used such a service to derive its valuation, either disregard it or, if you have a nose for investigation, check out the service—ask where the website gets its "comparables" data and how they manipulate the numbers entered by the company. If the answers are not forthcoming or are unsatisfactory, do not rely on this kind of valuation estimate.

Some automated valuation tools may be legitimately useful, but the good ones charge a fee. If the service is free, it is probably not worthwhile.

We conclude our discussion on valuation with a contrarian view written by Paul Graham, the CEO of tech accelerator Y Combinator:

> *There is no rational way to value an early-stage startup. The valuation reflects nothing more than the strength of the company's bargaining position. If they really want you, because [either] they desperately need money or you're someone who can help them a lot, they'll let you invest at a low valuation. If they don't need you, it will be higher. So guess. The startup may not have any more idea what the number should be than you do.[7]*

*Fully diluted valuation.* Often the valuation will be described as "fully diluted." This means the valuation was estimated as though all convertible preferred stock has been converted to common stock, all stock options and warrants have been exercised, and the company's option pool has been increased as needed for future employees. The conversions and exercise are hypothetical (although the increased employee option pool should be actual), but it lets investors know what will happen to the valuation—and, therefore, the value of their shares—when those dilutive actions occur in the future.

In the case of LLC membership units, the percentage of ownership may be stated "on a fully diluted basis." See more about dilution and antidilution provisions later in this chapter.

---

[7] Graham, op. cit.

If the term sheet does not specify that the valuation is fully diluted, ask the issuer what the fully diluted valuation would be. And make sure the issuer has, in fact, reserved a sufficient pool of options for future executives and key employees, as such options not only create incentives for employees to work hard and be loyal, but also aligns their interests with that of investors. Or, at a minimum, ascertain whether the company could make a future decision to dilute your ownership percentage (e.g., by issuing more shares in the future) without a vote of the equity crowdfunding investors.

Option pools typically represent 10 to 20 percent of outstanding shares. If the issuer waits until after the equity crowdfunding round to issue options, everyone's share value will be diluted.

**Investment increments.** Often the issuer specifies not only a minimum investment, but investment increments as well. So if the minimum is stated in terms of dollars, the allowed increment will be dollars; if the minimum is stated in terms of shares or units, the increments will be in terms of shares or units. For example, an issuer specifies a minimum investment of $500 (which represents 750 shares), and investors can add increments of $100 (for 150 more shares).

**Minimum and maximum raise.** Some offerings simply state a target amount to be raised by a certain deadline (known as the closing date). If enough investors commit to the deal and the target is reached by the closing date, the deal closes and investors receive their equity. Other offerings state a minimum and maximum amount; if investors collectively commit to the minimum or higher by the closing date, the deal closes on that date. If the maximum is reached before the closing date, the deal closes as soon as that amount is committed.

**Use of proceeds.** The company must state what it intends to do with the capital it receives from investors in the equity crowdfunding round. This can be quite general: "The net proceeds of this offering will provide working capital." Or it can be specific: " . . . will be used to expand our sales and distribution capabilities," or " . . . to purchase or lease computer terminals for the electronic ordering and sale of our products." The issuer might instead (or in addition) state it this way: "We believe the net proceeds will be sufficient to fund our operations for 10 to 14 months." To be more reassuring to investors, the company should include this sort of disclaimer: "The net proceeds will not be used to repay any indebtedness or deferred salaries."

How specific do you need the use-of-proceeds statement to be? Too much specificity can be restrictive in situations where flexibility is needed, while not enough specificity might inspire a lack of confidence. We can't give you a narrower rule of thumb; you just have to be comfortable that the managers are smart and conscientious, and will use the proceeds to increase the value of your equity. Note, however, that (1) some of the proceeds might have to be used for unanticipated costs, such as a spike in the price of fuel or raw materials, and (2) if the company promises to use the proceeds for one purpose and uses it for something else, it may be in violation of securities regulations, and/or investors may have a basis for a fraud lawsuit.

**Capital structure.** Somewhere among the offering documents—usually in the term sheet, but not always—the company must disclose the total number of securities it has issued; the names, positions, types of securities owned, and equity percentage of major shareholders; the sources and amount of current debt; and the proportions of debt, convertible debt, and equity financing. Most of this information would be found in the capitalization table.

## CONTROL TERMS

As an equity crowdfunding investor, you will probably hold a hyperminority share of the company in which you invest—that is, a tiny percent of the equity—among dozens, hundreds, or thousands of other investors in your funding class. Hyperminority ownership has two consequences. First, the deal terms of the equity crowdfunding round (we can call it Series CF) will give you, as an individual, very little control over, or participation in, the governance and day-to-day management of the company. That doesn't mean the company can ignore the interests of small investors. In fact, in all 50 states the officers, directors, managing members, and general partners of companies have a fiduciary duty to act in the interests of their company rather than in their personal interests. So, for example, officers and directors are generally not allowed to engage in self-dealing, which includes buying and selling supplies and services between themselves without competitive bidding, or hiring each other's relatives when they are not the most qualified candidates.

Gaining even a small amount of control should not be one of your goals when you invest in equity crowdfunding deals. The deal terms will probably not give you much control *unless* you distinguish yourself by making a very large investment and becoming the virtual lead investor. As lead investor you *may* have the necessary clout, by virtue of your large equity stake, to achieve modest strategic goals, such as participating in the management of the company, most likely in a narrow way.

If you are really interested in gaining significant control of a company, you should either buy into a later round of angel financing—where you will be one of just a few angels who each invests tens or hundreds of thousands of dollars—or start your own company.

A lack of control should not, however, discourage you from investing in equity crowdfunding deals that let you achieve your social and/or financial goals.

The second consequence of being a hyperminority shareholder is that if you are able to sell your shares in the secondary markets (after the mandatory one-year holding period), the price will be discounted due to the lack of control. In other words, if your share is 0.1 percent of the company, and the company's valuation is $2 million, your shares are actually worth somewhat less than $2,000 (.001 × $2,000,000).[8] That's a simplified scenario, but it gives you a feel for the added risk of investing in a minority share of a private company. (The consequences are different in an exit scenario such as an acquisition of 100 percent of the equity. In that case, there are no discriminate discounts or premiums on the share values.)

**Seat on the board of directors.** Ultimate control of a company rests with its board of directors. The board can hire and fire the CEO and vote on the most important decisions to be made by the company, the nature of which is spelled out in the company's bylaws or operating agreement. In the seed stage of development, companies typically have three-member boards consisting of the founder(s) and CEO, and possibly one outside board member. An outside member is one who is neither a founder nor an employee, who has experience in the industry in which the company operates, and who can provide oversight and an independent perspective on management strategies. The outside member is, ideally, a professional adviser such as a lawyer or accountant with domain expertise, or a successful entrepreneur or former executive in the industry.

Beyond the seed stage, a startup company might have five board members (always an odd number so that tie votes can't bog down the governance process): one or two founders, the CEO, an outside member, and a seed- or startup-round equity investor. Later-stage companies may have seven or nine board members, sometimes including two or three investors from successive angel and VC rounds of equity financing.

How do investors get seats on boards of directors? When a group of angel investors or a VC firm invests millions of dollars in a startup or early-stage company, this large investor naturally wants the right to elect a member of the board of directors, in order to protect its investment. They want to make sure that the company negotiates smart contracts with suppliers and customers, for example, and prevent the founders from squandering funds on exorbitant salaries, expensive company cars, high-rent offices,

---

[8] By contrast, if one principal shareholder owns 51 percent of the equity, which is considered a controlling interest, that majority share will probably be valued at a premium above $1.02 million (.51 × $2,000,000).

first-class travel, or reckless acquisitions (which is not unusual, especially with first-time entrepreneurs who are unaccustomed to having lots of money at their disposal). These angel groups and VCs can negotiate board representation because (1) they have strong bargaining power thanks to their large investment and deep industry expertise and connections, all of which the issuer covets, and (2) they are a cohesive enough group to elect a board member from their ranks in an orderly fashion—usually a lead angel investor or VC partner in charge of the deal. The members of this angel group or VC firm know each other and have probably already selected their board representative before entering into negotiations with the issuer.

In more than half of angel deals before 2002, the angel investors did not receive a seat on the board of directors, according to a study by Andrew Wong at the University of Chicago's Booth School of Business.[9]

Now imagine an equity crowdfunding deal where there are hundreds of small Series CF investors, collectively investing no more than $1 million, who don't know each other from Adam, and who may or may not have relevant expertise. How will this crowd elect a member to represent them on the board of directors? From the issuer's point of view, it's a potential train wreck, and that is why there is very little chance that the deal terms will include board representation for investors.

We expect that Congress will amend Title III of the JOBS Act to allow equity crowdfunding portals to pool investors' funds into a single entity (probably a limited liability company) to invest in an issuer as an agent or "nominee," similar to a VC fund. Portals would have the option to form a pooled-investment entity for some offerings and not others. This kind of arrangement is common on Regulation D offering platforms (see Chapter 2) and some equity crowdfunding sites in the United Kingdom, such as Seedrs. A funding portal acting as nominee may be better able to negotiate a board seat as well as voting rights on behalf of the investors, who buy LLC memberships instead of investing directly in the issuer.

As part of your due diligence, if you are interested in possibly investing in a company you should look at the composition of its board of directors. If an issuer's board does not have an outside (independent) member, that may be a red flag for investors, possibly a sign of poor governance or an indication that the board will merely rubber-stamp the CEO's proposals instead of giving them due care and consideration. If a seed-stage or startup company's board is too large—more than seven as a rule of thumb—that would also be a red

---

[9] Andrew Y. Wong, PhD, "Angel Finance: The Other Venture Capital," University of Chicago, Booth School of Business, January 2002. Wong is now a principal in the Analysis Group in Chicago.

flag, because more directors usually results in more complexity in decision making at board meetings. Another red flag is a board with a "vanity seat," that is, a director who serves on the board because he or she just wants to feel like a big shot, or a "nonvoting observer" seat, which can be disruptive because observers might rant and rave even if they can't vote.

**Protective provisions.** Absent a seat on the board of directors, neither you as an individual investor nor your class of Series CF investors collectively should expect to have any appreciable control over day-to-day operations and management decisions. However, the terms of the deal should afford your class, collectively, a measure of control over a narrow set of actions that relate to the long-term value of your equity shares. This narrow area of control will be in the form of *protective provisions,* also known as veto rights.

The wording of a typical set of protective provisions in an angel investment looks something like this:[10] As long as [a minimum number of] Series CF shares remain outstanding, consent of the holders of at least a majority [or a supermajority such as two-thirds] of the Series CF shares shall be required for any action, whether directly or through a subsequent round of financing or a merger, that:

- Adversely alters the rights or preferences of the Series CF Preferred.
- Increases the authorized number of shares of common or preferred stock.
- Creates any new class or series of shares having rights or preferences senior to Series CF Preferred.
- Results in any merger, corporate reorganization, sale of control, or any transaction in which all of the assets of the company are sold.
- Results in the redemption or repurchase of any shares [other than pursuant to the company's right of repurchase at a specified cost, if so provided by the terms].
- Changes the authorized number of directors on the board.
- Liquidates or dissolves the company.

These are some of the more common protective provisions in angel deals, and there are others. Any given angel or VC deal may have several, but rarely all, such provisions in the term sheet. In an equity crowdfunding deal, you might be satisfied with the first one, or maybe the first three, on this list. The administrative work of keeping track of hundreds or thousands of investors

---

[10]Adapted from SeriesSeed.com (recommended by the Kauffman Foundation), accessed August 2014, and Brad Feld and Jason Mendelson, *Venture Deals,* 2nd edition, John Wiley & Sons, 2013, pp. 64–65.

and collecting their votes might make more than a few of these provisions too unwieldy for a small company.

It is possible for a cohesive group of Series CF investors to use the veto power to exercise "affirmative control," as David Rose observes:

> *If, for example, the company needs to take in another round of investment, but the investors want the company to pivot its business model, they can refuse to approve taking the new investment unless the board votes to pivot the model.*[11]

But without a very influential lead investor, cohesion is not likely to be a feature of the Series CF class of investors.

**Voting rights.** Protective provisions are essentially negative voting rights. What about positive voting rights? In some VC and some angel deals, investors in preferred stock get the right to vote along with common stockholders in various matters as specified in the bylaws or operating agreement. Common examples are election of new board members and approval for the company to incur debt exceeding a certain amount. In those angel and VC deals, the investors are often a single entity (a special-purpose vehicle formed by the angel group or VC fund), which makes it easy for the company to contact the investment entity and collect its votes. Moreover, the issuer is familiar with the investors and their expertise because of face-to-face negotiations, so the issuer welcomes the investor's input in the form of a vote—if that weren't the case, the deal would not get done.

For reasons discussed here, granting voting rights would not be as easy in equity crowdfunding deals, unless all investors remained aggregated on the site where they made their investment, so they could respond quickly to notifications and requests for votes. There is no assurance that hundreds or thousands of investors will remain engaged on a regular basis. Moreover, while the investors are appreciated for their financial support, their votes may not be so welcome because their expertise is probably not on the same level as that of angel groups and VCs.

## TERMS RELATING TO LIQUIDITY EVENTS AND FUTURE FINANCING

The most important factor that drives your return on investment is the consistent growth in profitability of the company in which you invest, or at least

---

[11]Rose, op. cit., p. 125.

the potential for such growth, which in turn makes it a good acquisition target or IPO candidate. Along the way, however, several other factors can strangle your return on investment in large and small ways. Those factors include dilution of share value caused by the issuance of new shares for future financing rounds, the distribution of whatever proceeds might be available in the event of the dissolution of the company, and a sale of the company at a price that is lower than the CF series valuation. Those are three examples of liquidity events that could result in a disappointing return, if not an actual loss, for investors.

To protect equity crowdfunding investors, who are often in the first round of equity financing outside of friends and family, from the potential constrictions of those kinds of liquidity events, the term sheet should include at least the first one of the following terms.

**Liquidation preferences.** If you invest in 10 equity crowdfunding deals, chances are that you will experience a few liquidations. When a company calls it quits, whether voluntarily or otherwise, it must liquidate its assets in order to pay salaries and wages owed to employees first, repay its creditors and note holders second, and return money—if there is any left—to its investors third. As we explained in Chapter 10, holders of preferred stock generally have priority over common stockholders.

Liquidation preferences spell out the amount of money, stated as a multiple of their original investment, that preferred shareholders receive in the event of a dissolution or sale. In the worst case, if the company is "wound down" with very little left for investors, then remaining funds are distributed to preferred shareholders in proportion to their equity ownership. Only after preferred receives its full amount will common (including the founders) get any leftovers. The typical liquidation preference is stated like this:

> *In the event of any liquidation or winding up of the Company, the holders of Series CF Preferred Stock shall be entitled to receive in preference to the holders of the Common Stock a per-share amount equal to the greater of: (Option A) the original purchase price plus any declared but unpaid dividends, or (Option B) the amount such holder would have received had the shares of Preferred Stock been converted into Common Stock immediately prior to the liquidation or winding up (the "Liquidation Preference").*
>
> *After the payment of the Liquidation Preference to the holders of the Series CF, the remaining assets of the Company shall be distributed to the holders of the Common Stock on a pro rata basis.*
>
> *A consolidation, merger, acquisition, sale of voting control, or sale of all or substantially all of the assets of the Company in which the stockholders of the Company do not own a majority of the*

> *outstanding shares of the surviving corporation shall be deemed to be a liquidation or winding up for purposes of the Liquidation Preferences.*[12]

This is known as a 1x liquidation preference, because the first option gives preferred shareholders the amount of their investment (purchase price) multiplied by 1, plus any unpaid dividends. In deals where investors have a strong bargaining position, the liquidation preference might be 2x or higher.

Note also that the second option—in the case where the company is sold at a much higher valuation than in the Series CF deal (we'll call this an "upside" acquisition)—lets preferred shareholders convert their shares to common stock in order to benefit from the capital gain that common shareholders enjoy. Remember (as we explained in Chapter 10) that common stock prices rise and fall freely with market valuations, whereas preferred stock prices are protected—and restrained—from market volatility. In fact, based on the language of the liquidation preference, Series CF preferred is converted to common automatically if it results in a greater payout to Series CF investors. Later in this chapter we will discuss how preferred is converted to common.

Besides dissolution and upside acquisition, there is another possible scenario: a downside acquisition. That is where the company is sold at a valuation lower than CF Series valuation. In other words, the company lost value since you invested in it, but instead of being dissolved, it got sold. In this case, the proceeds of the sale are distributed according to the same order of preference as if the company had liquidated: employees, creditors, preferred stockholders, and common stockholders.

Here is an example to show you the benefit of the liquidation preference in this latter scenario: Suppose you invested $2,000 in Series CF preferred stock, in return for 0.1 percent of StartupZilla, Inc., when the valuation was $2 million. Later the company is acquired for $1 million, which is half the Series CF valuation. Without the liquidation preference, you would get back a maximum of 0.1 percent of the acquisition price, amounting to $1,000. With the liquidation preference, however, you still get back your full investment amount of $2,000—assuming StartupZilla has sufficient cash to pay employees and creditors with enough left for preferred shareholders. The founders would be at the bottom of the "liquidation waterfall," along with all common stockholders, and would not get a dime until you received your $2,000.

So the liquidation preference gives early investors, as a reward for taking a big risk, the best of both worlds: the downside protection of preferred

---

[12]Adapted from TechStars, "Open-Source Model Seed Financing Documents," drafted by Michael Platt and Noah Pittard, attorneys at Cooley LLP, www.techstars.com/docs/. Accessed August 2014.

combined with the upside benefit of common. Yet one study found that only about half of the deals in which accredited angel investors participated featured liquidation preferences in the event of downside acquisitions, compared with a "vast majority" of venture capital deals.[13]

Liquidation preferences can get complicated over several rounds of equity financing if some investor classes are "senior" to others and the preferences are "stacked." The simplest way for an issuer to structure this is to give all preferred shareholders equal preference, formally known as *pari passu* (Latin for "at an equal rate").

**Full participation.** Full participation means that in the event of a liquidation, after you (and all other preferred shareholders) receive your liquidation preference (the amount of your investment plus unpaid dividends), you will also share, on either a pro rata or a "capped" basis, in the distribution of the remaining proceeds to common stockholders. Don't count on seeing this provision in an equity crowdfunding term sheet. Founders, who are typically common stockholders, will certainly resist offering full participation (which they perceive as a "double dip") to equity crowdfunding investors, as it cuts into the founders' recovery in the event of a dissolution or their reward in the event of a sale of the company. The only reason for an issuer to make such an offer is to attract a specific strategic investor, not a crowd of mostly strangers.

If your liquidation preferences include conversion rights, you can simply convert your preferred to common shares in the event of an upside acquisition, so full participation would not be a critical advantage.

## DILUTION: THE DARK SIDE OF EARLY-ROUND INVESTING

If you watched the 2010 movie *The Social Network*, a fictionalized version of Facebook's startup years, you saw the harmful effects of dilution on the value of Eduardo Saverin's shares in 2004, when Mark Zuckerberg converted the company from an LLC to a corporation. Saverin was one of Facebook's cofounders. Although the movie is fiction, Saverin's lawsuit against Facebook, on which the movie was based, did in fact hinge on the dilution of Saverin's shares. If the whole dilution concept flew over your head, here is a simplified explanation of how dilution happens, and how it can affect early investors in a more typical, less spectacular scenario.

---

[13] Shane, op. cit., p. 89 (citing Amis and Stevenson, *Winning Angels*, FT Press, 2001; Van Osnabrugge and Robinson, *Angel Investing*, Jossey-Bass, 2000.)

XYZ Company is a startup. Its articles of incorporation created 100,000 shares of company stock and gave 60,000 shares to Founder F. In the first round of external equity financing, XYZ sold the remaining 40,000 shares to two outside investors. Investor A and Investor B each paid the same price for 20,000 shares.

After the first round of equity financing, F held a majority of the shares (60 percent), while A and B each owned 20 percent of the equity.

Some months later, XYZ needed to raise more capital. The company's board of directors authorized XYZ to issue 16,000 new shares of stock. XYZ sold the new shares to Investor C.

After the second round of equity financing, the total number of equity shares held is 116,000 (100,000 + 16,000). F still owns 60,000 shares, amounting to 52 percent of the new total, which is still a controlling share. A and B still own 20,000 shares each, which now represents 17 percent equity each (20,000 ÷ 116,000). Investor C's 16,000 shares represents 14 percent of the equity (16,000 ÷ 116,000).

Let's focus on one of the early outside investors. Look what happened to Investor A's equity after Round 2: It dropped from 20 percent to 17 percent, although A's number of shares has not changed. We say that A's equity percent has been diluted as a result of the subsequent round of equity financing. The same is true of B's investment.

Before you say Investor A was screwed, consider that an investor's percent of equity is not necessarily the most important issue for the investor. What's most important is the value of those equity shares. The value of each share depends on the valuation of the entire company.

So what happened to XYZ's valuation as a result of Round 2? If you view Company XYZ's valuation as a pie, then the question is: When Investor C bought into XYZ in the second round of financing, was the pie bigger than it was in the first round of financing when A and B invested? If so, then Investors A and B now own smaller percentages of a bigger pie. And whether or not they got screwed depends on how much bigger the pie got. (It's also possible that the pie got smaller, i.e., the valuation fell.)

### Three Scenarios for Investor A: Win, Lose, Draw

Let's go back to Round 1 and disclose some more information. When A and B purchased equity in XYZ, they each paid $100,000, or $5 per share, for 20,000 shares (20 percent of the company). Based on those transactions, XYZ was valued (premoney) by the transacting parties at $500,000 ($100,000 ÷ .20).

**Investor A wins.** Here is an upside Round 2 scenario. Between Round 1 and Round 2, Company XYZ's actual revenues greatly exceeded its projected revenues. Investor C is willing to pay more for XYZ shares than Investors A and B paid. Let's say C pays $6 per share for 16,000 new shares (14 percent of the new total shares), for a total investment of $96,000. The company's new valuation, as a result of Round 2, is $686,700 ($96,000 ÷ .14). Investor A's equity percent has been diluted to 17 percent, so the total value of A's 20,000 shares is now $116,740 ($686,700 × .17). The value of A's investment has increased from $100,000 to $116,740 as a result of Round 2. In other words, A has a slightly smaller piece (in terms of equity percent) of a much bigger pie (in terms of valuation). So dilution of equity percentage has not screwed A.

This is, in fact, the upside scenario that Eduardo Saverin found himself in. Although his equity percentage was substantially diluted, he still became a billionaire when Facebook went public in 2012.

**Investor A loses.** On the other hand, let's look at a downside scenario, where the company has struggled and Investor C is willing to pay only $4 per share in Round 2 (a dollar less than A and B paid). The company really needs the capital, so, OK, it accepts C's offer of $4 per share. To skip a lot of math, the company's new postfunding valuation is $457,000. Investor A hopes the company rebounds in the future, but for now A's investment has lost value—a smaller percentage of a smaller pie.

This downside scenario, where the Round 2 price per share is less than the Round 1 price, is commonly referred to as a "down round." In a down round, A's equity is diluted not just in terms of equity percentage, but in terms of price as well.

**It's a draw.** Somewhere between Investor C's share price of $4 and $6 would be a break-even point for Investor A, where A's diluted equity percent multiplied by the new (post–Round 2) valuation would equal A's original investment of $100,000. That break-even point is about $5.07 per share.

You can see that early investors' equity percentages may be diluted in subsequent funding rounds. If the company's valuation grows significantly, then early investors may still earn positive returns on investment even with diluted equity. But if the company's valuation fails to grow enough, then dilution is bad news for early investors.

Title III equity crowdfunding offerings may include *antidilution provisions* in their deal terms that compensate, at least to some extent, for later-round dilution.

**Antidilution provisions.** As Facebook cofounder Eduardo Saverin learned the hard way (see sidebar), the equity percentage held by early-round investors can be diluted when the company issues more stock for later-round equity financing. Remember that your equity percentage is calculated by dividing the number of shares that you own by the total number of outstanding shares. As the total number of shares increases, your percentage decreases (unless you buy more shares). If the company grows like Facebook did, you can still earn a spectacular return on your investment even if your equity has been diluted, which certainly eased the pain for Saverin. But without spectacular growth, dilution can throttle your return on investment in a more painful fashion.

As the sidebar shows, your investment can be diluted in two ways: first in terms of equity percent, and second—in the case of a down round, where the Round $N+1$ valuation is lower than the Round $N$ valuation—in terms of price as well.

That is why VCs and sophisticated angel investors try to negotiate favorable antidilution provisions when they invest in early rounds. The Crowdfunding Professionals Association (CfPA) includes an antidilution provision in its model term sheet for Title III equity crowdfunding offerings[14] (although the TechStars Series AA model term sheet does not). Because these provisions can be complicated, however, and because they may be perceived as disadvantageous to later-round investors (and to common stockholders, for that matter), angel investments do not always contain antidilution clauses.[15]

The way antidilution provisions work, if you are fortunate enough to make an investment that is protected by one, is by adjusting the ratio according to which you would convert your preferred shares to common shares at a later time. That is, if a down round occurs, for example, where new investors pay a lower price per share than you paid in an earlier round, then your conversion ratio will be adjusted to give you more common shares than you would otherwise get when (and if) you convert later (when the company is sold in an acquisition, for instance). In other words, to compensate you for being diluted, the company will give you more common shares than you originally bargained for—if, that is, things go well and you have an opportunity (and/or an incentive) to convert.

The method by which the conversion ratio adjustment is calculated is what makes this provision complicated. The "full-ratchet" method, which is

---

[14] "Title III Equity Crowdfunding (Section 4[a][6]) Investment, Essential Termsheet Model," CfPA, July 2014.

[15] Shane, *Fools Gold?*, op. cit., Oxford University Press, p. 88, citing (among others) Wong, "Angel Finance: The Other Venture Capital," op. cit.

most favorable to first-round investors (and which is rarely seen these days), uses a conversion ratio that essentially restores your original equity percentage at the time of conversion. The CfPA recommends a "weighted-average" method, which is more favorable to issuers and later-round investors than a full ratchet. The weighted average is a compromise between full ratchet and no antidilution protection at all. The calculation is too complicated to explain here; a good explanation is provided in Chapter 4 of *Venture Deals*, by Brad Feld and Jason Mendelson.[16]

Full ratchets were seen more often around 2001 to 2003, when down rounds were quite common because of the bursting of the tech bubble. If such a bubble happens again, in tech or another industry, full ratchets could become more popular than they are today.

There are two ways to avoid dilution if the term sheet does not contain an antidilution provision. One is to buy more shares in the later round of financing. The other is to exercise your collective veto power if you have it, to prevent the company from issuing more stock in anticipation of a down round. On the other hand, if you use your veto to stop the company from raising money, the whole venture might sink and your shares will be diluted, so to speak, down to pure water.

Should you avoid offerings that do not provide antidilution protection? Not if you really like the company, its founders, their product or service, and the other deal terms. You can look at dilution as just another risk that can be mitigated by consistent profit and growth, and, if the company fails, dilution (unlike liquidation preferences) is irrelevant.

**Right to participate pro rata in future rounds.** This provision gives you the option, but not an obligation, to buy more shares in future rounds of equity financing. This is only fair, since you provided the seed or startup capital that enabled the company to launch; you should not be excluded from opportunities to participate further when the company is growing—if, that is, you are still bullish on the company and can afford to invest more at the price and terms being offered in the subsequent round. This right is especially important if the terms do not include antidilution provisions, because it gives you a chance to bring your equity percentage back up if it gets diluted. (This is why we said in Chapter 8 that you should reserve "dry powder" for future rounds.)

In Latin, *pro rata* means "in proportion." The pro rata aspect of this provision means that you have a right to invest as much as necessary in a

---

[16]Brad Feld and Jason Mendelson, *Deal Terms*, 2nd edition, John Wiley & Sons, 2013, pp. 56–57. The identical weighted-average calculation is shown on Feld's website: http://www.feld.com/?s=anti-dilution.

future round to restore your original equity percentage, if it otherwise will be diluted. The issuer does not want to give you an unlimited right, because it doesn't want early investors to crowd out new (possibly more strategic) investors.

**Pay to play.** This provision compels early-round investors to invest more money in later rounds. In this respect, the issuer encourages early investors to continue supporting the company when it needs additional capital. The typical pay-to-play provision states that if the Series CF investor does not participate in subsequent equity offerings on a pro rata basis, then that investor's preferred stock is converted to common stock and he or she loses the liquidation preferences and other rights that came with preferred shares.

If a company is thriving and has no trouble attracting later-round investors, then it might waive this provision and let early investors sit on their preferences and rights. Like full-ratchet antidilution, pay-to-play is seen more often after asset bubbles burst.

**Drag-along agreement.** This is another provision that you will probably not see in equity crowdfunding term sheets. It gives the Series CF preferred shareholders the power to force the company to liquidate, if more than 50 percent of the shareholders in this class vote to do so. In other words, the class of Series CF preferred can drag everyone else, even the controlling common stockholders (including the founders), along on a dissolution or sale.

This radical provision comes into play if the company is failing and the founders refuse to liquidate because the company's value is lower than the liquidation preference of preferred stock—so that the common stockholders wouldn't see a dime out of a dissolution or sale. In that case, preferred stockholders can force the liquidation.

Drag-along provisions can be written to benefit other classes of shareholders, even common stockholders, instead of Series CF. In such cases, it is possible for preferred stockholders to convert some or all of their holdings to common in order to vote for or against a liquidation. So life can get complicated when you are dragged along.

## OTHER TERMS

The deal terms in this group are no less important than the preceding ones; they just don't fit neatly into any of the aforementioned categories. The first two, conversion and transfer rights, are, in fact, quite important.

**Conversion rights.** In addition to the conversion rights spelled out in the liquidation preferences, preferred shareholders may be granted the right to convert their shares to common stock at any time (or perhaps after a given date, such as one year after the closing of the Series CF round). You might wish to exercise this right if you want to vote more actively with the common shareholders, for example, or if you think it would be easier to sell common shares on the secondary markets. Once you convert to common, you can't revert to preferred.

Whether conversion is at the investor's discretion or only upon liquidation, this provision sets the conversion ratio—that is, the number of common shares the investor receives for each preferred share on conversion. The typical ratio is 1:1, unless it is adjusted according to an antidilution provision or a stock split (which is rare for startups).

The conversion provision also states that preferred shares will be converted to common automatically (1) if a majority of the Series CF investors consent to such a conversion at the request of the company or (2) in the event of an IPO where the capitalization is above a certain dollar threshold, usually in the tens of millions. (IPOs were not covered in the liquidation preferences because, unlike dissolutions and sales, IPOs are not liquidations.)

**Information rights.** A typical term sheet in a Regulation D offering states that the company shall provide, at the very least, annual financial statements (reviewed or audited, depending on the amount raised) to each investor within a reasonable time. This provision may be unnecessary in equity crowdfunding deals because Title III requires issuers to do so anyway—although some members of Congress have proposed changing this requirement. Aside from Title III issuers, private companies are not obligated to share financial records with anyone unless compelled to do so by the terms of a securities offering, institutional debt financing arrangement, credit application, or certain legal or forensic proceedings.

Some later-stage deal terms require the issuer to provide monthly or quarterly financial reports in addition to annual financial statements.

**Dividends.** Angel investment offerings may or may not include dividends for preferred stockholders. The CfPA Title III model term sheet does not provide dividends. The TechStars Series AA model term sheet contains this provision for dividends:

> *The holders of the Series AA shall be entitled to participate pro rata in any dividends paid on the Common Stock on an as-if-converted basis. Dividends are payable only when . . . declared by the Board of Directors.*

Dividend rights can be cumulative, meaning amounts promised but not paid in one year must be added to the deferred dividends owed to preferred stockholders. Those deferred dividends must be distributed to preferred before any dividends may be paid to common.

Some term sheets provide that dividends are "paid in kind," meaning in equity rather than cash.

Because dividends are rarely declared in the early stages of company development, and they are usually nominal if they are declared, this term should not be a point of contention for early-stage investors.

**Redemption rights.** Redemption is when the company buys back preferred shares from shareholders. Some VC and angel capital deals require the company to redeem outstanding shares at their original price, plus unpaid dividends, five years (or some number of years) after the deal closes. This provides an exit, although not a capital gain, for investors in cases where the company has become successful but is not growing enough to be an acquisition or IPO candidate. Redemption rights may be contingent on some major milestone being achieved by the company, rather than a number of years, and in those cases the redemption price could be higher than the original price, providing investors a more successful exit. This latter option solves a liquidity problem for investors in middle-market companies whose shares are not in demand on secondary securities markets.

*Voluntary redemption* gives investors an option, rather than an obligation, to sell shares back to the company in a redemption event. *Involuntary redemption* obligates the investor to accept redemption or convert to common shares in order to avoid redemption.

Of course, the issuer can offer to buy your shares back at any time, even during the first-year holding period, and you are free to accept or reject the offer. One reason the company might want to redeem preferred shares—at a price that is attractive to investors—before you convert them to common is to avoid the dilution of common stock that would result from conversion.

Redemption rights are limited by law in some states. California, for example, prohibits redemption unless the company uses retained earnings (rather than capital from later investors) to redeem shares of early investors.

**Right of first refusal.** Some term sheets use "right of first refusal" (ROFR) to mean the same thing as "right to participate pro rata in future rounds" (see previous discussion). First refusal could alternatively apply to a situation where a shareholder in the Series CF class wants to sell his or her shares and receives a bona fide offer from an outside buyer. In that case, the company (or designated owners) would have a right to step in and buy those shares at the same offering price. This provision works well when there are just a few investors in the class, but probably *not* in equity crowdfunding.

Rights of first refusal can work in other ways: Investors might negotiate the right to buy shares of other coinvestors who want to sell to outside parties if the company does not exercise its ROFR, for example.

**Cosale right.** Investors have the right to sell shares to an outside buyer when the company's founders or executives offer their shares for sale. This is also known as tag-along rights or "If you get out, we get out."

**Vesting of founder stock.** Some venture capitalists want to make sure the company founders stick around when the going gets tough and don't bolt for an irresistible job offer, leaving the company in the hands of executives who don't share the founders' vision and passion. So in some VC deals, founders' stock and options vest over a period of years, typically four years. If a founder leaves before the end of the first year, he or she forfeits the shares entirely. Typically, 25 percent of the founders' shares vest after the first year, and the rest vests monthly during the second through fourth years. In the event of a merger or acquisition (or other trigger event or combination of trigger events), the vesting schedule may accelerate. Vesting provisions are not as common in angel capital deals.

**Restrictive covenants.** Company founders and executives can't quit and start a competing business.[17] They can't quit and take employees with them to start a new business even if it doesn't compete. Restrictive covenants cover all the specific things investors don't want founders to do that might hurt the company's chances for success and investors' ROI.

**Cancellation.** The CfPA's model term sheet contains this provision: "Each investor (and issuer) shall have the right to cancel investment commitment (or offering), for any reason prior to closing date, and receive (or provide) full refunds of all monies proffered." In other words, the deal is not done until it's done.

**Expenses.** A term sheet usually clarifies that any expenses incurred by the investors prior to the closing date—including legal and financial advice and due diligence—shall be paid by the investors and not charged to the company. In rare instances, the company agrees to pay those expenses for investors after closing.

## EVALUATING DEAL TERMS

You naturally wish for deal terms that are most advantageous to investors, such as strong protective provisions, 3x liquidation preferences, full participation, antidilution protection, and voluntary redemption. But remember that more advantages for you often means more disadvantages for the issuer. You don't want to put the company in a very disadvantageous position; in fact, you want it to have advantages so it has flexibility to make smart strategic decisions without undue constraints and demands placed on it by investors. So the best deal is always a compromise between your interests

---

[17]This kind of restrictive covenant might be found in founders' employee agreements if it is not in the term sheet. In an employment agreement the restriction typically covers a specific period of time, and sometimes a specified geographical area as well.

and the issuer's interests. Another way to look at it is that your interests and the company's interests are (or should be) aligned.

Some issuers will adapt model term sheets, while others will build their term sheets from scratch. Even when models are used, no two offerings will look exactly the same—terms will be customized based on the financing needs of the issuer and what kinds of investors they want to attract. If you study and understand all the terms in one offering, that doesn't mean you will understand the terms in other offerings, even if they are in the same industry or listed on the same equity crowdfunding site.

For a deeper dive into the meaning and uses of deal terms, we recommend the "Term Sheet Series" of blog posts by Brad Feld at www.feld.com/archives/2005/08/term-sheet-series-wrap-up.html. Feld is an angel investor, managing director of the Foundry Group (a venture capital firm in Colorado), and coauthor of *Venture Deals*. If you plan to build a diversified equity crowdfunding portfolio, you should take the time to study the terms. You might even find it fascinating.

## THE JOYS OF DUE DILIGENCE

In Chapter 12 we will explain the due diligence process. Not all equity crowdfunding investors will have a desire to conduct due diligence before investing. It might seem like a daunting challenge for a new angel investor. We are not preaching that you absolutely must do some professional level of due diligence. But you should at least read Chapter 12 so that you will know what due diligence looks like, so you can better evaluate the comments and opinions of other people who have (or who claim to have) conducted their due diligence on a particular offering.

As an equity crowdfunding investor, you will depend on other members of the crowd for information, opinions, and insights about a deal. Unless you are a sociopath (in which case, you would be better off investing your money in your own mental health), you will feel a responsibility to contribute valuable ideas in the discussion forums where the crowd members collaborate on due diligence. If you don't feel qualified to conduct a broad range of due diligence, maybe you can zero in on a narrow range of it—such as market research, technological feasibility, cash flow projection analysis, intellectual property rights, product or prototype testing, local or regional economic outlook, or founder integrity—and contribute as a specialist in that area.

You may find that conducting due diligence, like being an investigative journalist or private detective, is a very satisfying aspect of angel investing (sniffing out fraud can be fun!), even when it leads you to decide not to invest in a deal. More important, it helps you select suitable deals in which to invest.

# CHAPTER 12

# How to Invest, Part III: Due Diligence

**B**efore you buy a house, you would walk through the premises and the grounds to make sure (1) the property will meet your requirements and (2) there are no undisclosed problems that would cost an arm and a leg to fix. The seller of the house has a duty to disclose problems that he or she knows about. But in most cases, if you buy the house and *then* find a serious problem, unless the seller claimed specifically that no such problem existed, then it's your problem to fix because you failed to discover it before the deal closed. That's why home buyers are keenly observant during their walk-throughs, study the neighborhood and local schools, and hire building inspectors to make sure any problems are exposed before the deal is closed. This is the real estate due diligence process.

In the context of investing in securities, due diligence is the research and investigation that an investor conducts into the issuer and its associated industry and market before buying its debt or equity securities. Investing in private securities is like buying a home in the respect that you spend a significant amount of money for something that you plan to live with for years.

Securities due diligence includes making sure the issuer is properly incorporated or registered with the state, confirming that it has the necessary permits to make and sell its product or provide its service, testing out the product or the service, digging into the backgrounds of the owners and key managers, evaluating the business plan to see if it makes sense, and so forth. Any investor needs to conduct due diligence before investing, or ensure that someone has done it reliably.

The due diligence process is different for various types of investments. There is no single due diligence checklist or set of procedures that investors always undertake. How much investigation you do depends on a number of factors. When Warren Buffett buys a railroad for billions of dollars, he has lawyers at an expensive law firm spending weeks scouring every offering document. No average "retail investor" (nor even Warren Buffett) will spend that much on due diligence when investing $1,000 or so in a startup. That's why the legal definition of due diligence is the investigation that a *reasonable person* would do in the administration of his or her own affairs. As a reasonable person, you will not accept on faith every statement, claim, and representation an issuer makes. Not that most issuers will be intentionally deceptive or evasive (some will), but there will occasionally (or often) be inadvertent mistakes, inaccuracies, and miscalculations.

Simply reading the offering documents and disclosures that a company is required to produce and confirming that it has indeed produced them is a good and important first step, but it is not the same as due diligence. Securities law stipulates the information—including financial data and risk disclosures—that the company must produce, and you should certainly read it and confirm that it has been produced. But someone still needs to evaluate the disclosed data and risks and make a decision as to whether the investment is a sound one. Evaluating that information is a key element of due diligence.

## DIY, OUTSOURCE, OR COLLABORATE

Who is qualified to conduct due diligence? Some angel groups have designated reviewers. Law firms can do due diligence, but they are generally too expensive for investors seeking crowdfunding offerings, given the low dollar amounts involved.

The crowdfunding intermediary is obligated to have a reasonable basis for believing the issuer has met the requirements to offer securities under Section 4(a)(6) of the Securities Act,[1] but you can't always rely on the intermediary to conduct thorough due diligence. Some equity crowdfunding sites take additional steps, such as establishing an antifraud department or hiring a third party like CrowdCheck to conduct due diligence. This level of due diligence focuses mainly on compliance, rather than the potential return on investment.

CrowdCheck is a premium due diligence service, charging about $1,000 for the most basic report (which provides assurance that the offering complies with the law), up to several thousand dollars for a comprehensive report. Some platforms or issuers hire CrowdCheck to conduct due diligence, advise the company on how to get into compliance where needed, and issue a report, which the company can then post on the equity crowdfunding

---

[1] 78 Fed. Reg. at 66, 556 (Proposed Rule 301(a)).

site (and only on that site) to share with prospective investors. Investors need not pay for access to the report.[2]

More affordable third-party due diligence ranges from automated systems that come up with a numerical rating or a thumbs up/down at the end of the evaluation to law firms willing to conduct due diligence at a discounted rate or with a narrow focus. In between, various independent financial advisers and consultants specialize in conducting due diligence for small offerings and can offer high-quality evaluations, but always check their credentials and experience before you hire someone who professes to conduct due diligence for equity crowdfunding offerings.

You can conduct due diligence yourself, or learn how to do so—you don't have to be a securities lawyer or a member of an angel group. We will help you get started in this chapter, and you can dig deeper by reading how-to books for angel, VC, and private equity investment that offer tips on due diligence.[3]

Incidentally, securities laws do not require issuers that make offerings under Regulation D[4] to produce as many disclosures as issuers in Title III equity crowdfunding offerings, although the Reg D offering platforms may establish more stringent disclosure policies of their own.

As the equity crowdfunding industry develops, various types of off-platform analysis will be available—that is, websites independent of crowdfunding sites that offer reviews, reports, background checks, and ratings of issuers, some subscription-based and some supported by advertising, including reports and ratings and other "due diligence checks." After you review the following discussion of what due diligence is, it may become clear that some of these forms of review, often marketed as "due diligence" products, do not amount to thorough due diligence. Background checks and examinations of an issuer's social media or other online presence, for example, are only part of the picture, although they may be useful elements. In the case of ratings services, consider how the ratings are put together, what calculations or formulas are used to derive a rating, and whether the input comes from crowdsourcing or from informed professionals. In the case of services that give numerical rankings to offerings, research whether those rankings are on the basis of objective or subjective factors, and whether you agree that those factors are important and properly weighted.

---

[2] The founder and CEO of CrowdCheck, Sara Hanks, peer-reviewed each chapter of this book. The authors believe CrowdCheck is highly reputable and authoritative, but have no obligation to mention or promote CrowdCheck in the text.

[3] We recommend *Venture Capital Due Diligence*, by Justin J. Camp, John Wiley & Sons, 2013.

[4] Including 506(b) and 506(c) offerings; the latter are also known as Title II offerings.

Not all data is reliable or predictive; numbers can be used to deceive as well as illuminate.

If anyone is offering "investment advice" online, which under securities law is a very broad concept and includes whether or not to invest in specific securities, bear in mind that investment advisers must be registered with the SEC and/or state securities authorities. And steer clear of so-called advisers or consultants who should be registered but aren't.

## The Crowd

This is crowdfunding, after all, and you will have an opportunity to collaborate on due diligence with other investors on the equity crowdfunding site. We discussed the wisdom (and madness) of crowds in Chapter 6. We will emphasize a few points about crowd wisdom here.

First, the input of any crowd member is valuable only if his or her knowledge, expertise, or experience is relevant, so read each member's profile and make sure they use their real names so you can check them out off-platform, via other social networks, search engines, and/or their own (or their employers') websites. Investors who have deep industry and market knowledge will dig up facts and express insights that lawyers and financial consultants will not. If a crowd member offers a surprising or dubious fact, ask him or her for the source of that information, and then check the source to verify. Whenever someone uses faulty information, be sure to challenge it and issue a correction, not only to help the crowd members but also to establish your own credibility and authoritativeness. In fact, some crowdfunding platforms and off-platform analytical websites will rate investors based on the perceived usefulness of their comments and questions.

Second, you will have to use your good sense to ascertain whether comments made by other "investors" are genuine and useful and contribute to illuminating the issues being discussed, rather than intended to hype or sabotage the offering.

Third, perhaps the most valuable input from many of the crowd members is that they are potential consumers of the product or service that the company is selling and can evaluate its potential in the marketplace (and the potential size of the market) as well as—maybe better than—anyone else. Their enthusiasm for the product and the market, as well as the company's plans and strategies, is worth more than the thumbs-up opinions of analysts and experts.

One final caveat regarding the social aspect of crowdfunding: Do not accuse an issuer (or anyone else) of fraud, or any other crime, unless you have hard evidence to prove it. You can be sure that any careless accusations you make will follow you in cyberspace and brand you as an unreliable source of information at best, and get you effectively banned from good offerings at worst—in extreme cases you could be sued for defamation. On the other hand, do not hesitate to ask probing questions that could expose fraud—don't simply walk away from a suspicious deal without alerting your fellow investors, who will welcome your participation in other offerings and reciprocate with their valuable input.

## Three Buckets: Legal, Financial, Business

Due diligence on an equity crowdfunding issuer can be divided into three buckets: legal, financial, and business due diligence. You do not have to approach due diligence in that order, as long as you (and the people with whom you collaborate) touch all three bases. At the very least you must make sure that someone you trust has looked into the issues in the list that follows, even if you aren't reading the documents and disclosures yourself.

You are certainly free to, and some people will, invest money without conducting all three categories of due diligence. If that is your approach, your odds are not good; you might have more fun at a casino.

## LEGAL DUE DILIGENCE

First and foremost, you want to avoid frauds. A legitimate business may or may not fail, but a fraudulent enterprise will absolutely fail. Fraud avoidance actually spans legal and financial due diligence, but we will broach the subject here. Most investment platforms work hard to exclude obvious fraudsters, but a sophisticated fraud is not always easy to screen out. You should watch for signs of false claims, intentional misstatements, material omissions, and guarantees that are too good to be true. Use off-platform search engines to check the profiles of founders and key management team members, looking for lawsuits, criminal convictions, and disciplinary action taken by state and federal securities agencies.

Do not hesitate to ask issuers questions about any of the above that you dig up, and see if their explanations are satisfactory or not. Also check with the professional and trade associations that founders say they are members of, to see if they are in good standing. Once you make an investment, if the deal turns out to be fraudulent, you may be able to recover some or most of your investment (if the fraudsters are still in this hemisphere) but you'll lose a lot of time at the very least. You're much better off spending the time now to check the accuracy or credibility of the issuer's information and profiles.

Due diligence to combat fraud is only one part of the story. Many small businesses fail for reasons that have nothing to do with fraud. Failure rates are high among startups, even if everyone involved is honest and well intentioned. Beyond the question of fraud, the objective of due diligence is to assess how likely it is that a business will be successful. We look for signs that the business concept might be flaky or incoherent, the operation disorganized, or management dysfunctional.

## Corporate Information

One very important point is that all the registrations, documents, accounts, rights, and contracts discussed in this section must be *in the name of the company,* not in the names of the founders. This includes bank accounts, websites and Internet domains (the part of the URL that follows "www."), and intellectual property such as patents and trademarks. This is essential because in the excitement of establishing a new company, the founders can neglect to distinguish themselves from the company—frequently, mere oversight rather than deliberate attempts to defraud investors. However, if there is a falling out among the founders later on (which happens frequently in startups), it is important to establish that the key assets of the company are in the company's name, and that one or more founders cannot simply walk away and establish a new, rival company.

Some of this information may be available on the company's or intermediary's website, and some you may need to request from the company, if you think it is essential to your investment decision.

No company should ever provide one investor access to information that it doesn't provide to all investors, so the company may need to post additional information on the intermediary's site upon your request. If a company declines to provide information, it may simply be because it's too much of a burden to handle individual investor requests, which is one argument in favor of third-party due diligence, where the company has to deal with just one set of requests. Following are more areas of inquiry:

- *Proper incorporation and good standing*: You'll want to know that the company has been duly incorporated or organized as an LLC in the applicable state and that it is in "good standing," which means that the company has filed all the paperwork and paid all the fees required by that jurisdiction. A company typically must be in good standing before it can legally issue securities. In large securities offerings, the company's lawyers issue a formal legal opinion that the company is in good standing, but it can be very expensive to get such an opinion, so that's unlikely to be a common practice in crowdfunding offerings. The cheapest way to check a company's standing is to look the company up on a public database maintained by the state. In some states this is a problem because their databases are updated only once a year. Startups themselves frequently fail to file their paperwork and pay their fees on time, so the chances of the database being out-of-date are high. If the company does not include a certificate of good standing with its offering documents on the equity crowdfunding site, the only reliable way to know that a company is in good standing is to apply to the secretary of state's office for a recent (no older than a few weeks) certificate of good standing, for which the state will charge a fee. Bear in mind that even if a company is in good standing it may still have other problems, such as bankruptcy, litigation, or SEC enforcement action.

- *Business entity*: Is the company a C corporation, an LLC, or other entity? This will make a difference to how the company is governed and who has the ability to make decisions on behalf of the company, as discussed later. Note the date the company was started—the date should be stamped on the formation documents, such as articles of incorporation—that helps to establish how old the company is, and you can evaluate whether the company is performing as you'd expect it to. In addition, check that the company's "business purpose," as stated in the articles of incorporation or LLC operating agreement, is not limited in any way, to ensure that the company is not acting *ultra vires*, a legal term for "outside its authority." Most companies' stated purpose is "any legal business" or something along those lines, depending on the state, but if the company's purpose is limited to a specific industry or operation, you'll want to know that.

- *Bylaws or operating agreement*: C corporations have bylaws, and LLCs have operating agreements. These establish basic rules under which the company will operate and how decisions are made in the company's name. The reason to check these documents is to make sure that the directors are properly appointed and that important decisions such as previous capital raises have been made in compliance with the company's internal governance documents. This might be hard for an amateur to do, so average investors might limit themselves to checking that the company does have bylaws or an operating agreement. One of the most important issues to understand is that LLCs are very flexible in terms of how they are governed. Unlike corporations, which tend to have a narrow range of operational options, LLCs are basically created by contract (the operating agreement is the document, signed by all members, that explains the rights and duties of the various parties to the agreement), so pay particular attention to the operating agreement and how or whether it grants rights to the group of investors. If you are not familiar with the variations that typically are built into the structure of LLCs, don't be afraid to ask questions or bring in people who have experience in these areas until you are acclimated. Make sure you understand the tax implications of investing in an LLC: Will the company pay taxes itself, or will it "pass through" all taxable income to its investors?

- *Minutes of meetings of the board of directors or managing members*: Review the minutes, sometimes called resolutions or "action by unanimous written consent" forms, which form the record of decisions, actions, and votes taken at meetings of the boards of directors. These documents show whether the board is complying with the company's internal management documents. Again, this may be difficult for a nonprofessional, who might want to just make sure that there is some indication that meetings are being held on a regular basis and that someone is keeping a record of those meetings, so that future disputes (for example, as to whether a decision to acquire another business was authorized by the board) do not arise.

## Operational Information

- *State and local registration, relevant permits*: Most states and counties, and some municipalities, require that companies doing business there register to do business or obtain licenses or permits. Some types of businesses, such as those in which professionals need specific qualifications or training (architects, veterinarians) or could affect the public's well-being (bars, food importers), require special permits or licenses. If the company doesn't obtain them, it won't be able to carry on its business. You'll want to establish that the company has researched what licenses or permits it needs in all locations where it operates and has taken steps to obtain those documents; once it does, it must renew them regularly. If the company doesn't offer this information, you may be able to establish for yourself what licenses are needed, by doing a simple search of the state, county, or municipality website.

- *Website and domain ownership*: For some companies, their website is an essential part of their business. It might be the first thing that the founders establish when they set up the company. For that reason, it is often owned by the founders as individuals, not by the company. If the person owning the Internet domain were to leave the company, still owning the domain, how damaging would it be, and how much goodwill would the company need to rebuild when it launches a site under a new domain, or even another name? Check that the company owns the rights to its website, not just as a matter of fulfilling its business plan, but also as an indication of the company's general professionalism and operational savvy. You can obtain a receipt from the domain registrar showing registration of the domain in the company's name.

There is no legitimate reason why a company would want to maintain an anonymous registration (which can be done) if it is issuing securities to a crowd of investors.

■ *Separate bank account*: It is crucial that the company has a bank account separate from those of the founders, and that the funds raised from equity crowdfunding are deposited into that account. Note how long the company has had its bank account—ideally from the time of the company's inception. Keeping clear records as to what belongs to the company and what belongs personally to the founders is essential, especially when it comes to money. If the bank account is new, ask how the company kept business funds separate from personal funds before the account was created.

This step is critical, for reasons beyond good accounting practices. If the founders commingle personal and company funds, the corporate veil that protects investors from liability may be pierced, exposing investors to lawsuits if the founders are sued. This kind of legal action is sometimes known as an alter-ego lawsuit.

## Potential Liabilities

■ *Litigation*: You should investigate whether the company is involved in any litigation, especially where the company is a defendant (i.e., where someone has accused the company of wrongdoing). A search of federal electronic databases will show if the company is involved in federal lawsuits. Start with Public Access to Court Electronic Records at www.pacer.gov and Justia Dockets & Filings at www.dockets.justia.com. State litigation records are more difficult to obtain. Many companies face litigation at various points in their life spans, whether they are plaintiffs or defendants. You want to consider the specific circumstances of any litigation and evaluate how the litigation may impact the potential value of the company. While litigation does not necessarily mean that the company is not a good investment, small companies, and especially startups, do not typically have the resources (especially in time and cost) to divert to managing a contentious litigation. You could hire a lawyer experienced in the appropriate area of litigation to review the legal filings to get an idea of whether the claims being made against the company have any merit. In general, avoid any small company that has more than one lawsuit filed against it. It might not be the company's fault (or it might), but even if the company has a good chance of prevailing in court, a small business cannot spend the time and money necessary to defend itself, especially in a complex case. If the company is the plaintiff in a suit, on the other hand, you should ascertain whether it is taking necessary, aggressive legal action against an injurious wrongdoer (if so, that's a good sign) or whether it is pursuing an expensive resolution to a problem that should have been avoided or mediated.

- *Bankruptcy*: Any history of bankruptcy disclosed by the company, or revealed through a background check, raises a red flag. Investing in a company that is emerging from bankruptcy or reorganization (which investors might do as part of a recapitalization or rescue package) is something that should be done only by experienced investors who know clearly what value they expect to get from the company (for example, if it still holds valuable patents or hard assets). If you consider yourself smart enough to evaluate such a company, keep in mind that many small businesses have worked their way out of bankruptcy and gone on to be successful, having learned how to correct previous mistakes.

- *Taxes*: Some companies are not required to file tax returns if they are pre-revenue startups with very low revenue levels. But you want to make sure the company has researched the issue and made any filings that are necessary. Many companies must file tax returns even if they have no taxable revenues, and they may face penalties if the filings are not made. In California, for example, every company must pay annual franchise taxes, whether profitable or not. The fact that a company has filed a tax return may be evidence that it is a legitimate company that has taken steps to consider its tax obligations.

- *Liens*: A lien is a legal claim against property or other assets of the company, by which the company can secure a loan. If the loan is not repaid, the property or asset must be turned over to the lender (similar to a mortgage). The company's valuation should not include the full value of assets that are subject to liens. Most formal background checks include lien checks.

## Intellectual Property

An intellectual property (IP) audit includes intangible assets such as patents, trademarks, and copyrights. While it might be obvious that a tech company will need to have a patent for a product or process that is the basis for its business, don't overlook the need for intellectual property protection in some other areas, such as the design of the company's website or the copyright to its content. It is common for early-stage companies to postpone or ignore protection until it is too late! If the company can't afford the services of an IP lawyer, it can use online self-help services such as Traklight, which will at least point the company in the right direction.

- *Patents*: There are few advantages for investors more powerful than a well-written patent—that is, one that confers broad protection. In effect, a patent is a federally granted monopoly for an inventor to use a new idea exclusively for two decades. In some cases, this is the only way a small company can enter a market and fend off giant competitors that could otherwise devote massive sums to reverse-engineering and mass-marketing a similar product, often at a lower price. Owning valuable patents or other intellectual property can greatly increase its valuation. Check that patents are assigned by the inventors to the company (this is usually done through employment contracts, formal assignments, or bulk bills of sale) and that any patents claimed by the company are filed with the U.S. Patent and Trademark Office (PTO). You can search the PTO for registrations at www.uspto.gov. In light of the fact that patents are often challenged, think about whether the patent claimed is actually reasonable.

  A patent is supposed to be issued only for products and processes that are not "obvious." But occasionally an inventor manages to get a patent that is later challenged in court and rescinded for being obvious. If you have any doubts about the value of an issuer, you can hire a freelance engineer to evaluate whether a patent is solid or obvious.

  Be careful if the issuer says that it has applied for a patent or has a "patent pending." There is no assurance that the patent application will be approved and granted by the PTO, and that process sometimes takes two or three years. If receiving a patent is a linchpin of the business, then ask the founders for an opinion letter from an independent IP lawyer suggesting the likelihood of a successful application.

- *Trademarks and copyrights*: Trademarks cover nongeneric brand names and distinguishing designs such as logos and slogans. Trademark protection prevents competitors from using identities that are confusingly similar. Check that the company has at the least filed for trademark or service mark protection of its name, logo, and any other marks that are important to its business. Just as important, make sure that a startup is not infringing on another company's registered trademark, which you can search for on the PTO's website: http://www.uspto.gov/trademarks/.

  Copyrights protect words and music expressed in a fixed medium such as books, periodicals, website content and digital media, CDs and DVDs, packaging, and advertising. Unlike patents and trademarks, companies do not need to file applications for copyright protection prior to engaging in commercial activities. As soon as the copyright owner inserts a copyright notice (© 2015 Company Name, Inc.) within the materials, they are protected by law. Registration with the U.S. Copyright Office confers additional legal rights in the event of an infringement action. If the issuer is engaged in publishing original works (rather than aggregated or repurposed works), it should routinely apply for copyright registration of its content.

- *Licenses*: If the company is licensing technology or designs produced by a third party, consider whether the terms of the license are appropriate and whether the company will have the use of the license for a sufficient period of time. If the company licenses its own IP to others, you should have access to those written agreements.

## FINANCIAL DUE DILIGENCE

Financial statements are reports that companies make periodically to summarize their financial activity and condition. The information in a company's financials is presented mainly in terms of quantities, dollars, and ratios rather than expository text. Established companies typically issue their financials annually and quarterly.

Financials are used internally by owners and managers to assess the company's fiscal health, determine its ability to generate cash and cover short-term operating expenses and longer-term debt, and plan for the future. Financials for small businesses usually include three items:

- The income statement (also called profit-and-loss statement, or P&L) summarizes income and expenses throughout the period. The difference between income and expenses is a profit or a loss (net income) for the period.
- The balance sheet shows the assets, liabilities, and ownership equity on the last day of the period.
- The cash flow statement shows the change in a company's cash balance from the beginning to the end of the period. It breaks down cash inflows and outflows into three categories: operating, investing, and financing transactions. Where the income statement is prepared on the basis of accrual accounting, a cash flow statement backs out items that don't involve the payment or receipt of cash, so that investors can gauge how much actual cash the company has.

It is important to understand the difference between cash and accrual accounting. The majority of small businesses keep their financial records on a cash basis. This means that when they get paid for something, they consider that payment as income as soon as it's received.

Accrual accounting attempts to match income and expenditure, so that you get a better idea of the company's profitability. With accrual accounting, you may be "recognizing" in your financial statements payments that you haven't made yet and income that you haven't received yet. Consider the operations of a bakery. It buys flour in bulk at the beginning of the year. If it similarly buys supplies to last all year in the first quarter, its financial statements on a cash basis might show a big loss in the first quarter and then high profits the rest of the year. But if it keeps its financial records on an accrual basis, it would "recognize" the expenses for flour as the flour is used up to produce its products throughout the year, and as it gets paid for those products, it matches the income with the costs. This would give you a better idea of whether the operations are profitable.

The SEC has proposed requiring the financial statements for companies making offerings under Title III to be produced on an accrual basis. It is possible the final rules may permit some relief from this requirement for some very-early-stage companies. (Companies making offerings to accredited investors under Title II are not subject to any requirements with respect to their financial statements: They don't have to provide them, and if they do produce financial statements there are no rules about whether they should be produced on an accrual basis.) So one important early step in preparing to review financial statements is making sure you know what basis of accounting is being used.

## Financials Required for Equity Crowdfunding

For Regulation D offerings where investors are accredited (including Rule 506 offerings online), issuers are not required by law to produce financial statements, although offering platforms may require them to do so. If financial statements are available they will probably not be audited. Seed-stage companies may produce "projected" financial statements, calculated by reference to the (sometimes overoptimistic) forecasts, estimates, and assumptions of the company's management.

As we explained in Chapter 3, for equity crowdfunding offerings under Title III there are different requirements, depending on the amount of capital sought. If a company is raising less than $100,000, then only tax returns (of the company) and financial statements certified by a company officer are required to be posted on the crowdfunding site. If a company is raising between $100,000 and $500,000, then the financial statements must be reviewed by a CPA. If a company is raising more than $500,000 (up to $1 million), then audited financial statements are required.

The next thing investors should consider is whether the financial statements are reliable, that is, whether they give an accurate picture of a company's financial condition. In general, financials are more reliable when an independent (outside) accountant has been involved in their preparation and/or review. If the company has not used an outside accountant, find out whether the company officer producing the financials has an accounting qualification. If not, the company financials might not give such a clear picture of the company's position. That doesn't necessary mean the company has done anything wrong, but producing financials is complicated, and it's not surprising if small companies sometimes make mistakes. Investors should ask more questions about the financial condition of a company that has produced its financial statements completely by itself.

There are three levels of involvement of outside accountants: compilation, review, and audit.

*Compilation.* The company may use a CPA to help "compile" its financial statements. Here, the CPA assists company management in presenting their financial information, but does not give assurance that the financials are free from material errors.

*Review.* The purpose of a review is to provide "limited assurance" that the statements are compiled in an appropriate form and are free of any obvious material errors.[5] If the independent accountant conducting the review is aware that any information supplied by the company for the financial statements is incomplete, unclear, incorrect, or misleading, he or she should request additional, clarified, corrected, or revised information from the company. But the reviewer generally does not examine any underlying records that support the financials (such as paid bills, sales orders and receipts, bank deposits, canceled checks, general ledgers, employee time sheets, or reconciled bank statements).

*Audit.* Audits are conducted by certified public accountants or CPA firms, are much more thorough than reviews, and (if all goes well) result in the highest level of assurance possible. The auditor must maintain an "attitude of professional skepticism" in order to determine whether the financials are free of material misstatements and are fair and accurate.

An audit involves researching the underlying records of the company (such as outgoing and incoming invoices, receipts, purchase orders, and

---

[5]The American Institute of CPAs uses the term "limited assurance" in its 2010 publication *What Is the Difference between a Compilation, a Review and an Audit? Comparative Overview.* This publication defines a review thus: "Reviewed financial statements provide the user with comfort that, based on the accountant's review, the accountant is not aware of any material modifications that should be made to the financial statements for the statements to be in conformity with the applicable financial reporting framework."

payroll records), or at least a representative sample of them, to support the figures used in the financials. The auditor may direct inquiries not only to management but also to third parties (e.g., suppliers and customers) and is expected to conduct a physical inspection of the company's operations. The CPA must look into the company's internal control structure and assess the risk of fraud.

Results of an audit are summarized in a formal audit report that expresses the auditor's professional opinion as to whether the financials are presented fairly. The auditor may issue a disclaimer of opinion or an adverse opinion when appropriate; that means there will be a paragraph in the auditor's report saying, in effect, "These financial statements are not reliable." Title III offerings will not be permitted to be made in the event the auditor's opinion is not "clean," that is, there are any qualifications or disclaimers. The financial statements presented to angel and VC investors are often not reviewed or audited, but if they are, a qualification or disclaimer would raise a red flag.

Unless you have an accounting background, the details and nuances of these financials may be hard to grasp. If you plan to be an active angel investor, it would be worthwhile to take a course in or otherwise study how to read financial statements. As a starting point, read the SEC's excellent *Beginners' Guide to Financial Statements*.[6] Beginners can simplify the analysis by focusing on three numbers:

- *Net profit (or loss)*: If the company is profitable, are the profits improving from one accounting period to the next? If it is not yet profitable, are the losses at least decreasing over time?
- *Total revenue*: If revenues are healthy and the company is reinvesting income to grow market share, expand capacity, or fuel development in other ways, then profitability is not necessarily the key number to watch in a period of rapid early growth.
- *Profit margin*: This reflects the costs of producing revenue. High margins can eventually lead to strong profits even in a relatively small local market. Tight margins require high sales volumes to achieve strong profits.

You can use the financial statements to build your knowledge about the company and its prospects. Consider these issues:

- *Compliance*: If the company is making a crowdfunding offering above $100,000, it must produce financial statements. The platform should

---

[6] http://www.sec.gov/investor/pubs/begfinstmtguide.htm

check that the financials have the right level of review, but so should you. If it turns out that the offering was supposed to have audited financial statements but they are merely reviewed, that's a signal that not just the offering but the platform it's listed on, too, is unreliable.

- *Financial conditions and trends*: Note what the company's anticipated expenditures are (employees, lease, raw materials, etc.) and its anticipated profits. Note how the company plans to deal with any large payments it may need to make in the future, how it anticipates its financial results will change in the future, how its financial results are recorded, and any recent changes in operations or in financial condition. Can you identify a trend? Will it continue?

- *Burn rate*: This is the amount of money the company is spending in the pre-revenue or startup phase—money it spends in order to get to the point where it can produce revenue to offset expenses. It is important to get an accurate picture of how much the company is spending and what it is spending on, what it anticipates for future expenses, what it will do if something unexpected happens, and what it will do if it runs out of money before reaching certain milestones. Investors should evaluate how long it will take for the company to use the funds, and whether that is a reasonable rate. New companies frequently underestimate how much money they need and overestimate how long funds will last. Investors should ask the company (1) what assumptions they used to estimate how long the money would last and (2) what it would do if those assumptions turned out to be false. Where would it get more money?

- *Projections*: If the company is presenting projected financial statements, it should explain the assumptions it is relying on to make those projections. Do you agree with those assumptions? For example, if it is assuming getting a specific market share, do you think that is reasonable? Do you agree with its pricing? Don't be afraid to ask questions about assumptions (or anything else).

- *Previous capital raises*: It is useful to evaluate how the company raised money in the past, and how it used the funds. That includes loans, rewards-based crowdfunding, venture capital rounds, Reg D offerings, and so on. How much did the company get and how did it use the money? If the company raised money previously from a VC or other institutional investor, consider whether a current crowdfunding round signals desperation, or if there is a strategic reason for crowdfunding. For example, a consumer products or retail company might genuinely want to have thousands of investors on its capitalization table, all of them helping to promote the brand.

■ *Subsidiaries*: A subsidiary is a different company that the issuer (the company you are investing in) owns an interest in. If there are any, they should be identified in the financials. Clarify the relationship between the different companies. If a subsidiary borrows money, that money has to be repaid before the parent company (the one you are investing in) gets any money from the subsidiary's operations. If a subsidiary isn't wholly owned by the parent company, then other shareholders of the subsidiary will have rights that differ from yours. This would be a red flag if you were investing in convertible debt or straight-debt securities.

## BUSINESS DUE DILIGENCE

Even inexperienced investors can do some basic business due diligence. Use your own life, education, and business experience. Consider first investment opportunities in your own line of work. Is this a product or service that you would use, and what would you pay for it?

If the company sells its product or services to consumers in your area, test it out. Buy the product, eat at the franchised restaurant, use the software. Is it just good, or is it exciting? Is it better than the competition? Is there or will there be a demand for it? Will the market ever be huge; if not, will margins (price minus cost to produce) be high enough for the company to thrive in a small market? Will the novelty of the product require consumer education? If it's a local company, be sure to swing by its location. Is the business really there, and are people really working there (as opposed to occupying space for the sake of appearances)?

What problem does the product or service solve? Or how does it solve the problem better than any other product or service? Does the company differentiate its product or service in terms of higher quality, lower price, quicker delivery, more convenience, ease of use or maintenance, and so on? Is the product's or service's advantage easy to comprehend, or will the company have to educate consumers (and at what cost)?

If the product is innovative (and if it is not patentable), how soon will competitors crop up like weeds and fight for market share? Will there be large competitors with virtually unlimited capital that can produce and market the product faster and cheaper? What are the barriers to entry? What is the company's plan for preempting the competition or differentiating to protect market share?

### Founders and Management Team

Some successful angel investors care more about a company's people than its product or business plan. "Bet the jockey, not the horse," they say. Other angels believe that a strong product in a growing market will make a hard-working entrepreneur look like a genius. It really doesn't matter whether you believe the jockey or the horse is more important—you need both to win a race. We will talk about the people first, because evaluating people can be more intuitive (you've been doing it all your life) than evaluating business plans. You basically want to determine if key members of the management team have track records as entrepreneurs, and if they are capable, resilient (i.e., they will persevere through hard times), and adaptable.

First, it is important to understand who the key team members are. Often one person will take on multiple roles, and it is important to understand how dependent a company is on such a person, in case he or she leaves or becomes incapacitated. In addition, seek to understand the relationships between the key players. Did they study together at college? Are they closely related? Consider whether those relationships will last, or could prove problematic in the future. Following are the people who will have a strong influence on the company's direction and, ultimately, success. Consider whether you recognize or know any of them and, if so, if there is any reason you would not want to play on the same team:

- *Founders*: Those who started the company, typically own most of the stock of the company, serve on the board, and have appointed other board members, so they have a great deal of control.
- *Directors*: Members of the board of directors, who vote on important decisions of the company.
- *C-level officers*: Chief executive officer, chief financial officer, and the three highest-paid other officers. Typically, the CEO serves on the board.
- *Shareholders*: The capitalization table shows the company's ownership and capital structure, identifying individual shareholders who own 20 percent or more shares in the company.
- *Advisers*: Some companies have high-profile advisers, some of whom are paid. Confirm that each of these relationships is useful, the advisers are credentialed, and their service is not gratuitous window dressing. Entrepreneurs need good advice, and advisory boards should not carry deadweight.

Now we will focus on founders and officers, the people who will be running the company day in and day out. We will look at three aspects of evaluating the team members: individual characteristics, group dynamics, and conditions of employment.

## Individual Characteristics

Equity crowdfunding intermediaries—the portals and broker-dealer platforms—are required to conduct background checks on officers (as well as directors and 20 percent shareholders), as a means to reduce the risk of fraud. Intermediaries must disqualify an issuer if one of its officers is a "bad actor," which we defined in Chapter 3.

You look for the following information about each founder (if still active in the company) and officer. If the issuer's offering documents do not contain this information, inquire directly and/or search online:

- *Employment commitment.* How long has each person been with the company? If someone is key to the company's operations, what mechanisms are in place to make sure he or she has incentives to stick around (e.g., employment contracts, vesting schedule for stock options) and will not bolt for a competitor (e.g., enforceable noncompete agreements, which specify that an individual may not work for a competitor in the same industry over a finite period, sometimes within a limited geographical scope)? Check for any exorbitant severance provisions (golden parachutes) that might strain the company's finances when a key person leaves the company. Also check to see if the company has a procedure for terminating the contract of (i.e., firing) an employee who violates the terms of the employment agreement or "for cause."
- *Education and previous employment.* Check with schools to confirm graduation and degree status, and check with prior employers to confirm the jobs, training, and accomplishments claimed in the individual's profile.
- *Previous entrepreneurial experience.* The phrase "serial entrepreneur" frequently comes up in biographies; establish what this means *exactly*. How many previous startups has the entrepreneur been involved in, how many of them are still in business, and/or at what stage did they flounder? Of course, much is learned from failure, and some angel investors would rather see an unsuccessful venture in an entrepreneur's past than none at all. But past entrepreneurial success is unequivocally the best predictor of future success.[7]

The following factors are more subjective, requiring you to make judgments based on your experience, education, and understanding of human nature. First, David Rose wrote in his book *Angel Investing* about three traits that founders should exhibit:[8]

---

[7]A Harvard Business School study found that the success rate for first-time entrepreneurs is about 18 percent, failed serial entrepreneurs had a success rate of about 20 percent in later ventures, and entrepreneurs with successful track records had "predicted success rates" of almost 30 percent in new endeavors. (Zack Miller, "Investing in Future IPOs," Benzinga.com, October 28, 2013.)

[8]David S. Rose, *Angel Investing*, John Wiley & Sons, 2014, pp. 70–79.

- *Realism and pragmatism.* "I have no problem with optimism as a trait, but it has to be optimism based on a realistic understanding of how things work," Rose says. "I don't want to hear vague, rosy promises like, 'We'll attract 10 percent of our addressable market.' Instead, I want to know who the first customer is. The second. The third. Through which channel they will each be recruited, and at what cost. And will they reorder?"
- *Flexibility.* "In all cases," continues Rose, "something is going to go not as planned, and the entrepreneur needs to be able to adapt and pivot if necessary to deal with problems and take advantage of opportunities. That's how startup Tote turned into blockbuster Pinterest."[9]
- *Knowing when to back away.* Founders should be willing "to step away from the CEO role if it becomes apparent that this would be best for the company."

Conversely, Rose points to these warning signs of a weak founder:[10]

- Lack of integrity, "an instant deal-breaker."
- Unrealistic assessment of market size, competition, competitive advantages, execution challenges and costs, financial projections, valuation expectations, or timing.
- Lack of execution track record, domain expertise, technical expertise if needed, long-term vision, leadership capability, communication skills, or willingness to accept advice.

Another angel investor, Paul Graham (CEO of Y Combinator, the tech accelerator), looks for the following traits in founders:[11]

- *Determination.* "This has turned out to be the most important quality in startup founders," Graham says. "We thought when we started Y Combinator [in 2005] that the most important quality would be intelligence. That's the myth in [Silicon] Valley." The founder is going to run into many obstacles and "can't be the sort of person who gets demoralized easily."

---

[9]Note, however, that the stated use of proceeds may not allow a pivot unless the issuer notifies investors in advance that a pivot is possible, defines the alternate plan in advance, and keeps investors informed during a pivot." See Sara Hanks, "The Perils of the Pivot," May 6, 2013, http://www.crowdcheck.com/blog/perils-pivot.
[10]Rose, op. cit., p. 75
[11]Posted on Graham's blog, October 2010, http://www.paulgraham.com/founders.html.

- *Imagination.* "In the startup world, most good ideas seem bad initially. If they were obviously so good, someone would already be doing them. So you need the kind of [imagination] that produces ideas with just the right level of craziness."
- *Cohesiveness.* Most of the successful startups have two or three founders, Graham points out. "The relationship between the founders has to be strong. They must genuinely like one another and work well together. Startups do to the relationship between the founders what a dog does to a sock: If it can be pulled apart, it will be."

We will add three characteristics based on our own observations of entrepreneurs and startups over the past few decades:

- *Modesty.* You would be amazed what happens when some young entrepreneurs who never had much money all of a sudden get a million dollars deposited in their company bank account. Too many of them rush out and buy expensive sports cars and start flying first class—this happens more often than you might think. Unfortunately, such a transformation is hard to reverse, and extravagance becomes a way of doing business.
- *Strong sales experience.* No explanation needed.
- *Confidence, not passion.* A candidate for buzzword of the decade, *passion* has become an overrated cliché. In many cases it can be equated with overzealousness, which "blinds entrepreneurs, leading them to get overconfident and make bad choices at the worst times—potentially dooming even the most promising startup. Only then do founders appreciate that the origin of the word 'passion' is the Latin word for 'suffer.'" That quote appeared in a 2014 article titled "How an Entrepreneur's Zeal Can Destroy a Startup," by Noam Wasserman.[12] A visiting professor at Harvard Business School, Wasserman based that opinion on his study of 16,000 founders.

Wasserman further states, "Founders believe in their ideas so strongly they throw aside comfortable jobs and risk their life savings to chase their dreams. They have such contagious enthusiasm they can convince others to sign on, whether it's co-founders or venture investors or early-adopting customers." That's the positive aspect of entrepreneurial zeal. On the other hand, "Another constant I've seen is that if there's anything that can sink a new business, it's passion." Wasserman calls this "the paradox of entrepreneurship."

---

[12] *Wall Street Journal,* August 25, 2014, p. R1.

Signs of overzealousness in a founder include:

- Appearing to be on a mission to change the world rather than deliver a better product or service to people who need it.
- Getting defensive when advisers point out flaws in their product or strategy.
- Neglecting to conduct market research to assess consumer demand. "Obsessed with their own ideas," founders are at risk of believing that others will love their product as much as they do, Wasserman warns.
- Hiring friends and family members who are not well qualified, because better-qualified people do not buy into the founder's vision.

## Group Dynamics

Paul Graham points out that pairs of cofounders tend to be much more successful than solo founders. But, of course, anytime you have two or more founders in a company there is a possibility of disagreement. "If there are any signs of discord, steer clear," warns Naval Ravikant, a prolific angel investor and founder of AngelList.[13]

In the midst of cohesiveness on the management team, look for diversity as well, especially in companies whose markets are global or very large and diverse. For example, in a market where men and women are customers in roughly equal numbers, make sure there are both men and women in key positions. In fact, regardless of market demographics, gender diversity on the board of directors may lead to superior performance. A 2012 study of public companies by Credit Suisse Research Institute found that "the share price of large-capitalization companies with at least one woman on the board outperformed companies with no women on their board by 26 percent. For small and mid-capitalization stocks, the outperformance was 17 percent."[14]

Watch out for related-party transactions, where contracts with outside companies are entered into only because of personal relationships between the parties' officers. This tends to be common in startups. Note especially purchases of goods or services that could be obtained more reliably from an unrelated third party but are instead obtained from a relative of one of the controlling persons. Renting space from an in-law is very common. Related-party transactions are not necessarily bad if they're economically sensible and not too prevalent, but you have to consider what might happen if something goes wrong in the relationship. If the CEO gets divorced,

---

[13] Christina Farr, "Get Funded!" *Venture Beat*, November 19, 2012.
[14] "Gender Diversity and Corporate Performance," August 2012, Credit Suisse AG, Zurich, Switzerland.

does the company still get to rent from the now-former father-in-law? If a related party gave the company a "sweetheart deal," is that transaction the only reason the company is making a profit? Consider how things might be different for the company if the transaction had been "at arm's length," in other words, at market rates.

## Business Operations

If the company is already operating, investors should consider the following issues:

- *Complete management team*: The existing staff should have all the skills it needs to operate successfully. If the team is not complete, does the company plan to fill the holes?
- *Employee and management compensation*: Note who (or what committee) determines the amount and type of compensation for senior officers. See if management incentives align with the best interests of the company and its shareholders. For example, if key employees receive stock options or incentives based on profits, that is usually good for investors. If executive bonuses are tied to short-term goals such as gross sales or revenue rather than profits, that could be bad for investors.
- *Customers*: Ask the company to identify its major customers. Contact them—are they happy with the company's product and/or service? Note whether any of them are crucial to operations. If the company seems to rely heavily on one particular customer, ask what would happen if the company lost that customer. Are key customers locked into long-term contracts, or is it likely that they could be?
- *Suppliers*: Identify the company's primary suppliers, sources of raw materials, and vendors. Are they reliable? What happens if supply of raw materials is cut off or a manufacturer fails to deliver under its contract? What are the company's alternatives?
- *Lease*: A lease that is current and paid regularly can serve as an indication that a company is legitimate. However, many legitimate companies do not lease space for their operations. Tech startups, especially, are known for operating out of the founder's basement or garage (e.g., Hewlett-Packard). Consider whether the company's office or factory or other space is adequate to its current and future needs.
- *Insurance policies*: Insurance helps the company minimize financial risks associated with unexpected events such as lawsuits, natural disasters, property damage, or theft. The kind and amount of insurance a company is required to have by law varies from state to state. Workers' compensation, unemployment, and disability insurance are usually required for

businesses with employees, and commercial auto insurance is usually required if a vehicle is used for business purposes. Consider what kind of insurance the company should have, and find out whether it has policies in place. Are there expensive assets that need property insurance? If the company relies on the unique skills of one person, it should have "key man" insurance.

■ *Material contracts*: If a company relies to a great extent on a particular contract (a license to use technology, for example, or a franchise agreement), try to get a copy and review it. Do any of the terms strike you as unreasonable (e.g., fees, length of contract term, exclusivity or noncompete clauses)?

## Business Plans

Whether or not the company is operational today, you want to know what its plans are for the future. More precisely, how will it create generous margins, gain market share, and provide a return for investors? The company should spell out its strategies either in a formal business plan or in a less formal set of offering documents, which may include a videotaped pitch. Either way, the founders' vision should be clear, well organized, tightly focused, and logical so that you can evaluate the company's long-range potential and the possible risks and rewards for investors.

Companies can prepare business plans according to fairly standard outlines or use one of several online business plan templates or "generators." The plan should not sound like boilerplate, though—it should express the company's distinctive voice, indicating that the executives put a lot of thought into the plan and how to present it.

The plan should describe current and planned operations (including the product or service, management team, and other items already covered here), analyze its market and competitive advantages, make projections and forecasts about financial performance (even if it has no operating history yet), and articulate a likely exit strategy whereby investors will earn a return.

The company's grand vision should appeal to you viscerally. It should excite you; otherwise, you shouldn't be willing to take a risk on it. Grand is good. Just make sure the plan's forecasts and projections, while optimistic, are not fanciful.

## Market Analysis and Competitive Advantages

After defining the customer base and identifying specific customers (as we've discussed), you should estimate the size—and potential growth—of the market in terms of people and dollars spent each year. Is this market relatively untapped, or is it overcrowded with entrenched competitors? If the market is untapped, this could be a huge opportunity; or it could mean that nobody else believes there is a market for such a product or service. You must answer this question. If you are not familiar with the industry, talk to people who are knowledgeable in the field, and conduct research by reading industry reports and analysis.

Some markets are already saturated, such as the energy drink market, and any new entrant would have to be spectacular—in terms of superior quality and low price—to compete.

It is always wise to approach with skepticism claims that the startup has "first mover advantage." That means it believes it is the first to enter the market with a new product, and it can gain a lot of loyal customers before competitors enter the field. Being the first entrepreneur in a new industry or with new technology has advantages, but (even with a patent) it is never sufficient. Microsoft Internet Explorer was not the first Web browser, and few people remember the earlier "first movers" Mosaic and Netscape. Google was not the first search engine, and many young people today have never heard of InfoSeek, AltaVista, and Lycos. "It doesn't really matter being the first," said Andy Bechtolsheim, founder of Sun Microsystems and seed investor in Google. "What matters is to solve the problem the best way. Then comes ongoing innovation to keep it up."[15] Thus, the key to the business plan is how the company will solve the problem the best way, and then how it will stay ahead of the competition.

Part of the plan should be how the company will attract new customers, what is the cost of acquiring each one, and in what quantities and for how many years will the average customer purchase the product or service. What will it cost to make and deliver each unit or provide the service? Are sales and distribution channels already established, or are they only theoretical? After these questions are answered, the company can forecast market share and volume, and project revenue, profit, and cash flow over a period of 6 to 10 years—that's how long it usually takes to achieve an exit for investors, although that varies with the industry.

## Forecasts and Projections

To judge whether estimated costs, sales forecasts, and financial projections are reasonable, it helps to compare them with industry averages, which most trade associations publish yearly. Key ratios can also be compared with

---

[15]Andrea Bechtolsheim, speaking on the history of venture capital in 2011, https://www.youtube.com/watch?v=4bbkp0pFcmk, accessed December 20, 2014.

industry averages, including revenue per employee, margins, growth rates, lifetime customer value, and so on.

Even if the company's projections seem optimistic, the important thing is that the company has gone through the exercise of figuring what it has to do in order to make a profit. "Out of 90-plus investments in my portfolio (including several that eventually generated 5x to 12x returns), not one beat its original projections," says David Rose. "So take the financial projections . . . with a grain of salt. But by all means take them! Impressive charts of future revenues and profits may be of doubtful accuracy," but they show that the founders have thought through their business sufficiently.[16]

Similarly, the company's valuation ought to be optimistic but not crazy. Its intended use of proceeds (the capital raised through this round of equity crowdfunding) should be specific, and it should estimate how long the proceeds will allow the company to operate if profits are not forthcoming. If the proceeds will be used up before the company is profitable, will it need another round of equity financing? If so, check the deal terms to see if you have antidilution protection. (We covered valuation, use of proceeds, and antidilution provisions in detail in Chapter 11.) If the company claims that it will become profitable and self-sustaining without the need for further financing, does that seem realistic?

## Exit Strategy

In most cases, the business plan should touch on a likely exit strategy or a range of possible exit plans. If it doesn't take this topic seriously, then the company is not considering the interests of its investors. If the company predicts that it will be acquired within four to seven years, *who* might acquire it and *why*? Except in cases where a conditional acquisition candidate has been identified, this is pure speculation at this point, but it is an important part of the grand vision.

On the other hand, some businesses are, by their nature, truly long-term holdings and not focused on exits. Some examples might include existing apartment complexes and franchise businesses with high-profile brands.

As we pointed out in Chapter 8, there are many reasons why an established business might want to buy an early-stage company: to expand its sales territory or product line, to achieve vertical integration, for access to proprietary research, to acquire patents or other intellectual property, to bring in a brilliant founder or stellar management team (also known as an acqui-hire), to gobble up future competitors preemptively, and other motivations.

---

[16]Rose, op. cit., p. 86.

If the company says its goal is to file an IPO, well, good luck with that. The odds are very slim, but it does happen. What are the chances that the company will (1) grow at a phenomenal pace and (2) fend off tempting acquisition offers? To achieve that level of success, the company will probably need subsequent rounds of venture capital financing. If you invest solely on the basis of IPO potential, you are in for a bumpy ride.

If the company says in its business plan that its goal is to be a middle-market business and level off in terms of growth, rather than grow into an acquisition or IPO, then this is not a good candidate for return on investment. You might be happy owning a share of the business and receiving dividends, but don't count on huge capital gains.

Once you understand the deal terms (see Chapter 11) and have conducted or collaborated on due diligence, you are ready to make a decision about whether to invest in a company.

# CHAPTER 13

# How to Invest, Part IV: Funding and Postfunding

**I**f you are investing in startups and early-stage companies in a systematic way, with your objectives being portfolio diversification and maximum return on investment, then you will complete the following steps before you commit to an equity crowdfunding deal:

- Decide what percentage of your overall investment portfolio you will devote to angel investments via equity crowdfunding. Plan to invest in a variety of equity crowdfunding deals over three to five years, and create an equity crowdfunding budget for the coming year. (These steps are covered in Chapter 8.)
- Identify your primary motives for investing in startups and early-stage companies. Select one or more appropriate equity crowdfunding portals and/or broker-dealer platforms and search for investment opportunities that match your (1) motivation for investing, (2) business or industry expertise, and (3) risk/liquidity profile. (These steps are covered in Chapter 9.)
- Select offerings that you may want to invest in, understand the kinds of equity securities being offered (most likely stock, LLC units, and/or convertible debt), and make sure the terms of the investments are as favorable to investors as possible while still being fair to issuers. (These subjects are covered in Chapters 10 and 11.)
- Conduct (or collaborate with the crowd on) due diligence for each offering that you want to invest in, or ensure that due diligence has been completed by a reliable party who is looking out for the best interests of investors. (Due diligence is covered in Chapter 12.)
- Remind yourself one last time that investing in equity securities issued by startups and early-stage companies is riskier than investing in most public securities. Your expectations for liquidity and ROI should be

realistic. (See Chapter 6.) Deciding to invest in a company via equity crowdfunding should leave you hopeful, not anxious—just before you click on the "Invest" button. That is your final stress test.

When you make the decision to invest in a private company, you have done most of the hard work. The transaction—transferring money into escrow to purchase equity shares—is easy, thanks to Web technology. But your work is not quite finished. Assuming the issuer reaches its funding goal and the equity crowdfunding round closes, you still need to monitor your equity crowdfunding investments and possibly take action in the event of a liquidation (including dissolution or bankruptcy), subsequent equity financing rounds (e.g., more equity crowdfunding or venture capital), and exit opportunities (such as acquisitions and IPOs). You also might have an opportunity to sell your shares back to the issuer or, after a 12-month holding period, to another investor on a secondary market.[1]

In this chapter we will talk about the investment transaction, your rights and obligations as a shareholder, and how to monitor and manage your equity crowdfunding portfolio. We discussed liquidations and exits in previous chapters. We will discuss secondary markets next, in Chapter 14.

On most equity crowdfunding sites, the first step to making an investment is clicking on a button on the issuer's offering page that says something like "Invest Now." This is the beginning of a process that includes commitment, verification, and transfer of funds into escrow. After committing to invest, you may have to wait hours, days, or weeks to see if the issuer reaches its all-or-nothing funding goal by the stated deadline; if it does, then the round closes and your status changes from a commitment to a transaction. Following are details about the steps in this process:

1. By clicking on "Invest Now" and entering the dollar amount of your investment on a commitment form, you are making a promise to invest that amount in the issuer *if* the funding round closes. Refund policies may vary from one crowdfunding site to another, but once the funding round closes you will not be able to get a refund unless the issuer has violated the law or failed to comply with securities regulations.
2. You will be required to "e-sign" the relevant offering documents, including the term sheet. Crowdfunding sites typically use secure, third-party services such as DocuSign to ensure that signatures are legal and enforceable in court.

---

[1]Even during the 12-month holding period, as established by Title III of the JOBS Act, you may sell shares to accredited investors, or to family members in the event of a divorce or death.

3. Having registered as an investor on the crowdfunding site, you must now "self-certify" that you are qualified to make the investment you are committing to, based on your income and net worth. We summarized the annual investment limits in Chapters 3 and 7.

   The crowdfunding site can check its own files to see if you have made other investments in the previous 12 months on that particular site, but it cannot check other crowdfunding sites for that kind of information. In that respect, you alone are responsible for complying with your annual Title III investment limit—the crowdfunding site may not always be able to enforce that limit. If the SEC later discovers that you have exceeded your annual limit, your investment transaction may be canceled; it is unlikely (but not impossible) that you will be criminally prosecuted, since the regulations are, after all, there to protect investors. But the crowdfunding site or the issuer may be liable for your violation if they reasonably should have known that such violations were occurring, and they could thereby be in a position to sue you for damages (also unlikely but not impossible) if the offering is seriously disrupted by your violation.[2]

4. On some sites, you will have an option to purchase an insurance policy (from independent providers such as Asurvest) that covers your investment in the event of dissolution or bankruptcy of the issuer, for a limited period—typically up to 18 months after closing. This service is integrated into the crowdfunding site seamlessly; you do not have to visit the insurer's website unless you want to check it out. We covered this option in Chapter 8.

5. The portal or platform will provide instructions for securely transferring your funds (the investment amount plus insurance premium, if any) into escrow. You will have an option to mail in a check or make a wire transfer. If the crowdfunding site is a broker-dealer platform, then the broker-dealer can act as escrow agent and charge a fee to the issuer (at no cost to investors). If the site is a non-broker-dealer crowdfunding portal, then investors transfer funds to an independent escrow agent. The escrow agent's fee comes out of the issuer's funds. Crowdfunding portals do not earn any portion of the escrow agent's fees.

6. At this point, some crowdfunding sites will provide a "sharing tool" that lets you notify your off-platform social network (via LinkedIn, Twitter, or Facebook, for example) that you just invested in [name of issuer here] on the [name and URL of portal], and encourage your friends and colleagues to explore the same opportunity. This little marketing ploy promotes the

---

[2] The SEC will further clarify portals' responsibility in this regard.

crowdfunding site, attracts more potential investors to the offering that you invested in, and helps ensure that the issuer reaches its funding goal. But you have to decide whether you want to involve your social networking contacts in your investment life. (There is no way you can earn referral fees for steering new investors to an offering, as it is illegal under Title III.)

If the issuer's funding goal is not achieved by the stated deadline, then the escrow agent returns all funds to the investors; the issuer walks (or perhaps limps) away with nothing, and the crowdfunding site receives no fee.

If the issuer does achieve its funding goal by the deadline, then the funding round closes. The escrow agent disburses investors' funds to the issuer (and to the insurer if applicable) and takes a fee from the proceeds, and the crowdfunding site earns a percentage of the capital raised, typically around 6 to 10 percent. Then the issuer countersigns the offering documents and makes them available in PDF format through each investor's dashboard. You should copy and store these executed documents on a computer hard drive or another memory device and/or print and file them away for future reference. The crowdfunding site promises to maintain document archives indefinitely, but there is no guarantee of that.

Finally, you *might* receive a certificate of stock ownership or LLC membership from an SEC-approved stock transfer agent, another outside party contracted by the crowdfunding site. The SEC does not require issuers or platforms to provide such certificates, however. It requires only that shareholder records be kept by issuers, and in some cases that will be evidenced only by a "book entry," which eliminates the need to issue paper certificates.

After a deal closes, most crowdfunding sites leave a private, secure communication channel open between the issuer and its investors. The crowdfunding site's staff does not interact with either party via that channel, and it's not accessible by anyone except the issuer and its investors. Issuers can disseminate reports, newsletters, updates, and other information to investors through this channel. Investors can seek to have discussions with the issuer, and with each other, through the same channel, which each investor can access through his or her dashboard on the crowdfunding site. This channel is to be left open indefinitely by the site, or until the issuer decides it would rather maintain communication channels with investors through its own website.

Issuers have business incentives, as well as legal obligations, to keep lines of communication open with investors. A community of investors can come to the aid of a company that needs help spreading the word about a new product or job openings, for example, or retweeting company news. And if the company needs to raise a second round of equity capital, its first-round investors are the logical place to start soliciting funds. A smart company will harness the power of its investor base, and to do that it must keep investors engaged. Likewise, by supporting the company and helping it succeed, you have an opportunity to boost your return on investment. Of course, you also have the right to be a passive investor and not respond to requests for help or input.

## YOUR RIGHTS AS A SHAREHOLDER

Companies that raise capital via equity crowdfunding must file annual reports with the SEC and make those reports available to investors, in compliance with Title III. Annual reports should include financial statements—profit-and-loss, balance sheet, and cash flow, at a minimum—as well as a discussion of next year's opportunities and challenges, and how the company plans to reach its near-term goals.

In addition to Title III requirements, corporate law requires that companies notify equity investors of annual shareholder meetings, certain kinds of legal proceedings that affect shareholder rights, and any liquidation (dissolution, bankruptcy, merger, or acquisition) or IPO.

Any additional rights of investors would be spelled out in the terms of each deal. Your company (yes, it is your company, as you are now an owner) may be required to provide quarterly reports or progress updates, for example, and/or notify shareholders when their approval is required, whether by majority vote or by absence of a veto, to take certain action such as changing the bylaws or incurring debt above a certain dollar amount. The deal terms might also require the company to notify shareholders of subsequent equity funding rounds (whether via crowdfunding or in traditional Regulation D angel deals) and give early investors the opportunity to participate in later rounds at favorable prices. You may have the right to convert your preferred stock to common stock at any time—which you would not want to do until (1) the company is consistently profitable; (2) the company is about to experience a major liquidity event, such as being acquired; or (3) you want fuller voting rights.

The terms of an investment in preferred stock may entitle you to quarterly or annual dividends based on a percentage of the share price that you paid, even if the company is not profitable. If the company does not have the cash flow to pay such dividends, they would be deferred until the company could pay them cumulatively—if ever. You should keep track of those accumulated dividends if you are entitled to them.

We recommend that you review your term sheet for each investment at least yearly (and study each company's annual report), as a reminder of the options you may have as your company develops and changes.

## MANAGEMENT PARTICIPATION

As a company owner, you have a right (along with the company's customers and everyone else in the world) to contact the founders and executives and ask questions, express concerns, or give advice. Do they have an obligation to respond to you? By law they are not obligated, although most companies want to maintain good relations with their investors. That can be time-consuming when the investors are numerous and some are demanding. One of the facts of life, unfortunately, is that some shareholders are nuisances; they want to be entrepreneurs vicariously. As a matter of fact, some real entrepreneurs (with the possible exception of the consumer products and retail fields) avoid equity crowdfunding finance because of the potential burdens of managing all the concerns and demands of the crowd.

Unless you are a board member or have a contractual right to participate in the management of the company in a specific way, then you should be circumspect about contacting executives and offering advice. If you have a personal relationship with a founder or executive, be careful to preserve the boundary between personal and professional interaction. Remember that the time it takes staff members to respond to their crowd is time they can't spend moving the business forward. Consider raising questions or issues with other members of the crowd first to see if they have answers and to see if they share your concerns or questions. If there is a pattern of questions in the crowd, then management needs to take the time to deal with them—if not, their lack of response may be emblematic of a broader problem, such as a lack of communication with customers.

By all means, if you strongly believe you have urgent or otherwise constructive questions or suggestions, do not hesitate to contact the management team. If in doubt, though, as a general rule you should not offer advice unless you are invited to do so.

If you suspect the management of your company is engaging in fraud, criminal activity (such as embezzlement or bribery), or violations of securities regulations, then you should get involved. First, try to obtain an explanation or relevant information from the company that might clear up any misunderstanding or, at worst, confirm your suspicions. If your request for information from the company is ignored, or it provides irrelevant or false information, then you can either (1) ask your lawyer to investigate, (2) ask other investors off-platform whether they share your suspicions, or (3) if you have irrefutable evidence of wrongdoing, contact your lawyer, the SEC, or the attorney general's office in the company's home state. Be careful not to make unprovable accusations that might get you sued for defamation (libel or slander). Something that may seem improper to you might have a legal basis, as in the example of a manager who uses company funds to buy a car:

This may be accounted for in the manager's employment contract or in general company policy. In fact, a car allowance, which is a deductible expense, is often used in lieu of a higher salary. That's why asking a lawyer for advice is always the safest way to go. In any case, the sooner you address these sorts of concerns, the more likely you will recover your investment (or part of it) if the company's founder is convicted of a crime or charged with civil fraud by the SEC—and the more likely you can recover from an insurance policy in the event of resulting dissolution or bankruptcy, assuming the coverage term has not expired.

Keep in mind that crummy management is not a crime. In general, for corporations, the legal standard by which courts will evaluate the acts of management is pretty low. Under the business judgment rule, actions by management are improper only if they are made (1) in bad faith, that is, with knowledge that the act is illegal; (2) with a lack of due care that an ordinarily prudent person in a like position would exercise; and (3) against the best interests of the company. For LLCs, those legal standards do not necessarily apply, as LLCs are governed by contract law rather than corporate law.

## MANAGE YOUR EQUITY CROWDFUNDING PORTFOLIO

Over the next few years, you may invest in more than one Title III offering and build a diversified equity crowdfunding portfolio. In Chapter 8 we discussed portfolio strategy and suggested that you build a portfolio of a dozen or so equity crowdfunding investments to diversify the risk.

You will have exits. Almost certainly, some will be downside exits, otherwise known as liquidation stemming from dissolution and/or bankruptcy. Not quite as certainly, some will be upside exits.

As you exit one or more investments, you should consider replacing it/them with further investments to maintain a fully diversified equity crowdfunding portfolio. Keep track of the amount you invest each year to make sure you do not (1) exceed the annual limit set by Title III, based on your income or net worth, or (2) exceed the percentage of your overall investment portfolio that is allocated to alternative assets like angel capital deals.

Equity crowdfunding sites provide tools that let you keep track of multiple investments, with dashboards that feature news updates, archived documents, and discussion forums (accessible only by issuers and investors). If you have various Title III investments all on one crowdfunding site, your job of managing your portfolio is easier than if your investments are spread over several sites. On the other hand, investing on only one site limits the number of offerings that are available to you and the opportunity for diversification. Ultimately, finding the best investments should take priority over minor administrative advantages.

If the company decides to raise more capital in subsequent rounds of equity crowdfunding, and you are not protected by an antidilution provision, you need to decide whether to invest more money in the company or let your equity percentage be diluted. If the company's valuation has increased dramatically between rounds, then dilution is not necessarily going to lower the value of your shares, but it might still be a good investment opportunity. If the valuation has dropped between rounds and you anticipate a down round (where the share price is lower than the previous round), then your shares will be diluted in terms of both equity percentage and price, and you need to judge whether the company can bounce back or not. If you think it can bounce back, a down round might still be a good investment opportunity because of the lower share price.

Another scenario is that the company decides to raise capital not via equity crowdfunding but through a Reg D angel deal, involving a small number of investors who each invest tens of thousands of dollars. If the offering is made under Rule 506(c), which allows general solicitation, it would be restricted to accredited investors only. This would be another magnitude of investing entirely. If the company skips a subsequent angel round and goes directly to venture capital, then you can no longer invest directly in the company; you would have to invest in the VC firm (if you are an accredited investor), which spreads your money over several portfolio companies. These scenarios might be too rich for your blood, but the good news is that the company you invested in is growing and might be on a fast track to an acquisition or IPO.

## RETURN ON INVESTMENT

You will not know for several years, maybe as long as 7 to 10 years, whether your equity crowdfunding portfolio is producing good returns on investment. Startups often need years just to break even and become cash-flow-positive, and then more time before they are acquisition targets. So failures will occur before successes.

Don't be discouraged when some of your portfolio companies dissolve within the first few years of Title III investing, while it takes several years to produce a winner or two. Losses will probably happen before gains, as a general rule, but gains can be bigger than losses because the upside is unlimited while the downside is limited to the amount you invested.

Successful angel investors find that, over a period of decades, a very small percentage of the companies in their portfolio will account for most of their total returns. According to Robert Wiltbank's 15-year study of accredited angel investors (which we introduced in Chapter 6), just 7 percent of their investments accounted for three-quarters of their total returns. This is known as skewed returns in a portfolio. Likewise, Luis Villalobos, a successful angel investor and founder of Tech Coast Angels in California (also introduced in Chapter 6), reported that 6 percent of his investment portfolio accounted for 84 percent of his returns. This data suggests there are a lot of failures, but the idea is to overcome the losers with high-performing winners.

When (we should probably say "if," but we are optimists) you do start to earn positive returns, you should compare your equity crowdfunding ROI with the returns on the rest of your investment portfolio, as well as the predominant market indexes such as the S&P 500. Your long-term goal is diversification of risk as well as absolute return. Remember that dollars are not the only cost of your investments—the time you spent selecting offerings and conducting due diligence should also be a consideration. If you spend a considerable amount of time managing your equity crowdfunding portfolio, then your returns must not only beat the benchmarks that you establish (whether they be your own portfolio or market indexes) but compensate for your time as well.

When you compare the return on Title III investments with returns on other investments, be sure to use annualized returns expressed as percentages, for an apples-to-apples comparison. Calculating annualized ROI is not simple, because of the time value of money—in other words, annual return rates compound. The easiest way to calculate annualized ROI is to use one of the many online "return rate calculators," to derive a *compound annual growth rate*. Investopedia provides a simple one at http://www.investopedia.com/calculator/cagr.aspx.

Some angel investors also calculate a total return multiple, the formula for which is:

$$\text{Return multiple} = \text{Exit value} \div \text{Cost of investment}$$

This is expressed as a number followed by "x." This does not take into consideration the holding period of the investment (i.e., the time value of money) or the time spent by the investor.

Sophisticated angel investors use more complicated formulas to determine their returns annually, involving the "fair value" of all assets, including Title III equity. This is beyond the scope of this book and not really necessary for an asset that costs less than, say, $10,000.

If after 10 years (this is what "long-term" means) the returns on your equity crowdfunding portfolio and other alternative investments are not keeping pace with your mainstream investments (public stocks, corporate and municipal bonds, mutual funds, residential real estate, money market funds, etc.), then you need to reassess your overall portfolio strategy and/or your alternative investment strategy. That's not to say you should quit equity crowdfunding investment necessarily, because the market is going to evolve—in terms of regulations, the kinds of issuers that participate, secondary (liquidity) markets, and platform technology—over the next decade. (Stay tuned to this book's website for updates in those areas: www.wiley.com/go/equitycf.)

If one of your equity crowdfunding companies goes public and you hit the jackpot, well, you might just graduate to larger venture capital and private equity deals. Or become a philanthropist.

Some Title III investors are not motivated primarily by financial returns. As we saw in earlier chapters, your motives may be primarily social. If that's the case, each year you should review the operations and accomplishments of the companies you invested in and make sure their performance is consistent with their stated mission and business plan, especially before you make later-round investment in the same companies. You should still undertake the same long-term evaluation of financial returns on investment, however. The satisfaction of seeing your companies doing good can be compounded by seeing them and their investors do well. But if you are losing money on equity investments, then you might be more satisfied by simply making charitable donations, which are tax-deductible.

## YOUR INVESTOR NETWORK

In the process of investing on an equity crowdfunding site, especially if you collaborate with crowd members on due diligence, you probably made valuable connections with other investors. Keeping in touch with them, whether on- or off-platform, is a good way to exchange ideas about new investment opportunities. We expect that equity crowdfunding meet-up groups will form in cities across the country, open to *all* investors, just as angel investing groups have formed for accredited investors only. As the equity crowdfunding industry matures, there will be educational conferences and networking events for investors, more books like this one, and maybe an equity crowdfunding channel on whatever medium replaces cable TV. You will be a member of an equity crowdfunding investor community.

# CHAPTER 14

# Liquidity and Secondary Markets

**Y**our primary motive for investing in private securities via equity crowd-funding is either social or financial. In the Title III world at least, you should not try to optimize your investment decisions in terms of both social and financial objectives, as we discussed in Chapter 8.

If you have invested in one or more Title III offerings for social purposes, your main concerns are the company's short-term survival, its long-term effectiveness in fulfilling its mission or achieving a particular social impact, and/or your satisfaction with being a member of the "team" (which may include both entrepreneurs and co-investors). This is a buy-and-hold kind of investment, rather than a mere trade. You certainly do not wish to lose the money you invested, so you hope that the company will someday return your money in the form of dividends, a capital gain, and/or perks and benefits. But a spectacular return on investment, in the event of an IPO, for example, is not your primary concern or expectation. Nor should you have high expectations regarding the liquidity of your equity shares—that is, your ability to sell the shares at any time after the one-year holding period.

If your motives are financial, on the other hand, ROI and liquidity are primary concerns. In Chapter 13 we discussed upside exits such as acquisitions and IPOs, where—after holding an investment for several years—investors can measure annualized returns (e.g., 20 percent per year) and return multiples (e.g., 5x). With respect to liquidity, in Chapter 11 we talked about the possibility of redemption of preferred shares, where investors may have a right or obligation to sell shares back to the issuer.

Redemption is not always a good avenue to liquidity for angel investors, however. "As the sole entity in charge of buying back shares, the company potentially could keep the valuation lower than what others might pay in the open market," explains Muhammed Saeed, a serial entrepreneur and developer of electronic trading systems for the securities industry (he was the founder of Firefly Capital, an electronic trading and brokerage firm in Boston that merged with Alivia Technology in 2008). "There is little or no incentive

**243**

at that time for the company to offer a higher price unless they are working with professional investors to 'take out' crowdfunding investors to clean up the cap table for an upcoming VC or institutional round." That is why some angel investors will not invest in private securities unless a secondary market is established that provides some prospect of liquidity.

In this chapter we will explain the role of secondary markets in providing more liquidity for investors in private securities. Before we go any further, we want to emphasize that, despite the existence of secondary markets, private securities are still quite illiquid relative to public securities. Public stocks of large companies are traded frequently in heavy volumes on stock exchanges, and share prices are published daily in thousands of newspapers and websites. Even small public stocks, often called over-the-counter (OTC) shares, while lightly traded, do have ascertainable values and ready buyers. In contrast, private shares may be subject to federal and state legal restrictions on trading, are infrequently traded, and are therefore highly volatile, and share prices are not widely reported.

Not only that, but the demand among average investors for shares of private securities (at least over the past eight decades) has been miniscule compared to the demand for shares of public securities. That low demand is due in part to restrictive securities laws that largely exclude nonaccredited investors, but also is due to a relative lack of disclosure and uncertainty about exit planning options for small, private companies—spooking many accredited investors.

So even if there is a secondary market and a reliably reported share price of a particular startup's stock, who will want to buy it (at any price)? Prior to the JOBS Act, reselling private securities was limited largely to accredited investors on both the buy and the sell side. The demand may remain weak for the foreseeable future, which can keep share prices depressed even for startups that seem to be doing well. Over the next decade, if tens of millions of average investors learn about the new opportunities to invest in Title III offerings, demand might surge and share prices could be lifted, but nobody can guarantee that will happen.

A good definition is provided by New York corporate and securities lawyer Mitchell Littman:

> A secondary market transaction is "a negotiated private sale of securities of an issuer whose securities are not publicly traded. Some transactions are effected directly from seller to buyer, and in some instances one or both parties may be represented by a broker-dealer who earns commissions on the sale or purchase. Buyers and sellers

*may find one another through networking, their individual brokers, or intermediaries.*"[1]

## RESTRICTIONS ON TRANSFERS

The JOBS Act imposes a one-year holding period (with exceptions) on securities issued via crowdfunding sites under Title III. During that first year, you may transfer (sell or donate) stock or LLC membership shares only (1) back to the issuer, (2) as part of an offering registered with the SEC, such as an IPO, (3) to an accredited investor, or (4) to a member of your immediate family upon divorce or death.

The main purpose of a holding period is to ensure that the first-level investors are not acting as "underwriters" who buy large blocks of securities solely to resell them in smaller portions at a markup.

Further, any resale of securities must be made in compliance with state and federal law. While federal securities law "preempts" state law requirements for initial offerings made under Title II or Title III (that is, federal law says that state laws may not impose registration or qualification requirements on them), there is no preemption for subsequent transactions. While federal law provides that Title III securities may be resold freely after the one-year period is up, state laws are a patchwork of conflicting requirements.[2] Some states do not regulate secondary sales; others permit them to be made freely if they are "isolated." Some permit resales freely to institutions. Until state laws are coordinated, the ability to create organized markets for secondary sales of Title III securities will be limited.[3]

In addition to Title III's first-year restrictions on transfers of equity crowdfunding shares, as well as state law restrictions, the terms of *your deal* might contain further restrictions and/or obligations regarding transfers of those shares even after the one-year holding period. For example, you will be obligated to notify the issuer of your intention to transfer shares, including the name of the transferee (you are the transferor), the price per share (or other valuable consideration) if you are selling the shares, and the date of transfer. The company needs to know who its shareholders are. If the deal terms include a right of first refusal, you must give the issuer an opportunity to purchase the shares at the same price and on substantially the same terms

---

[1] Mitchell C. Littman and Lesley A. DeCasseres, "The Secondary Market for Private Shares," Littman Krooks law firm, New York City, May 2012.
[2] See SecondMarket's "Blue Sky Report" updated January 31, 2013, at https://www.secondmarket.com/education/reports/secondmarket-blue-sky-report.
[3] Source: Sara Hanks, Virginia-based securities lawyer and CEO of CrowdCheck.

by which you intend to sell them to a third party. Some deals (such as Series Seed) include terms that give other Series Seed investors the same right of first refusal, so the notification process can be more complicated.

It is also possible that a company would simply prohibit any private sale of shares for a specified period. For example, a company could include a provision in the organizational documents stating that no investor can sell his or her shares for 36 months after the offering date. These customized elements of offerings remind us of the importance of reviewing deal terms before you invest.

## WHY SELL? WHO WILL BUY?

After the holding period, you may sell equity shares under Title III to any investor, either in a private transaction or on an established secondary market, if any such markets develop.

We will explain what a secondary market is and how it works, but first: Considering the unpredictable (and usually low) prices of shares in secondary markets, why would you want to sell your shares before an exit that might yield an upside ROI? Here are seven reasons:

- You unexpectedly need cash.
- An investor offers to buy your shares at a price that you can't resist.
- You decide to change your portfolio allocation strategy and need to sell shares of private securities (alternative assets) so you can rebalance in favor of less risky investments.
- You sense that the company is plateauing in terms of revenue growth, and even if it stays in business you do not expect the share value to go any higher than it is now.
- You believe the company has made a serious strategic mistake that will result in the share value being wiped out, or you perceive that there is excessive conflict among the factions of the company's management.
- The opportunity cost of holding onto an investment is too high, considering that you are aware of much more attractive investment opportunities.
- The company pivots, revises its business plans, and is no longer committed to achieving the community impact that motivated you to invest.

Now, if you really must sell, ask yourself: Who would buy my shares, and why? If the company is not growing, then the only reason another investor would want to buy in is if the deal were a bargain—in other words, the price is very low, perhaps less than you paid for the shares. If the company is truly profitable and growing, then investors should be interested in buying in at a reasonable price—but then you're better off holding onto the shares and waiting for an upside exit, unless you desperately need cash.

Maybe the company experienced fast growth for a few years and now its growth has plateaued, but it's not obvious whether the company will recover and resume its growth spurt, remain plateaued indefinitely as a stable "lifestyle" business, or slide into oblivion. You may believe the company will not grow significantly again, while other investors may still see strong potential in the company. This is one of those situations where, because the company has grown since the equity crowdfunding round, its valuation is higher and an optimistic investor might offer you a price for your shares that is significantly more than you paid. This is where your business experience can help you evaluate the company's potential and make a smart decision about whether to sell your shares.

There could be other scenarios, not necessarily involving plateaus, where your forecast diverges from that of other investors—namely, you believe the share price will go no higher and they believe the opposite—creating an opportunity for you to sell at a decent price. This, after all, is what happens every day in the public stock exchanges: One investor buys and another sells, based on their disparate expectations of the same stock.

Back to that question: Who are these buyers, and why would they want to buy your shares? They may be one or more of the following:

- Other equity crowdfunding investors, your cohorts, who invested as much as they could in the equity crowdfunding round based on the Title III limits for one year (that is, based on their income and net worth), but they really wanted to invest more in the company. So they waited until the holding period was over and now seek to invest more in the company via secondary markets or direct transactions with cohort seed investors.
- The company itself wishes to buy back shares from its seed round investors for any number of reasons, for example, because it wants to raise capital from venture capitalists who insist on a tidy capitalization table.
- New investors who were aware of the original equity crowdfunding investment opportunity but could not afford to invest in it at that time, or decided to wait and see if the company gained traction after that funding round, and now they decide they want to buy in.
- New investors, latecomers who were not aware of the original equity crowdfunding investment opportunity but now wish to be shareholders of the company for social reasons (e.g., their friends are shareholders) or financial motives (the company appears to be poised for strong growth). These investors are likely to hunt for bargain prices.

- Strategic investors who perceive value because the company is becoming a key supplier or innovator in the investor's industry. These are investors who won't necessarily wait for bargain prices to buy in; they are willing to pay a price based on fair or even optimistic valuations.
- Institutional investors who have been waiting to see how equity crowdfunding works out. These investors are more likely to invest at later stages, when early-stage companies graduate to venture capital rounds of financing, but they might invest in Title III shares for the sake of diversification, not to mention the upside potential of fast-growing companies.

You might find yourself on the buying end of that scenario: Another investor wants to sell shares and you believe the share value will increase, so you are happy to buy those shares, preferably at a bargain price but maybe even at a "reasonable" price (where the valuation makes sense to you).

The question then is how you and those diverging investors can find each other. The answer is, the same way that you and the company you invested in found each other: via an online intermediary. The postfunding intermediary is known as a *secondary market*. Because these are the early days of equity crowdfunding, secondary markets for Title III equity crowdfunding shares are not established, so the market mechanism—where buyers seek a low price and sellers seek a high price and the two parties meet somewhere in between to set a "fair" price—has not yet been fine-tuned. Title III secondary markets may be inefficient or even chaotic for some years to come. The only way these markets will evolve is for buyers and sellers to meet and set prices day after day, until the process becomes more efficient and prices more consistently fair. This is what we call free-market capitalism.

## SECONDARY MARKETS IN THE DIGITAL WORLD

The earliest electronic trading platforms for private securities emerged in the 1990s. Most of the early platforms were passive bulletin boards where sellers and buyers connected on-platform and then conducted transactions off-platform.[4] The first true, SEC-sanctioned[5] electronic secondary markets, where the transactions occurred on the platforms themselves, were launched

---

[4]Robert B. Robbins and Matthew Hallinan, "Private Trading Platforms for Restricted Securities," The American Law Institute, March 2013. The authors are securities lawyers, Robbins in Washington, DC, and Hallinan in San Francisco.
[5]The sanctioning was conveyed by the SEC mainly by no-action letters, which are provisional commitments not to take enforcement action.

in the late 1990s by Nasdaq, Goldman Sachs, NYPPEX, and others, and were limited to trading by "qualified institutional buyers," that is, institutions with $100 million portfolios.

So-called secondary funds emerged around 2000. These funds, the most prominent of which were Industry Ventures and Millennium Technology Value Partners, typically invested in venture-backed early- and growth-stage companies by purchasing shares directly from founders, employees, and angel investors. With almost $1 billion under management today, Millennium's investments have included pre-IPO shares of Facebook, Twitter, and Alibaba Group.

Partly in response to the slump in IPO activity after the recession of 2007–08 and the resulting demand for alternative liquidity options, Second-Market and SharesPost launched secondary market platforms for private securities in 2009.[6] These operate like eBay-style auctions where sellers can post their private shares, stating a minimum price; buyers who are accredited investors can bid for those shares within a stated period of time; and the highest bidder "wins." These platforms quickly drew strong interest from secondary funds, institutional investors, and individual accredited ("retail") investors alike.

Initially, SecondMarket allowed sellers—predominantly current and former employees of issuers—to sell their shares on the platform without the consent or participation of the issuers. But the platform evolved into a provider of "customized liquidity programs" for issuers, and SecondMarket now gives issuers (which it considers its customers) a lot of control over the secondary market transactions—and now sees itself primarily as an "M&A platform." For example, issuers can determine whether former and/or current employees may sell shares only to existing shareholders (so as not to increase the number of shareholders), set the maximum number of shares that can be sold per quarter, establish a minimum price, add a right of first refusal even if there is no ROFR provision in the deal terms, and so on.

SecondMarket requires that each company whose shares are traded post financial information, including audited financial statements, in its secure data room for eligible buyers to see. The platform sets the minimum transaction size at $100,000, and it earns at least 3 percent of the proceeds (with a minimum of $2,500) in each transaction. In the first six months of 2014, according to a SecondMarket report,[7] the platform's median transaction size was $27 million.

---

[6]SecondMarket actually began in 2004—then called Restricted Stock Partners—as a market for trading restricted securities of public companies.

[7]Source: http://blog.secondmarket.com/image/94718993867.

Keep in mind that these figures are all pre–Title III equity crowdfunding, and all buyers in these transactions were accredited investors—about 15,000 of whom were using the SecondMarket platform in 2011. At this point no secondary markets for Title III shares have been established, but we can expect that if and when they are, the minimum and median transaction amounts will be substantially lower and nonaccredited investors will be able to participate on both the buy side and the sell side.

According to SecondMarket's first-half 2014 report, sellers were predominantly current employees (83 percent) and former employees (15 percent) of the issuers, while only 1.6 percent of sellers were angel investors, and less than 1 percent were founders. The breakdown of securities sold showed that most transactions involved common stock (52 percent), while options (26 percent), preferred stock (20 percent), and warrants and restricted stock units (2 percent) accounted for the remainder. The average age of companies that participated was eight years from foundation. Another notable fact from the first-half 2014 report was that 67 percent of the transactions were third-party tender offers (primarily by mutual funds and hedge funds), while 33 percent were repurchases of shares by the issuers.

SecondMarket has shifted its business and is, in addition to operating secondary markets, offering enterprise technology that companies can use to conduct their own secondary share sales. Customers for this new service include SurveyMonkey, Square, and video-game developer Kabam.

In March 2013, SharesPost and Nasdaq OMX Group entered into a joint venture to launch a new secondary market trading platform, called Nasdaq Private Market (NPM), for private securities. Like SecondMarket, NPM places a strong emphasis on issuer control over the secondary marketplace.

Bloomberg reported that transactions involving sales of private securities by employees and angel investors reached a record $12 billion in 2013 and are expected to rise to $19 billion in 2014.

## TITLE III SECONDARY MARKETS

Some financial professionals believe that by giving issuers control over the secondary market, SecondMarket and NPM are stifling the market mechanism that tends to foster efficiency and price fairness. Many private securities are already saddled with constraining terms and restrictions, and allowing issuers to control the market only adds further constraints on sellers as well as buyers. We hope that secondary markets in the Title III arena, to the extent they develop, will allow shareholders to sell their shares (after a one-year holding period, unless they sell to an accredited investor during the first year) on such platforms without consent of or control by the issuers.

It is possible that some equity crowdfunding portals and broker-dealer platforms themselves will have built-in peer-to-peer secondary markets that let their registered investors trade the shares that they purchased on-platform. The Netherlands-based equity crowdfunding platform Symbid already does this. Founded in 2011, Symbid allows nonaccredited investors to participate with a minimum investment of €20 (and is the world's first publicly listed crowdfunding platform).

## CONCLUSION

Like the equity crowdfunding industry itself, the secondary market for Title III shares will evolve over the next several years. We will report on all new developments in Title III secondary markets on this book's website: www.wiley.com/go/equitycf.

Some sophisticated investors believe, as Saeed writes, that "without a robust secondary market there can be little or no primary market, since not every company that succeeds will go public or get acquired. And without liquidity, no equity investors small or large will be tempted to invest in a startup." For that reason, some investors might read this chapter first. And we hope they are encouraged.

# Epilogue: Trends and Innovations

**T**itle III equity crowdfunding sits at the confluence of (1) securities laws and regulations, (2) social media, and (3) a massive influx of "new" angel investors. All three of these areas will evolve over the next decade, resulting in greater efficiencies in the equity crowdfunding process for both issuers and investors.

With respect to securities laws, the U.S. House of Representatives has already proposed rewriting Title III of the JOBS Act to raise the funding limit and make equity crowdfunding less burdensome and costly for issuers. That would, in our opinion, improve the flow of good deals into equity crowdfunding portals, including later-stage companies with traction in the marketplace. We expect that the laws and rules that govern equity crowdfunding will improve over the next several years, partly to keep pace with other countries in which equity crowdfunding (for all investors) is flourishing, but, most important, to achieve the original vision of the JOBS Act: to promote economic development and create more jobs.

With respect to social media—which supports the technical infrastructure of all kinds of crowdfunding platforms—who knows what innovations will make life easier and less risky (and probably more fun) for new angel investors. But we all know it will happen: Social media is young; it will continue to evolve rapidly. We expect, as one example, that equity crowdfunding sites will soon have the capacity to let investors "pool" their efforts to negotiate deal terms with issuers, rather than being forced into an "in or out" decision.

With respect to new angel investors, you can expect many educational opportunities, including college courses, webinars, conferences, and more (and updated) books. You will have a chance to learn the ins and outs of private securities, portfolio strategy, deal terms, due diligence, and all the aspects of equity crowdfunding that will help you invest more wisely and achieve better returns. On the other side of the table, issuers will learn how to develop business plans and terms that provide more transparency for investors. Collectively, issuers and their lawyers will, we predict, create a new business entity—call it a Subchapter CF corporation—designed especially for success as a crowdfunded company. The CF corporation would deftly resolve, for example, the unique governance issues produced by having hundreds or thousands of small investors scattered around the country.

When equity crowdfunding gains traction of its own, you will see a growing number of entrepreneurs seeking equity capital (the supply side), and more investors seeking to diversify their portfolios into "alternative" investments (the demand side). Growing supply and growing demand lead to an explosive industry with relentless innovation and ever greater efficiencies.

You can keep up with trends and innovations in equity crowdfunding by keeping your eye on this book's website: www.wiley.com/go/equitycf.

# Equity Crowdfunding Resources

The authors have reviewed the following resources and believe they are informative, reliable, and unbiased. Please visit this book's website (www.wiley.com/equitycf) for a more comprehensive list, plus updates.

Because of the fast-changing nature of the Internet, some of the following URLs may disappear without notice.

## A. LAWS AND REGULATIONS

**Securities Act of 1933, including Regulation D and Other Amendments**

The entire 1933 act, as amended through 2012 (93 pages), in PDF format. http://www.sec.gov/about/laws/sa33.pdf

Concise summary of the 1933 and 1934 acts and each amendment (1939, 1940, 2002, 2010, 2012); published by the SEC. http://www.sec.gov/about/laws.shtml

Regulation D offerings: a summary published by the SEC. http://www.sec.gov/answers/regd.htm

**JOBS Act of 2012, Particularly Title III ("Crowdfunding Exemption")**

Jumpstart Our Business Startups Act (H.R. 3606), signed into law April 5, 2012; the entire original act (22 pages) published by the GPO. http://www.gpo.gov/fdsys/pkg/BILLS-112hr3606enr/pdf/BILLS-112hr3606enr.pdf

FAQs about the JOBS Act, published by the SEC (updated January 2014). http://www.sec.gov/spotlight/jobs-act.shtml

Summaries and analyses of the JOBS Act published by law firms:
Sullivan & Cromwell. http://www.sullcrom.com/files/upload/JOBS_Act_Presentation_PDF.pdf

Morrison & Foerster. http://media.mofo.com/files/Uploads/Images/Jumpstart-Our-Business-Startups-Act.pdf

Orrick Herrington. http://www.orrick.com/Practices/Equity-Capital-Markets/JOBS-Act/pages/default.aspx

Godfrey & Kahn. http://www.gklaw.com/news.cfm?action=pub _detail&publication_id=1176

Cooley LLP. http://www.cooley.com/66282

Title III of the JOBS Act (the "Crowdfunding Exemption"): the full text (PDF). http://www.freedman-chicago.com/ec4i/Title-III.pdf

Insightful commentary on Title III published by law firm Morse Barnes-Brown Pendleton (offices in Massachusetts and Utah). http://www. mbbp.com/resources/business/crowdfunding.html

Intrastate Securities Exemptions: please see www.wiley.com/equitycf

**2014 Legislative Proposal to Revise Title III of the JOBS Act**

Equity Crowdfunding Improvement Act of 2014 (discussion draft). http://financialservices.house.gov/uploadedfiles/bills-113hr-pih -crwdfnd-m001156.pdf

"Crowdfunding 2.0," a summary of the proposed Equity Crowd-funding Improvement Act, by Sheppard Mullin Richter law firm (published in *National Law Review,* June 25, 2014). http://www .natlawreview.com/article/crowdfunding-20-proposed-equity -crowdfunding-improvement-act-2014

## B. RELIABLE CROWDFUNDING NEWS AND ANALYSIS

**Crowdfunding Industry News Media**

Crowdfund Insider, published in Beachwood, Ohio, is updated daily and profusely. Andrew Dix is the CEO. http://www.crowdfundinsider .com/

CrowdFundBeat is a rich-media blog published by Sydney Armani in San Francisco, updated daily. Mostly aggregated from other sources. http://crowdfundbeat.com/

Crowdnetic Wire is updated occasionally. Crowdnetic is a "provider of technology and market data . . . to the global crowdfinance mar-ketplace." http://www.crowdneticwire.com/

*Entrepreneur* magazine's website has a section on crowdfunding. http://www.entrepreneur.com/topic/crowdfunding

Crowdsourcing.org has a section on crowdfunding, updated daily. http://www.crowdsourcing.org/community/crowdfunding/7

The CrowdCheck Blog, published by the due diligence firm Crowd-Check, offers occasional news and analysis. http://crowdcheck.com /blog

### Educational and Research-Oriented Sites

A Brief History of Crowdfunding: Rewards, Donation, Debt, and Equity Platforms, by David M. Freedman and Matthew R. Nutting (PDF). http://www.freedman-chicago.com/ec4i/History-of-Crowdfunding .pdf

CrowdPassage is a "community" with educational content covering donation, rewards, and equity crowdfunding and free membership-based networking. Founded by Matthew R. Nutting, a lawyer in Fresno, California, and a director of the National Crowdfunding Association. http://www.crowdpassage.com/

Crowdfunding research reports from the Fung Institute, University of California at Berkeley (Richard Swart, director of Program for Innovation in Entrepreneurial & Social Finance). http://www.funginstitute.berkeley.edu/publications?field_research_type _tid=7

Basics for Crowdfunding Investors (equity only) published by the National Crowdfunding Association. http://www.nlcfa.org/investor -information.html

## C. TRADE ASSOCIATIONS

Crowdfunding Professional Association (CfPA.org)

National Crowdfunding Association (NLCFA.org)

Crowdfund Intermediary Regulatory Advocates (CFIRA.org)

# About the Companion Website

Readers can access this book's companion website at www.wiley.com/go/equitycf (password wiley15).

On the website, readers will find:

- The most up-to-date version of the appendix "Equity Crowdfunding Resources" from the book
- Summary of final rules issued by the Securities and Exchange Commission under Title III of the JOBS Act
- Intrastate crowdfunding exemptions, details state by state
- Establishment of secondary markets for Title III equity crowdfunding shares
- And more

# Index